Studies in Military and Strategic History

General Editor: William Philpott, Professor of the History of Warfare, Department of War Studies, King's College London

Thomas R. Mockaitis
BRITISH COUNTERINSURGENCY, 1919–60

Bob Moore and Kent Fedorowich
THE BRITISH EMPIRE AND ITS ITALIAN PRISONERS OF WAR, 1940–47

T. R. Moreman
THE ARMY IN INDIA AND THE DEVELOPMENT OF FRONTIER WARFARE, 1849–1947

Kendrick Oliver
KENNEDY, MACMILLAN AND THE NUCLEAR TEST-BAN DEBATE, 1961–63

Paul Orders
BRITAIN, AUSTRALIA, NEW ZEALAND AND THE CHALLENGE OF THE UNITED STATES, 1934–46
A Study in International History

Elspeth Y. O'Riordan
BRITAIN AND THE RUHR CRISIS

G. D. Sheffield
LEADERSHIP IN THE TRENCHES
Officer–Man Relations, Morale and Discipline in the British Army in the Era of the First World War

Adrian Smith
MICK MANNOCK, FIGHTER PILOT
Myth, Life and Politics

Melvin Charles Smith
AWARDED IN VALOUR
A History of the Victoria Cross and the Evolution of British Heroism

Nicholas Tamkin
BRITAIN, TURKEY AND THE SOVIET UNION, 1940–45
Strategy, Diplomacy and Intelligence in the Eastern Mediterranean

Martin Thomas
THE FRENCH NORTH AFRICAN CRISIS
Colonial Breakdown and Anglo-French Relations, 1945–62

Simon Trew
BRITAIN, MIHAILOVIC AND THE CHETNIKS, 1941–42

Kristian Coates Ulrichsen
THE LOGISTICS AND POLITICS OF THE BRITISH CAMPAIGNS IN THE MIDDLE EAST, 1914–22

Steven Weiss
ALLIES IN CONFLICT
Anglo-American Strategic Negotiations, 1938–44

Studies in Military and Strategic History
Series Standing Order ISBN 978–0–333–71046–3 Hardback 978–0–333–80349–3 Paperback
(*outside North America only*)

You can receive future titles in this series as they are published by placing a standing order. Please contact your bookseller or, in case of difficulty, write to us at the address below with your name and address, the title of the series and the ISBN quoted above.

Customer Services Department, Macmillan Distribution Ltd, Houndmills, Basingstoke, Hampshire RG21 6XS, England

The Greater War

Other Combatants and Other Fronts, 1914–1918

Edited by

Jonathan Krause
University of Portsmouth, UK

First published 2014 by
PALGRAVE MACMILLAN

Palgrave Macmillan in the UK is an imprint of Macmillan Publishers Limited,
registered in England, company number 785998, of Houndmills, Basingstoke,
Hampshire RG21 6XS.

Palgrave Macmillan in the US is a division of St Martin's Press LLC,
175 Fifth Avenue, New York, NY 10010.

Palgrave Macmillan is the global academic imprint of the above companies
and has companies and representatives throughout the world.

Palgrave® and Macmillan® are registered trademarks in the United States,
the United Kingdom, Europe and other countries.

ISBN 978–1–137–36065–6 hardback
ISBN 978–1–137–36064–9 paperback

This book is printed on paper suitable for recycling and made from fully
managed and sustained forest sources. Logging, pulping and manufacturing
processes are expected to conform to the environmental regulations of the
country of origin.

A catalogue record for this book is available from the British Library.

Library of Congress Cataloging-in-Publication Data
Krause, Jonathan.
    The greater war : other combatants and other fronts, 1914–1918 /
Jonathan Krause, University of Portsmouth, UK.
      pages   cm. — (Studies in military and strategic history)
    ISBN 978–1–137–36064–9
    1. World War, 1914–1918—Campaigns. I. Title.
    D521.K818 2014
    940.4—dc23   2014025886

For Grayson, Madison, and those to come

Contents

Tables

Acknowledgements

The editor would like to thank the Joint Services Command and Staff College for the generous assistance it provided in arranging and funding the conference which led to this book. In particular the assistance, patience and guidance of Ashley Jackson, Karen Crouch, Lucy Fisher, Beverly Oliver and Lyn Reynolds were invaluable.

Contributors

Alex Bostrom is a doctoral candidate at Lincoln College, Oxford. His research focuses on industrial mobilisation and the production of munitions and artillery in France during the First World War, and governmental responses to the pressures of expanding domestic output.

Tony Cowan is a former British diplomat now studying for a PhD at King's College London. His thesis is on German operational command on the Western Front in 1917. He is a member of the British Commission for Military History and co-ordinates its activities on the First World War centenary.

Tim Gale is an independent scholar. He undertook his doctoral research on the French Tank Service (the Artillerie Speciale) at the Department of War Studies, King's College. His research interests centre on the French army in the Great War. He is a member of the First World War Operations Research Group (KCL) and he is Honorary Treasurer of the British Commission for Military History.

David Ian Hall is Senior Lecturer in the Defence Studies Department, King's College London, at the Joint Services Command and Staff College, part of the UK Defence Academy. He has a DPhil from the University of Oxford. He specialises in the cultural and intellectual history of Germany. He teaches an interdisciplinary MA special subject entitled 'Hitler Studies'. His current research, funded by the British Academy, is on the Bayreuth Festival during the Second World War.

Simon House is an independent scholar. He spent 32 years as an accountant with British Telecom, culminating with his appointment as CFO (Chief Finance Officer) BT Asia-Pacific, based in Sydney, Australia. After retiring in 2001 he began his PhD at King's College London, and in May 2012 was awarded a doctorate for his dissertation on the Battle of the Ardennes. He is currently in the process of expanding his thesis into a book.

Spencer Jones is Senior Lecturer in Armed Forces and War Studies at the University of Wolverhampton. In addition, he presently serves as the Regimental Historian of the Royal Regiment of Artillery. His research focuses on the training and battle tactics of the British Army in the First World War. Previous publications include *From Boer War to World War: Tactical Reform of the British Army 1902–1914* (2012) and the edited collection *Stemming the Tide: Officers and Leadership in the British Expeditionary Force 1914* (2013), which was runner-up for the 2013 Templer Medal.

Jonathan Krause is Lecturer in Strategic Studies at the Royal Air Force College, Cranwell, under the auspices of the University of Portsmouth. He has published a range of works on the First World War, including *Early Trench Tactics in the French Army: the Second Battle of Artois, May–June 1915* and *The Origins of Chemical Warfare in the French Army*. He won a 2014 Moncado Prize for his article in the *Journal of Military History*, 'The French Battle for Vimy Ridge, Spring 1915'. He is the Assistant Secretary-General of the British Commission for Military History.

Andrew Lambert is Laughton Professor of Naval History in the Department of War Studies at King's College London. His latest book *The Challenge, Britain versus America in the Naval War of 1812* (2012) won the Anderson Medal of the Society for Nautical Research as the best maritime history book of 2012.

Stuart Mitchell is Senior Lecturer in War Studies at the Royal Military Academy Sandhurst, where he specialises in learning, transformation and leadership in the British Army during the First World War. He is also a member of the Centre for War Studies at the University of Birmingham, British Commission for Military History, Western Front Association and the Institute for Historical Research.

Christopher Newton is a PhD candidate in the Department for War Studies at King's College London. His thesis examines the British Third Army during the Battles of the Scarpe in 1917. He has previously worked as a defence policy analyst and adviser.

William Philpott is Professor of the History of Warfare in the Department of War Studies, King's College London. He is a specialist on the operational history of the British and French armies and Anglo-French relation in the early twentieth century, subjects on which he has published widely. He is the author of the prizewinning reassessment of the battles of the Somme, *Bloody Victory: The Sacrifice on the Somme and the*

Making of the Twentieth Century (2009), and a new strategic history of the First World War, *Attrition: Fighting the First World War* (2014). He is on the Council of the National Army Museum, and is Secretary General of the British Commission for Military History.

B. T. Smith earned his Bachelor's degree from the University of California, Davis. He went on to study at the Naval War College, receiving a Master's in National Security and Strategic Studies, and at the University of Cambridge, receiving a Master's in Business Administration. He is an 18-year veteran of the US Navy and currently the Commanding Officer of a C-130 squadron station in Jacksonville, Florida.

Vanda Wilcox teaches Modern European history at John Cabot University, Rome. She completed a DPhil at Oxford University on morale and discipline in the Italian army and has published on various aspects of the Battle of Caporetto, on the experience and identity of Italian First World War soldiers, and on the memory of the war in Italy.

Introduction

Jonathan Krause

The advent of the First World War centenary has made it a topic of international discussion, with regular pieces appearing in newspapers, on television and across the spectrum of social media, to say nothing of the countless unrecorded discussions happening over coffee, tea, wine and beer the world over. As exciting as this has been (it is not often that one's particular historical niche is suddenly a popular topic of public discourse), it has not been without some disappointment. Thus far the public debates, and the events already planned to commemorate the conflict, have been largely confined to the national and local levels. International perspectives remain in the minority, which, sadly, is unsurprising. History is, after all, a distinctly national affair. When we are taught history as children we are taught first and foremost about our nation, our group, our people (however defined). The net may at times be wider, at other times less so, but it can only ever cover a limited cultural, religious and geographical area. At the end of the Cold War, Sir Michael Howard spoke of a similar phenomenon regarding power and culture in international politics. He elaborated on a concept attributed to the Norwegian Minister of Defence Johan Jørgen Holst of a 'European village' consisting of an old European core with other states and regions (such as the Europe-derived nations in North America and the Antipodes) having a closer or more distant relation to this 'core'.[1]

History, from a young age, tends to be taught and studied with this sort of downtown-and-suburb mind-set, with each nation being a core unto itself: when young we learn a great deal about the nation we come from, a fair bit about nations that are geographically, historically and culturally linked to our own, and rather less about nations with which we might share little more than a continent. About vast swaths of the world we learn absolutely nothing. Relating this phenomenon specifically to military history, Jeremy Black argued in his 2004 book *Rethinking Military History* that 'other states and societies appear primarily in order to be defeated...the "non-West" is misunderstood when it is not ignored'.[2] This was an unfortunate fact that needed pointing out and, despite a decade's worth of progress, it is still unsettlingly accurate for too many military history courses.

While Black was very right to assert that we need a much more global understanding of history, there are still steps we can take within the field of European history to broaden perspectives and open up a more international discussion about the past. In time this might grow into a much fairer appraisal and recognition of the history (military and otherwise) of peoples from all corners of the globe. One small step we can take to begin improving the discipline is to approach history from a more international perspective (the increasing number of international histories, and history posts, is reassuring). With the centenary of the First World War, historians have a unique opportunity to do just that, and to make serious inroads into what has thus far been a largely introspective memory centred on concepts of nationality. With the countless efforts to commemorate the Great War, there is inevitably going to be a point at which the general population is simply over-loaded with programming and publications about mud, blood and 'the ordinary soldier'. International historians have what may well be a once in a lifetime opportunity to showcase their knowledge of other aspects of the First World War in front of a population which is still interested in the conflict, but will very soon be hungry for new angles and perspectives. The UK is already at significant risk of over-exposure,[3] and is thus a ripe target at which to aim a broader narrative of the war.

The First World War seems to occupy a more prominent place in the national psyche of Great Britain than most of the other combatant nations.[4] This is in many ways an understandable reaction to what was an unparalleled cultural experience for Britons: never before had so large a force been raised, had so great a part of society been involved in the war effort. Never before had so many young men failed to come home alive and in one piece after a war. In response to this unique cultural experience, Britain and former Dominion states have produced a great body of art and literature informed by the First World War. This body of literature has evolved to become the primary means by which Britons engage with the First World War. This is not only a ramification of the inclusion of war poetry in school curricula, but also a result of genuine interest in the period; in recent decades historical fiction has reasserted its dominance in the public memory of the First World War.[5]

The most prominent of this new wave of war books is probably Sebastian Faulks' novel *Birdsong*. Since its initial publication in 1993 *Birdsong* has sold over three million copies, and has remained one of Britain's consistently best-selling novels since its release (to say nothing of its adaptations for screen and stage). The fact that this feat was achieved, at least initially, via word of mouth rather than critical acclaim should bear some witness to the immense fascination Britons have with the Great War. In the face of such popular success, the work of academic historians has been slow to permeate into the broader public debate. In 2001 Richard Holmes wrote in his foreword to Gary Sheffield's *Forgotten Victory* that 'we [have] at last reached a time when it [is] possible to make balanced judgements on a struggle which [has] polarised opinion for so long'.[6] Writing a year later, and referring to that same hopeful notion, Brian Bond had to admit that

> This hope and expectation has not been realized; indeed, the gulf between serious historical studies and popular misconceptions, encouraged by the media, may even be widening. This is a depressing state of affairs which historians must do their best to remedy. Public interest in the First World War has recently become more intense, due mainly to the development of a battlefield tourist industry, so there is certainly an audience and readership to be reached.[7]

Despite the opportunities presented by Britons' deep fascination (even obsession) with the trenches, the national discussion of the First World War remains staunchly inward-looking. This has been especially true regarding military histories of the war; the most prominent British catch-phrase in the military historiography of the Great War, 'the learning curve', has remained almost entirely national in its usage.[8] Worse yet, the historiographical debates have increasingly taken on a decidedly political tone, even if the denotation of 'right' or 'left' frequently has no relation to the personal politics of the historians in question.[9] This tendency was reinforced earlier this year by Education Secretary Michael Gove in his widely read article in the *Daily Mail*, 'Why does the Left insist on belittling true British heroes?' The article sought to promote a somewhat more positive interpretation of the conduct of the First World War (especially regarding British leadership, political and military), and tended to do so with good historiographical support.[10] Unfortunately, the Secretary's overt politicising of the historiography has served only to reinforce the idea that one's understanding of the First World War is an expression of political philosophy rather than an objective appraisal of historical research. It seems likely that Gove's article was merely a sign of things to come. Sir Richard Evans' riposte in the *Guardian* four days later thankfully made the case that the research of historians should be respected for what it is (rather than being politicised), but still did not seize the opportunity to remind readers that we are talking about a 'world' war, not an Anglo-German one. The purpose of this book is to do just that. In so doing, it will make a small contribution in favour of international history and bring a bit more balance to the prevailing Anglo-centrism in British accounts of the Great War.

This book began its life as a conference held at the Joint Services Command and Staff College, Shrivenham, in October 2012. The goal of the conference was to bring together historians of war whose expertise lies outside the well-worn ruts of the British army on the Western Front. The initial plan was to offer panels on a wide-ranging variety of topics which would look at perspectives from the Eastern Front and the Middle East to Africa, Asia and beyond. Unfortunately, reality set in: conference organisers can only create panels out of willing speakers. This led to a programme which featured panels on France, Germany, Morale (comprising papers on Italy and the Middle East), and the Americas. Transformed into a collaborative book, these essays, including additional chapters which expand on colonial aspects of the war not discussed during the conference, constitute a comparative international history of overlapping facets of the war, which will hopefully stimulate wider interest in the areas we have chosen to focus on. By pursuing a more narrow range of topics, the book can provide quite an ample survey of certain key aspects of the war, which should be of great utility for readers interested in exploring a more comparative approach to the First World War.

With any edited volume there is always the issue of theme and consistency. This book exists in a slightly awkward space, as it has no true over-arching theme aside from a desire to highlight work being done beyond the usual focus of the British on the Western Front. Within sections and across chapters, however, there are micro-themes that serve to link chapters and concepts together in a few important ways. The chapters on Germany are linked by their central focus on German culture and its importance in the German Empire. Being such a new state, having existed for only 43 years in 1914, Germany was still in the process of discovering itself. What did it mean to be German? This was a question not only of enormous cultural importance, but also of practical political and military relevance throughout both world wars (and beyond).

Whereas the German chapters focus on the important issues related to German *Kultur*, the chapters on France, together, tell a story of the evolution of French command and the army's adaptation to industrial warfare. These four chapters constitute a broad-ranging glance at the French army, spanning action from 1914 to 1917 (with references to the French in 1918 present in the chapter on attrition). The breadth and interconnectedness of the chapters make for an especially useful series of essays for any student of comparative history. Together these four essays represent the cutting edge of research on the French army in the First World War. The authors' research has largely evolved together, which gives the section a cohesiveness that is altogether rare in edited volumes of this nature.

The three chapters on Britain are also strongly cohesive, and operate best as a whole, focusing as they do (implicitly or explicitly) on the vast colonial dimension of the war. The chapters on Palestine and East Africa are, of course, rather overtly colonial in nature. Together they help remind readers not only of the global nature of the war, but also of the importance of empire in Britain's strategic and political goals during the First World War. The chapter on the British army in 1914 is really about the 'colonial police force' that Britain sent to war in 1914; Britain's pre-war military culture is unique in the First World War, and is therefore worth exploring as a product of colonialism and Britain's maritime empire. All three of the chapters serve to broaden perspectives on the British war effort and, above all, to remind readers that we are talking about a global conflict, not one confined to the narrow fields of France and Flanders. In this vein, the chapters on Italy and the United States further explore the experiences of armed forces which are too often overlooked, and yet are crucial to understanding the First World War. The book's sole naval chapter reinforces this point *par excellence*, linking together not only geographic areas far removed from the battlefields of Europe, but also time periods long past. As a work focusing on strategy it reminds us of the power of geography in shaping global strategy, lending a welcome *longue durée* vision to the work.

The book ends with a chapter on attrition. It is a subject that is fundamentally controversial: it offends human sensibilities to reduce war to a rote tally of enemy killed. Niall Fergusson's *Pity of War* in many ways exemplifies the emotional reaction that many have to the very concept of attrition. The military strategy of every side is painted as absurd and hopeless, leading to the inescapable conclusion that the slaughter was an act of futility. Nevertheless, his discussion of the concept in financial terms (i.e. the cost of killing an enemy soldier) is unique and provides an interesting way of looking at (and quantifying) the loss of life.[11] Despite his stated reasons for the analysis (to argue that Britain should not have become involved), there is still a chilling resonance in the analysis, and it needs to be grappled with by historians of the war. While the attrition chapter may seem out of place among a series of chapters defined by geography and nationality, it actually fits in thematically very well. Attrition is, after all, an aspect of the war that is too often side-stepped rather than being made the subject of a careful analysis. It is one more crucial component of the war without which we cannot properly understand what took place between 1914 and 1918, and why.

Notes

1. This argument was made in an interview with Sir Michael Howard for *Conversations with History*, a long-running interview series at the University of California, Berkeley.
2. Black, Jeremy, *Rethinking Military History* (Abingdon: Routledge, 2004), p. 67.
3. The BBC's four-year 'World War One Centenary' plan foresees a truly prodigious amount of programming on television and radio.
4. Todman, Dan, *The Great War: Myth and Memory* (London: Hambledon Continuum, 2005), p. 221; Hanna, Emma, *The Great War on the Small Screen: Representing the First World War in Contemporary Britain* (Edinburgh: Edinburgh University Press, 2009), pp. 7–9.
5. Hanna, *The Great War on the Small Screen*, p. 13.
6. Sheffield, Gary, *Forgotten Victory: The First World War: Myths and Realities* (London: Headline Book Publishing, 2001), p. xiv.
7. Bond, Brian, *The Unquiet Western Front: Britain's Role in Literature and History* (Cambridge: Cambridge University Press, 2002), p. 75.
8. Winter, Jay and Prost, Antoine, *The Great War in History: Debates and Controversies, 1914 to the Present* (Cambridge: Cambridge University Press, 2005), p. 75.
9. Ibid., p. 73.
10. Gove, Michael, 'Why Does the Left Insist on Belittling True British Heroes?' *The Daily Mail* (2 January 2014). http://www.dailymail.co.uk/debate/article -2532930/   MICHAEL-GOVE-Why-does-Left-insist-belittling-true-British -heroes.html (last accessed 17 July 2014).
11. Fergusson, Niall, *The Pity of War: Explaining World War I* (New York: Basic Books, 1999), p. 336.

1
The Battle of the Ardennes, August 1914: France's Lost Opportunity

Simon House

On 3 August 1914 France and Germany declared war on each other. It was an event for which both nations' armies had prepared for decades, France since her catastrophic defeat in 1870–1871, Germany on a continuous basis since the time of Scharnhorst, Gneisenau and Clausewitz. Preparation consisted of building, training and equipping ever-larger conscript armies, and of planning. Germany had her Schlieffen Plan, France had Plan XVII. History has dealt more kindly with Schlieffen and his successors than it has with Joffre, the owner and executor of the latest and last French plan.

For years Schlieffen's plan was regarded as a study of genius, a war-winning creation in the style of the elder Moltke, marred only by the manner in which the younger Moltke chose to execute it. It is only recently that revisionist research has questioned the 'given' of the past, that if Moltke had strengthened his right wing as Schlieffen had wanted, even at the expense of the left, then France would once again have fallen. Now we question it all: was there a Schlieffen Plan at all? Written as a *Denkschrift* in 1905, did it have any relevance to the military situation pertaining in August 1914? Did Germany ever have, or plan to have, sufficient army corps to execute the Schlieffen concept? Could even the most modern and best-trained army in the world sustain the supply lines and rudimentary communications needed to command and control the vast force – nearly three-quarters of a million men – marching on a 400-kilometre loop across Belgium?[1] Despite revisionist argument and analysis, the Schlieffen Plan lives on in popular history: France saved by a whisker at the 'Miracle of the Marne', due to human error in execution.[2]

Plan XVII has been criticised from the outset. In 1930 Liddell Hart called it 'a negation of historical experience, indeed, of common sense', 'a plan by which a frontal offensive was to be launched with bare equality of force against an enemy who would have the support of his fortified frontier zone'. And he accused General Joseph Joffre, commander-in-chief of the French army, of being no more than 'a lever' for the designs of a group of young staff officers peddling a disastrous new doctrine of *offensive à outrance*, or 'all-out attack'.[3] According to Cyril Falls, Chichele Professor of Military History at Oxford University from 1946 to 1953, the plan was based on 'a disastrous doctrine', 'a sort of fanaticism, a veritable *mystique* of the offensive' that caused the unnecessary slaughter of tens of thousands of young innocent French conscript soldiers.[4] In recent years, fresh research has thrown new light on the French army's planning and performance during the opening phase of the war, and a new, more balanced appreciation of Joffre and of Plan XVII is beginning to emerge.[5] But, just as it is hard to shift the popular image of the Schlieffen Plan, no matter how detailed and compelling the new evidence, so, too, there is a long way to go before Joffre will be rehabilitated. This chapter, in examining Joffre's little-known offensive in the Ardennes on 22 August 1914, seeks to add weight to a new understanding of Plan XVII, and to reveal details of a significant lost opportunity for Joffre's armies to inflict a first defeat on Imperial German forces.

Plan XVII was, in fact, no more than a plan for the mobilisation and initial concentration and deployment of the French army.[6] Unlike the so-called 'Schlieffen Plan', which embraced a military strategy and set of initial operational moves designed to force a battle of annihilation and German victory, Joffre's Plan XVII stopped once the armies were in place and was then superseded by a series of General and Specific Instructions issued by the commander-in-chief's office (GQG) to the army commanders for the conduct of operations in the field.[7] Far from demonstrating stubbornly inflexible adherence to a single stupid frontal attack on the German frontier defences, this was a most flexible system of command and control, which worked so effectively that it enabled Joffre to plan and execute successive attacks, from right to left along the whole north-eastern front (i.e., what we today call the 'Western Front') in France and Belgium, culminating in the successful counter-attack on the Marne in September 1914.

Most of Joffre's attacks in August 1914 ended in defeat, but that was more a matter of tactics, and of the comparative quality of pre-war preparation, than of grand strategy. And one of those attacks – the Ardennes offensive of 22 August 1914 – achieved, as we shall see, the much sought-after goal of strategic surprise, delivering superior forces at the decisive point without discovery by the enemy. So deep-rooted and widespread is the continuing popular misconception about Plan XVII and its execution that it is difficult to know where not to start but to stop detailed analysis in a short chapter such as this. It is necessary to limit ourselves strictly to the narrow constraints of the Battle of the Ardennes, and to the lost opportunity contained therein.

The Battle of the Ardennes commenced early on the morning of 22 August 1914, when two French armies advanced due north from their start lines on the rivers Chiers and Semois into Luxembourg and the Belgian Ardennes. It was conceived by Joffre as a counter-attack against the major German thrust in the north from Aachen and Liège into Belgium; in essence, it was planned to sweep aside the weak forces covering the Ardennes forests and swing round the then exposed German right flank, trapping the 'northern group of German armies' (as it was known to French intelligence) between the Meuse and Ourthe rivers, where it would, of course, be annihilated.[8]

The Ardennes counter-offensive was the last of the first phase of attacks envisaged by Joffre in his General Instruction No. 1, issued on 8 August 1914.[9] It had been preceded by a limited *attaque brusquée* by a strengthened army corps of the French permanent frontier protection force into Alsace on 7 August, and then by a major attack into Lorraine by two French armies – Dubail's First and Caslelnau's Second – starting on 16 August.[10] The Lorraine attack was Joffre's one outright offensive, unconstrained by what the Germans were doing and intended to seize the strategic initiative. It failed, and, in two bloody encounters at Morehange and Sarrebourg on 20 August, the French were forced to withdraw. It is worth noting in passing that Joffre had wished to open his attacks in Belgium (as, indeed, the Germans were doing), but the politicians forbade him to breach Belgian neutrality; therefore, since French grand strategy was predicated upon bringing the Russians into action as quickly as possible, and to do so Joffre had promised to launch his own attack at the earliest opportunity, he had no choice but to attack across the common frontier in Alsace and Lorraine.[11]

Emphasis has been placed in this chapter on Joffre's flexible approach to planning the opening encounters of the war. Nothing exemplifies this better than the troop movements, redispositions, that he ordered during the four days of 18–21 August. Even though the Lorraine attack was presented and perceived as the major French offensive that was to be executed 'with all forces assembled' and with all the *cran, élan* and spirit of *offensive à outrance* that the French troops and local commanders could muster, Joffre was already weakening the attack force before the battles of 20 August in order to strengthen his left wing. On 18 August two army corps (XVIII and IX) were ordered to leave Lorraine and move to the Ardennes front, reducing Dubail's and Castelnau's attacking force by fully 20 per cent.[12] It is the strongest possible indication to the modern historian that Joffre was not totally fixated on Alsace-Lorraine, as is all too often suggested.

Equally significant in this respect is the fact that Joffre altered the initial deployment of de Langle de Cary's Fourth Army from that set out in Plan XVII, and in a way that suggests a particular line of thinking. The French Fourth Army was, according to Plan XVII, the reserve army, concentrating and deploying behind the other four armies lining up along the frontier. Its initial dispositions saw its four army corps located between Reims and Verdun, facing north-east and perfectly positioned to support the front line armies either south-east or north-east of Verdun. But on 2 August, even as the first troop trains were in transit, Joffre ordered a change of orientation, so that Fourth Army would position itself facing north, between Fifth Army on the left and Third Army in the centre.[13] This order suggests that from the very beginning Joffre was thinking of action on his left as well as on the right, and that he was thinking of giving Fourth Army a major role. So when, on 18 August, Joffre moved troops from his supposed main offensive to strengthen de Langle's Fourth Army, it suggests that Joffre's flexible planning process was in full flow, and the Ardennes front was gaining in importance.

The burgeoning concept of a counter-attack through the Ardennes was driven by French intelligence about German intentions and actions. Given that Joffre and his staff have been castigated by generations of historians for intelligence failures, and given the assertion already made in this paper that Joffre achieved strategic surprise when he attacked in the Ardennes, a review and reappraisal of France's intelligence situation is clearly required.

The first source of intelligence about Germany's initial deployment came from information gathered in and around the railheads. In a key intelligence assessment issued on 9 August 1914, 21 of Germany's 26 active army corps were correctly identified by name and number at their detraining points.[14] Unfortunately for Joffre's long-term plans, one that escaped identification (VI Corps) had sent its advance guard to the Eastern Front as part of the mobilisation, and was tagged there by French agents, while its subsequent transfer to the west went unnoticed. It went on to spring a surprise of its own when it appeared, still undetected, on the battlefield in the Ardennes on 22 August. As an overall piece of intelligence gathering, however, the French Intelligence Bureau's first report was good work, based as it was on Plan XVII's pre-war *Plan de Renseignements* and implemented by members of the French Intelligence Bureau's *Service spécial*.[15] Joffre's agents at the railheads had identified a northern group of about five or six army corps with two or three cavalry divisions disembarking at Aachen: about 20 per cent of the regular, active strength of the German army. Two other groups were gathering in the centre, either side of the fortress of Metz, each comprising about four army corps and two or three cavalry divisions; together these two groups constituted about 30 per cent of the active army. The two groups around Metz facing Verdun seemed at that stage to constitute the stronger force and greater threat. The northern group would have a long way to travel through Belgium before reaching the French frontier; nor was it yet clear on which side of the Meuse the Germans would deploy their greatest strength; therefore, Joffre could feel confident in launching his own pre-emptive strike across the common border in the south in his attempt to gain the initiative. But it is clear that, from this early date of 9 August, Joffre was watching developments in the north, and waiting for events there to clarify.

Joffre sent his cavalry corps to take up the intelligence gathering where the secret *Service spécial*'s reach ran out.[16] General Sordet took his three cavalry divisions north into the Ardennes on 6 August in order to clarify the situation regarding the northern group of German armies: were they increasing in strength? Would they march south, and, if so, when and on which bank of the River Meuse? But Sordet's mission was a complete failure, for three reasons. First, an early lesson about modern warfare was learned: lightly armed cavalrymen could no longer penetrate a defensive screen whose fire power was boosted by modern rifles, horse artillery and mobile (wagon-borne) machine gun companies, especially in the large formations of horsemen used by the French; when Sordet came up to the security screen around the northern group of armies near Liège and Namur, his horsemen could not penetrate it and could gather no useful information as to size or intent.[17] Second, in the vast area of the central Ardennes there was nothing to find: until Liège fell and the way was clear to advance in force across the Meuse, the central groups of German armies remained safely hidden behind the German/Luxembourg border, several days' march from where Sordet was searching. It was not until 18 August that the general order was given by Moltke to commence the great offensive, and by then Sordet and his troops would be long gone. Third, French cavalrymen did not look after their horses very well, and, after ten days of long and hard riding that exhausted their mounts, the cavalry corps was withdrawn.

So Joffre's initial picture of the situation in the north remained blurred and incomplete, and he did not feel ready to make firm plans.

One of the most enduring criticisms of French intelligence during this period, and one of the most telling, is the failure to realise that the Germans would use their reserve divisions in the front line, thereby effectively doubling the size, if diluting the quality, of the forces that Joffre would face. The report of 9 August from the railheads ignored reserve units, simply because they were still all gathering in their barracks deep in Germany. Only when the first-line (active) divisions left to march to their entraining points did the next tranche of older reservists come flooding in to the empty barracks to form the reserve divisions. Later French reports would contain details of reserve unit movement, and considerable data about their whereabouts was gradually collected; but that is where errors in analysis and interpretation mistakenly drew incorrect conclusions from accurate information. There was a well-documented rift between Joffre's intelligence staff and his operations staff, the latter believing themselves superior in judgement.[18] Those operational staff officers could not believe that, as a matter of principle, the Germans would do anything that they themselves would not do. French reserve divisions were poorly trained and unfit to enter the line of battle; so, by definition, German reserve divisions had to be the same. French reserve divisions travelled in a second line behind the first to guard lines of communication, rivers, bridges; so, by definition, that was what the German reserve divisions would do. The French knew where the German reserve divisions were – drawn up in a second line behind the first – but the operations staff simply discounted their value when calculating the odds during planning.

The upshot of all the French intelligence gathering, analysis and interpretation, of all Joffre's deliberation and calculation, was that by 20 August the generalissimo was convinced that a surprise thrust through the Ardennes northwards onto the open right flank of the northern group of German armies had the potential for a stunning success. If he could get de Langle's army in secret into the open spaces north of the forests around Neufchâteau, he could drive in and around the flank of the northern German group, trap them with their backs to the River Meuse and annihilate them.[19] Joffre had strengthened de Langle's Fourth Army by the addition of two army corps, so that by 20 August it contained five infantry and one cavalry corps, with a sixth corps concentrating in reserve and with two reserve infantry divisions in a second line, guarding the rivers and bridges. He believed that there were no more than two or three German corps in the Ardennes between the Semois and the objective, and he aimed to put twice that number against them.[20] In fact, there was a whole army (Fourth Army under Duke Albrecht von Würrtemberg) of five German corps, where Joffre saw at most three; but two were reserve corps that Joffre had convinced himself would remain in a second line, and one was the active corps (VI Corps) that had totally escaped French intelligence. Luckily for him and de Langle, however (and such is the nature of chance in war), only three of the five German corps were close enough to the battle zone to take part in the fighting on 22 August. So Joffre's conclusion was correct if based on a false premise. Duke Albrecht's Fourth Army had over 100 km of difficult terrain to defend, and thus two corps were deployed so far north that they could not intervene in the centre during the day of the battle. On the specific front of de Langle's army on 22 August, the overall odds were nearly 2:1 in favour of the French.

On 20 August de Langle received an order to prepare for an operation in the Ardennes. There is a debate that still has a long way to run on the subject of military operational art. Clausewitz divided war into two – strategy and tactics – and use of the word 'operation' or 'operations' was initially used to describe the phase of strategy that delivered forces and material to the chosen battlefield. Gradually, over the decades either side of the turn of the 19th/20th century, the term 'operation' began to develop a deeper meaning, to include the manoeuvre of large units in a coordinated manner on an enlarged battlefield – a battle front; and, by extension, a commander's operational remit included the steps he took and the orders he gave to secure his force during the phase of operational manoeuvre. In this context, General de Langle and his staff conspicuously failed to plan and execute the Ardennes operation properly.

De Langle had been given a cavalry corps to scout in front of his army and protect it from surprise. On 20 August, two days before the attack, the cavalry flushed out major units of Duke Albrecht's army, engaging them in a five-hour skirmish on the open terrain northwest of Neufchâteau – the central objective of the forthcoming attack.[21] From prisoners it was ascertained that elements of two divisions from two separate German corps were present, and that an additional reserve division was entering Neufchâteau town.[22] This intelligence was passed to GQG, where it was included in that night's intelligence briefing. Within Fourth Army, however, there was no further reference to, or preparation for, the likely presence of two German corps in the path of the proposed advance; indeed, such was the absence of 'operational' direction that none of the columns that advanced through the fog on the morning of

22 August had been briefed to expect contact; hence the commonly held view that the French were taken by surprise. In a further error of judgement, on the afternoon of 21 August, de Langle's powerful cavalry screen retired to take up a position on the left flank, so the vital 12 hours leading up to the engagement left the infantry columns suddenly without any early warning system.

The offensive began early on 22 August, its initial phase an approach march through the forests to the open terrain on the far side of Neufchâteau. There was a thick ground mist all across the Ardennes that morning, occasioned by the heavy rain the day before and the humidity of the river valleys during those very hot summer days; de Langle's columns would march unobserved from the air until the sun burned away the fog. This was the major factor in the surprise achieved by Joffre's attack; that, and the unexpected northerly direction of the advance. Each of the ten and one-half divisions (the half was an independent Colonial brigade attached to the Colonial Corps) of the army was allocated its own road, or track, through the forests, with its own objective town or village at the other end in which to bivouac. The catalogue of errors made at what we would call today the 'operational' level – army commander de Langle and his staff – was topped by the way they set the army on its march forward: no more than simple route march instructions, times, itineraries, geographic objectives were issued; no further mention of the two or more German army corps known to have been located near Neufchâteau, their main objective; no orders for heightened alert, no contingency plan in the case of contact.[23] Left to his own devices, each corps commander placed his own interpretation on the orders received. The overriding impression of the way the columns marched was one of complacency, of an unwarranted sense of security. This is exemplified best by General Lefèvre, commanding the Colonial Corps, who seems to have deliberately given his troops the impression that the Germans were several days' march away and that they could look forward to a stroll through the woods and a warm bivouac in Neufchâteau at nightfall;[24] or General de Villemejane of 33rd Division, who allowed his artillery to descend into a narrow forest track in the middle of enemy territory with the tampons still blocking the muzzles of guns rigged for route march, not action, and with no flanking infantry to provide warning of an approaching enemy.[25]

Much of the later myth that the Germans were lying in ambush waiting for the French to march into a trap stems from the fact that, at battalion and company level, the French soldiers were indeed caught by surprise, though they should not have been if their senior commanders had prepared them properly; that, and the fact that the equally surprised German battalions and companies reacted faster and were in action more quickly when the clashes occurred. There is absolutely no doubt that at all levels (from army down to battalion and company) the German commanders were caught by surprise.[26]

Generalleutnant Charles de Beaulieu (a German with an impossibly French name) had been ordered at very short notice, just after midnight on 21/22 August, to march his 12th Division south from its billets a little to the south-east of Neufchâteau down to the Semois River at Tintigny, there to fill a gap that had opened up between the Fourth and Fifth Armies.[27] There was at that time no inkling among the German commanders that the French attack had already begun. Beaulieu's division was part of the aforementioned German VI Corps that had eluded French intelligence in the initial railhead count and had arrived undetected in the Ardennes; and the whole corps was on the move. Beaulieu's troops set out at about 04.00; by 07.00 they were approaching the river through the woods when the advance guard unexpectedly encountered French patrols. Beaulieu was forced to deploy his leading regiment across and to either side of the road, spreading into the woods, in order to stop the French; his artillery was halted, unable to manoeuvre, let alone unlimber and find firing positions, in a long five-kilometre column stretching back towards Neufchâteau whence they came. Beaulieu had encountered the head of the French Colonial Corps column (on its insouciant march); the confrontation occurred in the woods some two kilometres north of Rossignol, after which the encounter battle was later to be named, and by default its initial phase became a close and bloody infantry encounter in which tactics and training – and sheer fighting ability – would decide victor and vanquished. It was a classic case of both sides being surprised.

Elsewhere, for a similar example, the first that Generalleutnant von Rampacher, commander of 21st Reserve Division at Neufchâteau, knew of the approaching French was when rifle fire shot down the horses and escorts of his supply column travelling westwards out of the town.[28] The surprise on the German side throughout Duke Albrecht's Fourth Army was absolute, the reaction and response both immediate and effective.

De Langle's columns, which caused such shock and surprise to his opponent Duke Albrecht, were aligned along a start line that was about 60 kilometres wide from Sedan to Montmédy. On the far left, General Eydoux's XI Corps marched along two roads that wound through the edge of the deep impenetrable area of ravines and forests that stretched westward to the steep gorge of the River Meuse. Eydoux's objective was the village of Maissin, there to halt, consolidate and anchor the whole Fourth Army front against the forests in the west. Eydoux's two divisions would encounter and fight one German division – 25th Division of XVIII Corps. Alongside Eydoux, but echeloned a little to his rear right flank, marched General Poline's XVII Corps, also utilising a road for each of its two divisions: 34th Division on the left would join in the fight against the German 25th Division, which thus fought against odds of three to one; 33rd Division (whose artillery we have seen plunge unprepared into dangerous forests) would be caught in the flank by XVIII Corps' other division, 21st Division, at Bertrix. So poor was its march security that it would be decimated in a melée without shape or (on the French side) control. In the centre marched General Pierre Roques' XII Corps, with the independent 5th Colonial Brigade up in support. It was to Roques that the greatest opportunity for battlefield success would be offered, when he encountered a single weak reserve division at Neufchâteau; he had both quantitative and supposed qualitative superiority (regular French soldiers versus older German reservists), yet failed to capitalise upon that advantage. Roques' lost opportunity will be examined in greater detail below. On Roques' right was the French Colonial Corps, which, as alluded to by the brief references above, became locked in a bitter close-quarters fire-fight in the woods above the Semoy River, an encounter that became an annihilation when the bulk of the German VI Corps came up in a classic encirclement manoeuvre and trapped the French with their backs to the river. Finally, on the extreme right of de Langle's wide front, General Gérard's II Corps (3rd and 4th Divisions) marched in one single snake-like column stretching a dozen kilometres or more from head to tail. The rationale was sensible; acting as flank guard to the army, the long column could at any time wheel to confront any surprise enemy advance. However, General Rabier, commanding Gérard's 4th Division, decided to disobey specific orders that he was to reach the south bank of the Semois River before nightfall. His excuse was that his men were tired; he would make up the time in the morning, and be in position at dawn. Of course he failed to keep his promise, and arrived late. The consequences were truly catastrophic: the full force of the German 11th Division flooded unopposed down from the north into the valley, crossed the unguarded bridge at Tintigny and proceeded to encircle the French Colonials on their right. German artillery set up on the high ground, from where the guns proceeded to first block, then blow up, the only bridge linking the 3rd Colonial Division with the rest of the French army, thus sealing its fate. The annihilation of 3rd Colonial Division, which suffered nearly 80 per cent casualties in killed, wounded and prisoners, was an entirely avoidable action caused by Rabier's unprofessional attitude to war.

The two disasters at Bertrix and at Rossignol, both self-inflicted, dominated the battlefield reports sent back to de Langle's headquarters during the late afternoon; XVII Corps had been routed and 3rd Colonial Division annihilated. Accurate intelligence was hard to come by. Truth be told, the communications between army and corps were so poor that de Langle had no idea what was happening on his left until after 18.00 that evening; he had lost command and control over the units under his command. Bad news invariably travels fastest; by early evening de Langle knew of the rout of 33rd Division at Bertrix, and reports from Rossignol of the critical situation of the trapped 3rd Colonial Division understandably dominated his attention. In the middle of all the bad news, reports from General Roques' XII Corps, indicating a situation reasonably under control, were a reassuringly bland confirmation that there at least there was nothing for de Langle to worry about.

The absence of further disaster on Roques' front was hardly a positive note, but it was at the time the best that de Langle had to cling on to. The pity is, however, that we now know with hindsight that Roques could have, should have been reporting France's first tactical victory of the war. Had Roques handled his corps with, say, the minimum degree of competence expected in the doctrine and field regulations that governed the French army, then Duke Albrecht's Fourth Army should have been split in two; the Germans should have been forced to try to plug a ten-kilometre hole in their long front at a time when they had no immediate reserves with which to do so. The consequences of a Roques victory at Neufchâteau stray into the counter-factual; suffice it to say that Roques squandered a clear opportunity to defeat the enemy in front of him.

When Fourth Army advanced at 04.00 on 22 August, the two divisional columns of Roques' XII Corps were in the centre. Roques had been ordered to advance north, bypassing Neufchâteau to the west – 5th Colonial Brigade was to occupy the town – and advancing across the plateau to the nearby town of Libramont, where XII Corps would set up for the night. Libramont was an important railway junction and crossroads; the old Roman road from Sedan passed through on its way towards the German border; and, unbeknownst to the French, it was also the forward command post of Duke Albrecht. Occupation of Libramont might well have afforded de Langle the unforeseen dividend of the capture of his opponent commander. Standing in the path of Roques' powerful corps was a single German division – Generalleutnant von Rampacher's 21st Reserve Division of XVIII Reserve Corps – which had moved up into Neufchâteau during 20 and 21 August to fill the widening gap between the few German units in the central Ardennes. Furthermore, the bulk of Rampacher's division was still massing inside the town when the action started, and was fixed and held in place by the surprise attack of the elite 5th Colonial Brigade. Only two regiments of Rampacher's unit had marched out westwards when they were hit in the flank by Roques' two divisions.

Roques' two columns marched due north. Rampacher's single column headed due west, out of Neufchâteau on the road to Bertix. The two sides would encounter each other at about 10.00 (French time) on 22 August near the village of Nevraumont, some five kilometres west of Neufchâteau; they were converging at right angles to each other. This meant that Rampacher's advance guard – 81 Reserve Infantry Regiment, commanded by Colonel Jordan and supported by a battery (six guns) of field artillery and a squadron of reserve cavalry – would meet the oncoming juggernaut of General du Garreau de la Méchenie's 24th Division, supported in column by the corps reserve infantry brigade, the corps artillery group and the corps cavalry regiment: in all, six regiments to the German one, 84 guns to six, several thousand cavalry to just over 100 – overwhelming odds by any measure. Furthermore, when the German advance guard turned to face the enemy (a 90° turn from west to south) it found its right flank 'hanging in the air', inviting Roques' abundant cavalry to find the gap, and exploit to the rear, and for Garreau's superior numbers of men to overlap around the open flank and envelop the enemy. None of which happened, as we shall see.

* * *

Colonel Jordan had reached the first range of hills west of Neufchâteau, at Petitvoir, when his cavalry patrols reported contact on his left. He deployed two of his three battalions into line, keeping his third in reserve, and sent the firing line forward, its right flank hanging in the air. But his men fought hard, using fire and movement tactics, and digging temporary field trenches to protect themselves when stopped.

Seen from the French side, their cavalry had occupied the high ground at Nevraumont overlooking Jordan's column and pushed patrols forward down into the valley, where they encountered both cavalry and infantry. Reports were sent to Roques and Garreau (marching together in the middle of 24th Division's column) that contact had been made. French cavalry seldom acted as dismounted riflemen unless specifically ordered to do so, however, and they ceded the high ground to Jordon's infantry, and rode to take up their battle position on the left flank of their advancing foot soldiers. At this point we can dispense with the French cavalry, for it took no further part in the battle. French cavalry doctrine required that fighting patrols be sent out to probe ahead, seeking exposed flanks; on this particular battlefield there was a wide-open German flank to be found and turned, but the French regimental commander received no orders to do so, nor did he use his initiative and act on his own account. So the opportunity to turn Colonel Jordon's line was missed, and both Roques and Garreau continued with a straightforward frontal fire-fight. Even so, the superiority of French artillery (once it could be brought into action) and the greater numbers of French infantry should have ensured Roques victory. Colonel Jordon had no reserves to bring up; his third battalion, held back in the first instance, was ordered by Jordon's superior officer not to go forward. Instead, the brigade commander ordered Jordon to withdraw the whole regiment back towards Neufchâteau, where the German divisional commander was seeking to rally and concentrate his meagre forces. With Jordon's forces engaged in a fighting withdrawal, step-by-step eastwards whence they came, the way to the north was opening up in front of Roques' eyes (he had his forward HQ at St Médard, alongside Garreau and a mere two kilometres from the firing lines, perfectly placed to oversee the battle), and yet he was not pressing forward towards his objectives, nor was he even pursuing a retreating enemy with very much vigour. The forward French battalions followed up slowly, cautiously, and not in great numbers, merely fighting patrols. One is entitled to ask where was the much-vaunted French *élan*, the spirit of *offensive à outrance*, that characterised French doctrine at the time, and the way history was later written.

To answer this question, we must retrace our steps to the moment when Garreau's leading infantry battalion replaced the French cavalry screen on the heights. With the cavalry gone, its first task was to recapture the village dominating the terrain, Nevraumont, suffering many unnecessary losses from rifle fire (the Germans, being a reserve unit, possessed no machine guns) as they did so. Nevertheless, sheer weight of numbers rapidly told, and pushed Jordon's skirmishers back. Soon a whole regiment of three battalions was lining the open hillside at Nevraumont, confronting the two German battalions in an increasingly intense fire-fight. But the German infantry had taken advantage of cover on the edge of the woods opposite the village, and the French commanders then chose to wait until their artillery was ready, and call down fire on their opponent. In the meantime a second and then a third regiment of French infantry arrived on the hill, and extended a thick firing line in frontal confrontation with the enemy. The odds became an impressive 9 to 2 in favour of the French infantry. The French divisional artillery (5 to 1 in numbers) went to work, and the French infantry waited for the German fire to slacken. Gradually the weaker German line was forced back until, after about three hours, the senior French officer at the front, Colonel Descoings, commander of 50th Brigade, whose two regiments were in the forefront of the battle, was able to report that the Germans were retreating to the north-east and his men were in pursuit. It was 14.00 (French time), and it was the seminal moment of the battle. If Descoings had led his six battalions vigorously in a north-easterly pursuit, as he clearly intended, there is little doubt that before nightfall Garreau could have brought up the rest of the division and driven the Germans off the battlefield back to Neufchâteau; and the route to the north, to Libramont and the empty German rear areas would have been open.

But at about this time Descoings was wounded in the shoulder and had to leave the field. As was often the case in the French army of 1914 when a charismatic and forceful leader suddenly disappeared, the impetus drained from the attacking French soldiers. Valuable time was lost while a replacement for Descoings came forward, and he (brigade commander General Sorin) was clearly not of the calibre of his colleague. The next message that Roques received reported 'significant' German forces debouching from the woods in the north; in fact, examination of German records shows conclusively that there were no more than an outlying company of infantry, some cavalry and a few stragglers in that direction, and the main German force was five kilometres further east. Nevertheless, Garreau ordered a full-scale divisional assault on the village in the north – Rossart – which he presumed wrongly to be a German strongpoint. It should be recalled that the idle French cavalry regiment on the open flank could and should have tried to ascertain the position and strength of the enemy in and around Rossart, but did not move from its passive position. Hours passed while the artillery was brought up to fresh positions from which it could direct fire on Rossart; reserves of fresh infantry were brought forward until Garreau's full 12 battalions were assembled. Then, at around 18.00, accompanied by a powerful bombardment, the infantry surged forward and captured the undefended village of Rossart at the point of the bayonet. Roques' triumphant divisions settled down to encamp on the battlefield, victors and possessors of the ground. Rampacher's decimated division, away to the east, licked its wounds and waited hopefully for reinforcement.[29]

By the morning of 23 August, the whole situation had changed. During the night, situation and intelligence reports arrived at each army headquarters, and each army staff analysed the data and laid plans for the day ahead. Duke Albrecht was relieved to find that the men of his XVIII Reserve Corps at Neufchâteau had beaten off a major attack. Reinforcements were arriving in the shape of the two corps from the north that had missed the previous day's battle. Even so, it took until after midday for the mauled units to recover from the fighting; composite units had to be formed from arriving fresh troops and the least harmed survivors of the battle. The German follow-up, when it came, was by no means dynamic or incisive.

This was just as well for de Langle. All the news gathered during the night was bad, and it was clear that on his left wing both XI Corps and XII Corps were exposed by the rout of XVII Corps and the decimation of the Colonials. De Langle had no choice but to withdraw his whole army behind the River Semois, and hope for the time to regroup.

That, in brief, was the Battle of the Ardennes. De Langle's army on 22 August fought five separate encounter battles, none of which was coordinated or impacted upon the others until after the event. At Bertix and Rossignol, the French suffered individual defeats, the result of which was to force de Langle to decide in the evening to withdraw to his start line. However, despite the losses and despite the defeats, de Langle's army was not broken. It continued to fight, day after day, as it continued to withdraw, but this time on Joffre's instructions and in conformance with the general retreat of the whole Allied army. Even as his 33rd Division was being decimated at Bertrix and 3rd Colonial Division was being annihilated at Rossignol, de Langle had at his disposal significant reserves: IX Corps, the Provisional Cavalry Corps and two reserve infantry divisions. Until it became quite clear that XVII Corps needed time to regroup and that both XI and XII Corps had lost momentum and were in static positions fearful of their flanks, de Langle wanted to renew the attack. Joffre and GQG also wanted to renew the attack, despite the knowledge of the setbacks. But de Langle and his staff were still not in control, and could not organise further offensive action until they had regrouped. What might have made a difference was a local victory to offset the defeats and wrong-foot the enemy.

This paper presents arguments for at least a partial rehabilitation of Joffre's reputation in respect of Plan XVII. No commander-in-chief should be held responsible for the operational and tactical mistakes of his subordinates, only for the selection and appointment of those who made the mistakes. And Joffre freely admits that in July 1914 the 'weeding out' of the old and incompetent from the officer corps had only just started and would have to be completed during the initial battles.[30] General de Langle de Cary has largely escaped criticism for his role in the battle, and it seems to me that his share of the blame has instead fallen on Joffre's shoulders. To cite but three important points at which de Langle failed: he failed to secure the exits from the forests, despite specific permission from Joffre to send forward strong advance guards for that purpose;[31] he failed to ensure that his corps commanders took seriously the known presence of at least two German corps on their march route when setting levels of security for a march through closed woodland;[32] and he allowed his strong cavalry screen to withdraw to the flank for the crucial 18 hours prior to contact with the enemy.[33] Indeed, there was a fourth, important, point: he failed to instil professional reporting discipline in his subordinates, which left him starved of battlefield intelligence on vital sectors of his front for the vital hours of the fighting on 22 August.[34] Furthermore, the following points can be made in Joffre's favour: his transfer of troops from his right to his left during the period 18–20 August remained unnoticed by German intelligence and delivered local superiority for his commanders to utilise; his choice of the direction and timing of the attack delivered to his field commanders the invaluable asset of strategic surprise; and he correctly insisted that Fourth Army was faced by no more than two or three German corps on 22 August and expected his generals to use their superior strength to overcome them. None of the above, however, excuses the mistakes that Joffre and GQG did make – failing to utilise Sordet's Cavalry Corps more effectively; failing to recognise the German use of reserve formations in the front line; and, perhaps most damningly, failing to accept that the level of skill in the French army of 1914 was not up to the offensive tasks asked of it.

There is no doubt that a breakthrough at Neufchâteau by Roques would have changed the shape of the battle, and in favour of the French. How far the French generals might have been capable of exploiting success is uncertain. Exploitation would have required initiative, and it is a moot point whether the French officer corps as an institution offered scope for use of initiative. This is a big subject, worthy of a chapter in its own right. My research, however, suggests that the French system in 1914 was based on a top-down, hierarchical structure of orders and reports, leaving little scope for initiative. Furthermore, French officer training during the decade leading up to war had not been as sharp and focused upon skill in war as on social and political acceptability.[35] One has only to look at the number of general officers Joffre felt it necessary to remove from post and send to Limoges before the end of the first month of the war – 58, with more to come – to see that pre-war policy had allowed too many second-rate commanders to remain at the top.[36] On the other hand, if the system did not teach or encourage the use of initiative, it was loose enough to allow talented individuals such as Foch, Franchet d'Espèry – or even Colonel Descoings – to exercise their own initiative. The problem for the French in August 1914 was that such talent was scarce, and its application random.

It is, however, clear from official German sources that Moltke would not have allowed Hausen's Third (Saxon) Army to cross the Meuse in support of Bülow and Kluck until the threat to his lines of communication was eliminated.[37] Because Roques lost his opportunity, Hausen crossed the Meuse on 23 August, and proceeded to add the weight of his four army corps to the six corps of Bülow in the ensuing attacks on Lanrezac's Fifth Army. If Hausen had been delayed, even for one or two days while the Ardennes situation was cleared up, the balance of forces fighting west of the Meuse would have shifted in Joffre's favour. Would he have been able to take advantage of such a situation? What might have been the outcome in that event? Such questions take us into the realm of speculation. Professor Herwig, however, in his analysis of the lead-up to the battle of the Marne, writes: 'If either Bülow or Hausen failed to press the enemy hard at all times and allowed Lanrezac freedom of action, there was a danger that especially Hausen's Third Army could be driven by French Fifth Army against Langle de Cary's Fourth Army in the Ardennes.'[38] The argument presented in this chapter is that Roques had it in his power to create the very scenario that Professor Herwig envisages, and failed to deliver. Beyond that is speculation; Roques' conduct of his action at Neufchâteau on 22 August certainly constitutes a lost opportunity for France; however, the magnitude of the loss can never be conclusively measured, leaving it to individual opinion as to what might have been.

Notes

1. Among the voluminous bibliography on this subject, see in particular: Gerhard Ritter, *The Schlieffen Plan: Critique of a Myth* (London: Wolff, 1958); Terence Zuber, *Inventing the Schlieffen Plan* (Oxford: Oxford University Press, 2002); Terence Zuber, 'Terence Holmes Reinvents the Schlieffen Plan', *War in History*, Vol. 8, No. 4, (2001) pp. 468–476; Robert T. Foley, 'The Origins of the Schlieffen Plan', *War in History*, Vol. 10, No. 2, (2003) pp. 222–232; and the rest of the chain of articles in that periodical, including contributions by G.P. Goss, Annika Mombauer and Antulio J. Echevarria.

2. See: Holger H. Herwig, *The Marne, 1914* (New York: Random House, 2009), pp. 266–306, for an exposition of the 'myth' surrounding Colonel Hentsch's mission.
3. B.H. Liddell Hart, *History of the First World War* (London: Cassell and Company Ltd, 1970 edition), pp. 71–72.
4. Cyril Falls, *The First World War* (London: Longmans, Green & Co., 1960), pp. 15–16.
5. For example: Dimitry Queloz, *De la Manoeuvre Napoléonienne à l'Offensive à Outrance: La Tactique Générale de l'Armée Française 1871–1914* (Paris: Economica, 2009); Michel Goya, *La Chair et L'Acier: l'invention de la guerre moderne (1914–1918)* (Paris: Tallandier, 2004); Robert A. Doughty, *Pyrrhic Victory: French Strategy and Operations in the Great War* (Cambridge, Mass: Harvard University Press, 2005), chapters 1 and 2.
6. *Ministère de la Guerre, État-Major de l'Armée, Service Historique: Les Armées Françaises dans la Grande Guerre, Tome premier, Premier Volume* (Paris: Imprimerie Nationale, 1922) [hereinafter 'AFGG I/1'], Chapter I, pp. 33–91.
7. See AFGG I/1, Annexes for copies of every GQG Instruction issued from 3 August 1914 onwards.
8. Simon J. House, *The Battle of the Ardennes 22 August 1914*, Unpublished thesis (London: Kings College, 2012), pp. 46–48.
9. AFGG I/1, Annex 103.
10. French and German armies, corps and divisions bearing the same numbers appear continually in this chapter.
11. *Mémoires du Maréchal Joffre (1910–1917: Tome Premier)* (Paris: Librarie Plon, 1932), pp. 120–122.
12. AFGG X/1: Order of Battle of Second Army (p. 88), Fourth Army (p. 204) and Fifth Army (p. 266) in August 1914.
13. AFGG I/1, Annex 33: *GQG, Paris, 2 août, 19.30: IVe armée, variante à la concentration.*
14. AFGG I/1, Annex 125: *Groupement connu des forces allemandes actives.*
15. AFGG I/1, Annex 10: *Plan XVII Plan de Renseignements.*
16. AFGG I/1, Annex 59: *GQG, 5 août, 19.00: Commandant en chef à commandant corps de cavalerie, à Charleville.*
17. M. von Poseck, *The German Cavalry in Belgium and France, 1914* (Berlin: E.S. Mittler & Sohn, 1923, trans. Captain Alexander C. Strecker, US Cavalry and printed by US War Office [IWM Collection]), pp. 42–43.
18. Jean de Pierrefeu, *French Headquarters 1915–1918* (London: trans. Major C.J.C. Street, publ. Geoffrey Bles).
19. AFGG I/1, Annex 706.
20. AFGG I/1, Annex 749: *Armée de Stenay, Bulletin de renseignements No. 7.*
21. AFGG I/1, Annex 685: *Compte rendu de renseignements du 20 août.*
22. AFGG I/1, Annex 748.
23. For example, AFGG I/1, Annex 751: *Ordre particulier pour le 2e corps d'armée et le corps colonial.*
24. AFGG I/1, Annexes 793 and 794: *Corps coloniale bulletin de renseignements no. 2 & ordre general d'opérations no11 pour le mouvement du 22 août.*
25. General J. Paloque, 1914,*Bertrix* (Paris: Charles-Lavauzelle & Cie., 1932).
26. *Der Weltkrieg 1914 bis 1918, Die militärischen Operationen zu Lande, Erster Band* (Weltkrieg 1) (Berlin: Reichsarchiv, E.S. Mittler & Sohn, 1925), p. 316.

27. The following description of the Battle of Rossignol is an abridged version of that in: Simon J House, *The Battle of the Ardennes 22 August 1914*, Unpublished thesis (London: Kings College, 2012), pp. 222–239, where primary sources are cited.

28. A full description of this action can be found in: Simon J House, *The Battle of the Ardennes 22 August 1914*, Unpublished thesis (London: Kings College, 2012), pp. 124–131, where primary sources are cited.

29. The scenario of the battle at Nevraumont, described above, cannot be found in any other work. It is new research drawn from meticulous examination of both French and German archival material, at the Archives in Vincennes and Freibourg and from the foreign collection at the Imperial War Museum. For a full list of sources and citations, see: Simon J House, *The Battle of the Ardennes 22 August 1914*, Chapter 3, pp. 118–174.

30. *Mémoires du Maréchal Joffre (1910–1917: Tome Premier)* (Paris: Librarie Plon, 1932), pp. 301–302.

31. AFGG I/1, Annex 640: [Fourth Army] *Armée de Stenay,20 août 1914: Instruction personnelle et secrète aux commandants de corps d'armée de l'armée de Stenay.*

32. J. Moreau, *22 août 1914, Journal du commandant Jean Moreau, chef d'état-major de la 3e division Coloniale* (retranscribed and with commentary by Éric Labayle and Jean-Louis Philippart, Anvoi, Parçay – sur-Vienne, 2002) (Rossignol), p. 54.

33. General V. D'Urbal, *Souvenirs et Anecdotes de Guerre 1914–1916* (Paris: Berger-Levrault, 1939), p. 25.

34. AFGG I/1, Annex 927: [11 CA] *De Paliseul, déposé le 22/8 à 10.10: Général commandant 11e corps à commandant armée Stenay.* [Received at Stenay at 10.55]; and AFGG I/1 (1936), p. 414.

35. Hew Strachan, *The First World War, Volume I: To Arms* (Oxford University Press, 2001), pp. 226–227.

36. Ibid., p. 217: 'By 6 September 1914 Joffre had dismissed three army commanders, seven corps commanders, thirty-four divisional commanders and fourteen brigadiers.'

37. *Der Weltkrieg 1914 bis 1918, Die militärischen Operationen zu Lande, Erster Band* (Weltkrieg 1) (Berlin: Reichsarchiv, E.S. Mittler & Sohn, 1925), pp. 316, 334.

38. Holger H. Herwig, *The Marne, 1914* (New York: Random House, 2009), p. 161.

2

'Only Inaction Is Disgraceful': French Operations Under Joffre, 1914–1916

Jonathan Krause

The historiography of the First World War has been overshadowed by a single monolith for generations: the spectre of the war's roughly ten million military dead. That figure, unimaginably high, has for decades been treated as an argument in and of itself for the obvious futility of the conflict. One can trace the argument's lineage back to Remarque, the war poets, AJP Taylor, Joan Littlewood and the many other influential writers who have dominated public perceptions of the war. On a purely national level many Britons still wonder why they participated in a Continental war, and some argue outright that Britain should have remained neutral.[1] Around the world casual observers openly wonder with incomprehension why the entire war was fought at all. While the historiography concerning the causes of the First World War is very mature, and continues to fruitfully evolve, there is still work to be done to explain (if not necessarily to 'justify') why the war was fought in the manner it was.[2]

Ian Ousby, in his book *The Road to Verdun*, provides a case in point for the most commonplace interpretation of the Entente's conduct of the war. He lauds the Germans for remaining on the defensive on the Western Front, and contrasts this against the folly of the Entente, who he characterises as 'bone-headed at top and devoid of initiative below'.[3] Ousby goes on to state a common perception of the First World War, saying: 'attrition was always a flawed concept. Often it was deliberately muddled, the muddle providing convenient room for excuse after failure.'[4] Unfortunately, Ousby did not manage to find a good explanation for the Entente's seemingly inexplicable folly. This chapter seeks to do just that by explaining why the French army continually launched attack after attack in the first two years of trench warfare, despite repeated tactical setbacks (and, in some instances, disasters).

French strategy after the solidification of the Western Front was dictated by one unavoidable fact: France had been invaded and was occupied by some two million Germans. The only acceptable response was to attack the occupying forces and drive them out of France (this is the reason that Joseph Joffre, commander-in-chief of the French army from 1914–1916, was so vehemently opposed to 'side-show' expeditions to places like Salonika and the Dardanelles).[5] There was, of course, a serious problem with this: going over the top was exceptionally dangerous, and attacks brought with them a heavy price in life and limb. General Charles Mangin is said to have observed that '*Quoi qu'on fasse, on perd beaucoup de monde*': 'Whatever we do, we lose a lot of men.' It was a soberingly accurate comment from a man nicknamed 'The Butcher'.

Tactical commanders, especially those who lived and worked in the trenches (as brigadier and even some divisional generals often did), had to face this hard reality day in and day out. The more competent and attentive of them, therefore, did all they could to preserve the lives of their men. These efforts can be seen not only in standard procedures aimed at reducing 'wastage' (casualties inflicted piecemeal from a range of sources, some human and some environmental), but also in the tactical models used by many of these commanders. Herein lies the friction: strategic commanders like Joffre felt compelled to win strategic victories (this meant attacking the Germans), while good tactical commanders were doing everything they could to preserve the lives of their men, which meant only attacking if there was a good, clear purpose and a high likelihood of success (itself often dependent on receiving reinforcements from the reserves of men, guns and munitions held at army level or in general reserves). What follows is a brief look at how this friction played out in the first two years of trench warfare during Joseph Joffre's tenure as commander-in-chief.

The War of movement (and of casualties . . .)

The principal belligerents who would initiate the First World War had spent years planning for the eventuality of a conflict not unlike that which would erupt in August 1914. This was an inevitable response to the breakdown of Europe into two opposed camps (France and Russia allied against Germany, Austria-Hungary and Italy).[6] Unsurprisingly, there were ongoing efforts to align the strategy of the individual partners within these, at times awkward, groupings of nations.[7] The Central

Powers, for example, had to prepare for multiple concurrent two-front wars, in which each power had very different objectives. These differences made planning a co-operative war very difficult, and at times downright acrimonious.[8] Disagreement between Helmuth von Moltke, commander-in-chief of the German army, and his Austrian counterpart, Conrad von Hötzendorf, had reached such a pitch in 1909 that Conrad had outright threatened to sit behind the Carpathians and let Berlin fall if Germany refused to allocate more troops to the Eastern Front in the event of war with Russia.[9]

For France, war-planning was somewhat more straightforward. If a major European war came, it would principally be fought along a single front. While in theory this should have led France to develop more detailed war plans, in practice it did the opposite. France's Plan XVII was not the explicit, timetabled operational construct that its German counterpart was. Instead, it was a more flexible (some might even say 'vague') concentration plan, which did little more than set broad parameters within which the various French armies would operate.[10] Such a plan left an enormous amount of control over the use and deployment of armed forces in the hands of Joseph Joffre, a man who already wielded vast influence over military matters. In effect, Joffre would be able to improvise in the opening weeks of the war, and did so with remarkably little oversight.

With both the French and the Germans hoping for swift victory in 1914 (fearing that their respective societies would collapse under the strain of a lengthy war), the combat on the Western Front took on a highly aggressive character.[11] Into this maelstrom the French made heavy, but uncoordinated, thrusts. French formations groped their way forward with insufficient reconnaissance. The infantry was frequently sent into battle without artillery support, or even the support of neighbouring units.[12] Commanders too often made gross errors of judgement, preferring bold audacity to a sober assessment of their situation. Foch's (probably apocryphal) statement, 'my centre is giving way, my right is retreating; situation excellent, I attack', while commanding the elite XX ('Iron') Corps in Lorraine summed up the thought process of too many French commanders during the opening phases of the war.

Joffre had a monumental task before him. In the opening weeks of the war the Germans had taken most of Belgium and large swaths of north-eastern France, the nation's industrial heartland. The French army would suffer enormous casualties (1914's five months would claim 301,000 French lives, making 1914 the second deadliest year of the war for the French), and had found their tactical model severely wanting.

Joffre, early on, exhorted his subordinates to take more care in their operations, and to proceed without undue loss of life, but this was insufficient; it was clear that many officers at all levels were simply incompetent.[13] In a desperate attempt to right the ship Joffre began to remove officers seen as underperforming and sent them to Limoges, a small town far from the front.[14] By the end of the year 162 generals or colonels had been '*limogé*' by Joffre, representing 40 per cent of all higher-level commanders; 70 per cent of the French army's corps commanders were sacked between August and December 1914.[15] This ruthless house-cleaning made possible the French army's rapid rehabilitation; it also meant that a large number of senior officers directly owed their rapid promotion to Joffre, yet further increasing his power and influence within the army.[16] The French army which saved Paris during the 'miracle' of the Marne in September 1914 was already very different from that which had marched to war just a month earlier.

As the trench stalemate congealed along the Western Front in the last months of 1914, the improvement of the French army had only barely begun. Unfortunately, the demands of allies (especially Russia) and the political pressure which arose from the German occupation of French territory meant that Joffre could not wait for the French army to be fully ready before going back on the offensive. Thus, on 20 November Joffre telegraphed Foch to ask if the Eighth Army, part of Foch's Provisional Northern Army Group (*Groupe Provisoire du Nord*, GPN), would soon be ready to return to the offensive. Joffre argued that 'The enemy's passive attitude and the inactivity of his artillery... would appear to indicate that he is short of ammunition, or else that he is reorganizing his forces as a result of his heavy losses in the recent battles.'[17] Unfortunately, this sort of strategic optimism was common among senior commanders in the First World War. Falkenhayn thought that the French were at the breaking point by the end of 1915, and therefore felt confident that an attritional hammering at Verdun would force the French to sue for peace.[18] This impression was not shared by other senior German commanders, but was strong enough in Falkenhayn's mind to convince him he could 'bleed France white'.[19] Similarly, Douglas Haig at times indulged in overoptimistic projections of just how badly worn down the Germans were in 1916; the implication being that German forces were approaching their breaking point.[20]

Joffre's strategic miscalculations tended to be based on the simple observation that the Entente had a substantial manpower advantage over the Germans. The effect of this advantage was, at least in theory, magnified by its being spread out across several fronts. The basic concept, then, was to simply apply pressure on each of these fronts simultaneously. Eventually, somewhere, the German line would give. What Joffre's theory did not take into account was the ability of out-numbered forces to provide stiff resistance in the face of an attack, especially if that attack was poorly supported or conceived. Yet unaware of the magnitude of the tactical problem his army faced, and feeling that there might be a brief window of opportunity as the Germans sup-posedly 'reorganised', Joffre decided to act. On 30 November 1914 he released an official note stating his intention to return to the offensive at the nearest opportunity. The French would launch their first organised trench attack two and a half weeks later.

The first battle of Artois (16–18 December 1914) was an experiment. The French Tenth Army, under General Louis de Maud'huy, would seek to capture the hill of Notre Dame de Lorette, just a little over a kilometre north-west of Vimy Ridge. Having not yet planned an attack against such a defensive network, the French were faced with two operational models to choose from: the attack could seek to annihilate the enemy in a general offensive, or it could be a methodical battle, which would chip away at the enemy in a series of small, but secure, engagements. Foch was consistently in favour of a slower, methodical approach, saying: 'it is less important to advance rapidly, *but essential to move securely*, step by step, as each objective is gained'.[21] Joffre preferred to seek larger strategic victories, partially due to his need to show France's allies (and potential allies) the strength of French arms in battle. This debate between the methodical and the 'breakthrough' battle (in which the trenches would be overrun, and battle would be fought in the open) would be the central debate of the French army in the First World War.

First Artois would prove to be an unmitigated failure. Tenth Army did not have sufficient heavy artillery (or, indeed, many of the other cru-cial tools of trench warfare) to break the German trench lines. In an attempt to alleviate their lack of artillery, it was planned to launch the attack in stages so that each infantry attack could have the full weight of Tenth Army's artillery behind it. Tenth Army's three corps would make individual attacks across three days, the XXI *Corps d'Armée* (CA) on the 16th, X CA on the 17th, and XXXIII CA on the 18th. None of them proved successful. Nevertheless, it was an important learning exercise for the French army, and especially for three of its intellectual leaders: Foch, Philippe Pétain (commanding XXXIII CA) and Marie Émile Fayolle, commanding 70ᵉ DI (XXXIII CA). These gen-erals were early proponents of methodical, firepower-intensive battle organised to minimise the loss of life that was so endemic on the

Western Front (on average some 890 French soldiers died every single day of the war).[22]

The failure of First Artois notwithstanding, Joffre pushed for a return to the offensive as soon as possible. His reasoning for preferring to attack changed little over the course of his tenure as commander-in-chief. Joffre felt the need, strategically and politically, to drive the Germans out of France, to maintain the initiative over the Germans and also to help the Russians as much as possible.[23] This desire to help Russia is easily criticised, especially in regard to 1915. The French would launch an astounding number of offensives up and down the front in 1915 in Artois, Champagne, Les Éparges and the Woëvre, to say nothing of the countless small, local attacks occurring up and down the front (which Joffre referred to as *grignotage*: 'nibbling'). Ultimately, none of them provided any obvious assistance to the collapsing Russian army, which in 1915 made the single greatest retreat of the entire war (losing all of Poland and large swaths of Galicia, Lithuania and western Russia).[24] For the French, however, and for Joffre in particular, it was crucial to do what they could to try to save Russia. Joffre had laboured hard in the pre-war years to tie Russia into a binding military agreement that would compel the Russian army to act vigorously in the event of war with Germany; he could hardly rest on the defensive and also maintain his credibility when Russia was in such dire straits.[25] Of course, there were direct benefits to be gained by trying to assist the Russian war effort: keeping Russia afloat meant pinning down hundreds of thousands of Germans on the Eastern Front, thus keeping them out of France.

When discussing French strategy it is important to remember that the assistance France gave to its allies served ultimately to reaffirm its position as the principal Entente member (a position it held in respect of its contribution to the war effort, and its fighting on the decisive front).[26] This assistance came in many forms. Along the Western Front, the British and Belgians were both the regular recipients of materiel from France (everything from sandbags and corrugated iron to field artillery and ammunition), especially early on in the war.[27] Italy, Greece and Russia also received assistance at various times throughout the conflict. Of course, these exchanges should not be construed as charity (least of all for Britain, which provided substantial quantities of capital and materiel to its allies). Beyond the immediate military benefit of helping allies fight more effectively, some of the French exchanges were made on a *quid pro quo* basis. The provision of military assets to Italy, for example, was predicated on the creation of a mixed Franco-Italian military commission.[28] From a French perspective this would not only ensure that

Italy's efforts were more effective, but would also introduce a degree of French influence over Italian operations. The material assistance France provided to its allies naturally sat alongside the contribution of French forces to operations which were fundamentally of little importance to Metropolitan France. The presence of substantial numbers of French troops in the Dardanelles, Salonika and Italy attest to France's desire to support its allies and to justify its pre-eminence in the Entente.[29] That said, we should not overlook the more immediate and practical considerations that led to France's involvement in certain theatres, some of which were far from their existential fight on the Rhine. The deployment of significant French forces to support the Gallipoli campaign, for example, was calculated to justify territorial claims French colonialists wanted to pursue in the Middle East (notably in Syria) once the war was over.[30] French campaigns in the Cameroons were likewise conducted more with an eye towards territorial aggrandisement than in any hope that such action would weaken Germany's ability to fight a war in Europe.[31] There was often a blurred line between supporting, coordinating with and even competing against allied powers (mainly Britain) in many of these 'side-show' theatres.

It was thus not without a range of strategic imperatives in mind that Joffre ordered a return to offensive operations on the Western Front. The French army's next offensive would be in Champagne, a sparsely populated region of relatively flat chalk which would not pose the terrain difficulties of the hilly and populous Artois region.[32] As in Artois, local attacks were launched by the French and the Germans with daily regularity in the Champagne, seriously attriting the fighting capacity of both forces. Nevertheless, Fourth Army found itself outnumbering the Germans 155,183 to 81,500, by grace of substantial reinforcements from neighbouring units and French army reserves. Fourth Army could also boast the largest concentration of artillery yet (879 guns, 110 of which were heavies).[33] When the men of Fourth Army went over the top on 16 February they met with mixed results. Some units managed to take the German first and second positions in their initial rush, others were stopped cold; all suffered grievous casualties.[34] Local successes could not be exploited, as reserves were frequently kilometres away from the fighting by the time they were ordered to move forward. Follow-up attacks on the 17th and 18th met with a similar combination of minor local successes, widespread failures and heavy casualties.

Barely more than a week after the battle began, operation orders had given up on ingenuity, with some commanders simply ordering 'same troops, same objective' for days on end.[35] Artillery preparations were short (frequently 30 minutes or less) and largely uniform, thus leaving no room for misinterpretation by the Germans. Morale sagged as a result of heavy casualties and vicious winter weather; frostbite was common. Ignoring these legitimate concerns, General J.B. Dumas, commanding XVII CA, issued a directive on 9 March arguing that the attacks simply were not being pushed forward in earnest. He recommended pistol-whipping men who refused to go over the top.[36] Nevertheless, resistance to suicidal attacks was voiced throughout the middle and lower ranks. On 27 February Commandant Martin, commanding the 1st battalion (104e RI, *régiment d'infanterie*), was ordered to attack the trenches opposite him, despite having suffered heavy casualties in a failed attack the day before. He impressed on his regimental commander that his men were in no state to launch another attack. Casualties aside, he had been unable to establish any reliable contact with his neighbouring units, or with the artillery that was ordered to support his attack. Concerning the plan for the attack itself, he wrote:

> The operation, as it presents itself, does not appear to have been changed [from previous attacks] and it appears to me that the only result must be very high, inescapable losses for those engaged, the destruction of the troops who will take part [in the offensive]; this without the hope of conquering one metre of terrain and exposing ourselves to the [potential] loss of terrain already conquered.[37]

Despite Commandant Martin's protestations, the attack went in at 10.00 on 27 February. Due to the regiment's inability to liaise with its artillery, the advancing French troops suffered deadly friendly fire during the opening assault. A second attack was made at 17.00, but was cut down by German small arms fire.[38] No progress was made, and casualties were heavy; the lead sections suffered 75 per cent casualties in a matter of minutes. The only positive result of the day was the sacking of 104e RI's commander, and his replacement by Commandant Martin.

The beginnings of a functional doctrine

After a month of bloody failures Joffre had to accept that the Champagne battle was going nowhere, and on 15 March he formally brought the battle to an end. The French had suffered 260,000 casualties, and to no avail; the line had moved a mere three kilometres, and only in the most successful sector of the battle. Nevertheless, the initial attack had been a heavy blow to the Germans. A German document captured by the British stated that Karl Von Einem's Third Army felt at the absolute breaking point in the opening days of the battle. After the initial shock, however, German reinforcements began to arrive and the French attacks lost cohesion and impetus.[39] By 20 February the Germans no longer felt threatened, even though the battle would last a further three weeks; in the end the Germans would lose less than half as many casualties during First Champagne as the French.[40]

Most attacks in the First World War followed this predictable curve of diminishing returns. The opening day or two of an attack yielded the vast majority of the ground, prisoners and guns. Afterwards, tired troops, a stretched supply line and the arrival of enemy reinforcements would combine to sharply curtail the efficacy of any further attacks. After the initial window of opportunity was lost, battle descended into attritional slogging matches. Most senior commanders understood this phenomenon, and two different methods arose to try to overcome it. Joffre's response was to reaffirm his belief that 'the hour of success is fleeting'.[41] His proposed response was to do everything possible to put troops in a position to exploit momentary enemy weaknesses before they disappeared.[42] Foch, whose GPN was responsible for launching the next attack, approached the problem differently.

On 24 March Foch presented to Joffre his plan for a renewed offensive in the Artois region.[43] His plan saw the battle as developing in three distinct phases. First, the XXXIII and XX CA (situated in the centre of Tenth Army) would advance and take the villages between their position and Vimy Ridge. After that operation had succeeded, XXI CA would capture Notre Dame de Lorette and the village of Souchez, thus clearing the northern flank of the XXXIII and XX CAs. Lastly, the X and XVII CAs would attack along the southern flank. Only after all three operations had taken place would Tenth Army attempt to take Vimy Ridge. Foch made it clear that Tenth Army must 'consider these attacks from the point of view of their succession in time'.[44] Foch's response to the stubborn trenches on the Western Front was to capitalise on the initial superiority that the attacker enjoyed. Attacks would be short, sharp and supported by overwhelming firepower levelled against clear and discrete objectives. Foch was thinking at the yet-unnamed operational level of war, building several tactical successes into strategic victories. Commanders like Joffre were trying to get strategic results out of singular tactical victories, a goal better suited to the time of Napoleon than to the industrial wars of the 20th century.

Tenth Army, by this point under the command of General Viktor D'Urbal, would follow Joffre's strategic vision and attempt to capture

Notre Dame de Lorette and Vimy Ridge in one bound, rather than in a series of successive battles. Foch's methodical, three-part battle had been transformed into an all-out general offensive, a decision which had been beyond Foch's power to control.[45] His role at the head of the GPN was one of coordination rather than command. Foch was to liaise with the British and Belgians on the northern flank of the Western Front, and ensure that their efforts lined up with those of the French; despite his desire to improve tactics, he could not force his vision on to commanders who were nominally his subordinates. Foch's institutional inability to enforce a more realistic framework for the offensive would contribute to the ultimate failure of the attack.

Despite the battle's recasting as a general offensive, rather than a lengthy 'operation', it was initially very successful. On 9 May the 77th and Moroccan divisions (part of Pétain's XXXIII CA) advanced over four and a half kilometres in a mere hour and a half.[46] This feat was in part enabled by the use of new tactics laid out in a doctrinal note (*'But et conditions et d'une action offensive d'ensemble'*, 'Goal and Conditions of a General Offensive' or 'Note 5779'), which had been released in April.[47] Unfortunately, with Tenth Army's efforts spread along the entirety of its front, not every sector got the artillery preparation it needed, especially in the very difficult terrain around Notre Dame de Lorette to the north and the village of Neuville-Saint-Vaast to the south. These areas would not be taken in the initial assault, and so could fire upon the troops fighting atop Vimy from both flanks and even their rear.[48] Faced with such overwhelming fire, the 77th and Moroccan divisions would ultimately have to pull back, and give up their hopes of carrying the ridge in the initial attack. Subsequent efforts were launched on 11 May, and again from 16 to 18 June, without avail; the 'breakthrough' battle had failed once more.

Searching for a winning model

As the largest single advance the French had yet made against an established trench network, 9 May remained a topic of great interest. By 20 May GQG had produced an update for *But et Conditions...* based on the actions of 9–11 May (the first of several over the course of 1915). The report stated that Second Artois had 'entirely confirmed the value of the principles and procedures laid out in the note of...16 April 1915, notably in regards to the importance of a detailed preparation'.[49] This sentiment was shared by most commanders. The French art of attack would continually improve and be refined as the war progressed, but the basics had been firmly established and widely agreed upon. What became contentious, however, was the interpretation of what the near-success of 9 May meant for future operations.

After the battle, Joffre, Pétain (who had become an army commander in June), Foch and Castelnau (head of the new *Groupe des Armées du Centre*; the Centre Army Group) exchanged their thoughts on how the French army should proceed. Foch had been very pleased with aspects of Second Artois, but stated his opinion that the French did not yet have enough modern heavy guns or poison gas shells to pursue grand, general offensives like that of 9 May. In the meantime, Foch wrote, the French should focus on launching smaller attacks with clear objectives, which could be easily conquered with minimal loss of life.[50] In short, Foch was again proposing a step-by-step, methodical approach to fighting on the Western Front. Pétain broadly agreed, stating that the French needed to seriously scale back their ambitions for each attack, and to focus on discrete, firepower-intensive operations to capture individual key pieces of terrain quickly, and without too many casualties. Pétain seconded Foch's vision of a series of small, interconnected battles fought in succession, which would capitalise on the advantages held by the attacker in the initial two or three days of a battle.[51]

These views were opposed by Castelnau, whose *Groupe des Armées du Centre* (GAC) occupied the Champagne region. Castelnau felt that limited attacks could only ever yield small, meaningless results and that, instead, attacks should only be launched along large fronts, and have as their goal a 'breakthrough' of the enemy trenches.[52] He argued that, since Tenth Army had clearly demonstrated that the new French tactical system worked, the French should press home their advantage with a major, ambitious offensive which sought a serious strategic victory over the Germans. Castelnau even went so far as to boast that an attack launched by his GAC would yield 10–12 kilometres in the first 24–48 hours, and that the first enemy position would be taken 'with rifles at the shoulder'.[53] Foch strongly disagreed, arguing that Castelnau's proposed battle 'does not appear to offer an appreciable tactical result .... it lacks an aim. It will be a pure loss.'[54] Foch's opinion was shared by General Marie Émile Fayolle, the acerbic general who had succeeded Pétain as commander of XXXIII CA.[55] Joffre, still seeking a decisive victory, sided with Castelnau. He argued that Foch and Pétain's vision 'would entail a month of combat, with a maximum expenditure of ammunition; at what point would we be able to declare ourselves ready to attack? Maybe not next year, and probably never. We must act, for us and for our allies. As our regulations say: only inaction is disgraceful.'[56]

When Castelnau's offensive (the second battle of Champagne) went in on 25 September (supported by a further attack in Artois and the British Army's attack at Loos, which constituted the Entente's first use of chlorine gas) it met with some initial success, but ultimately bogged down and failed to deliver the great victory Joffre had been seeking; Castelnau's over-ambitious promises proved to be just that. The effect on French thinking about the war was profound. The French official history states that

> After the battles of Champagne and Artois a very clear evolution came to manifest itself in the minds of the command. For the first time, all of the participants [of the battles of 1915] were in accordance on the following capital point: *the rupture of an enemy front probably could not be realised in a single bound, but* [only] *by a series of successive and prolonged efforts.*[57]

Methodical battle came to be seen as the only possible means of fighting trench warfare. Armed with this belief, and a constantly improving tactical system based on Note 5779, the French would enter 1916 as arguably the most capable army on the Western Front.

1916: Year of attrition

In December 1915, with winter setting in and the armies on the Western Front in need of rest, the Allies met at Chantilly to discuss their plans for the coming year. This sort of 'summit' was still a relatively new concept: the French and British had only held their first such meeting five months earlier.[58] The Entente still had a long way to go before it began to operate in any sort of unified manner; it ultimately did not get there until 1918. Hoping to commit the Entente to a single, co-operative strategy, Joffre laid out his plan for 1916 before representatives from France's allies. Broadly speaking, Joffre's plan was the same as it had been for 1915: the Allies should make large, coordinated attacks to negate the German advantage of interior lines.

The subtle difference in Joffre's 1916 plan came in his explicit discussion of attrition as the means by which the Allies would achieve victory.[59] It was a word (*usure*) that Joffre had used before, but its importance had been growing in his strategic thinking since May 1915. Of course, Joffre was not alone in this. 1916 can reasonably be portrayed as the year of attrition; it was not only the year of Verdun but also of the Somme and of Brusilov (an offensive which, although not conceived along attritional lines, contributed greatly to the overall attrition suffered by the Central Powers that year).[60] Battles had never before, and would never again, drag on for so long (the Somme lasted five months, Verdun ten!). No longer would soldiers suffer the *grignotage* of 1915; instead they would be inexorably ground up in monotonous, industrial killing machines along the Somme, the Meuse, the Isonzo and across the expanse of Eastern Europe.

According to Joffre's plan, the Western Front's contribution to the great attriting of the German and Austro-Hungarian armies would take the form of a joint Franco-British offensive along the river Somme. As with all previous such offensives, it would be principally French, consisting of a forecasted 40 French divisions and 25 British.[61] Respecting the fact that Britain's New Armies[62] would not be ready before the summer, Joffre encouraged Britain to launch a series of smaller-scale 'wearing out' battles to begin the process of attrition while the Allies waited for the new British formations to train and take to the field.[63] Haig agreed in principle, and in early January ordered the preparation of such 'wearing out' attacks.[64] Nevertheless, he remained, understandably, unenthusiastic about the prospect of launching a series of attritional battles on his own. He sarcastically wrote in his diary that 'they [the French] wished the British to commence attacking in end of April with the object of, they said, "wearing out" the German reserves (a "bataille d'usure" as they are pleased to call it) – while they intend to do nothing until the enemy's reserves had disappeared!'[65] There were, of course, reasons for France's desire to reduce its exposure to casualties before the Somme was launched: France had lost 349,000 soldiers dead in 1915, its worst year of the war.[66]

The preparations for the Somme did not progress far before they were violently interrupted by the German attack at Verdun. Beginning with a vicious artillery bombardment on 21 February 1916, the Battle of Verdun would be the longest land battle in human history (although it would not even be the bloodiest battle of 1916: the Somme inflicted nearly twice as many total casualties). Erich von Falkenhayn, commander-in-chief of the German army, had noted that the Allied (primarily French) attacks in 1915 had left behind an uneven butcher's bill that favoured Germany. Cognisant of the Entente's inherent superiority in manpower and finance, Falkenhayn felt that Germany's only hope was to bring at least one of its major enemies to the negotiating table as quickly as possible.[67] Since a drive on Paris would be too costly (and might not even end the war), Falkenhayn instead decided that Germany's best chance of success lay in the strategic offensive, but the tactical defensive. If the French could be compelled to launch another series of costly attacks against well-fortified lines they might be 'bled white' and therefore forced to sue for peace.[68]

The initial phases of the battle caught the French army unprepared and instigated a panic throughout the command structure (a reaction not unlike that the Germans had at the beginning of most Entente offensives). The Fortified Region of Verdun (*Région Fortifiée de Verdun*, RFV) was particularly unprepared to absorb a major attack, despite the efforts of its commander, General Herr, and the influence of Colonel Driant, an officer stationed in the region and a member of the French Parliament. Months before the Germans launched their attack, the Verdun sector (and other fortified places) had been largely stripped of their guns and ammunition to supply the grand offensives of September 1915. In August alone the RFV had lost 20 heavy artillery batteries.[69] The demands were not just limited to heavy artillery; they extended to grenades, machine guns and other myriad supplies; eventually entire divisions were being pulled away from Verdun in preparation for Second Champagne. By October the RFV would be down to three divisions and 34 territorial battalions. When the borrowed infantry divisions came back from Champagne they tended to be severely mangled, and in need of significant rest and reinforcement before they would be of value again.[70]

Joffre had his reasons for stripping France's forts of so much of their artillery. The fall of the great Belgian forts of Liège and Namur in 1914 had swept away any remaining trust military minds could have had in the ability of static fortresses to withstand modern firepower. Combined with the relative inactivity in the sectors of the great forts (Toul, Verdun, Belfort), Joffre understandably preferred to put these guns into a position where they could be of real, immediate benefit to the French war effort. This starving of defensive efforts in favour of maximising offensive capabilities would mark Joffre's efforts throughout 1916. The stress that this would cause between Joffre and the man who would be responsible for conducting the frantic Verdun battle, Philippe Pétain, was the last great instance of friction between strategic imperatives and tactical capabilities during Joffre's tenure at GQG.

Philippe Pétain took command of the Verdun battle at midnight on 26 February, just five days after it had begun.[71] Arriving in the midst of a panic (Fort Douaumont had fallen on the 25th), Pétain rapidly reorganised the front and was instrumental in what would eventually become one of France's most important victories in the war. Principal among his improvements was the creation of a logistical network that would come to be called the '*Voie Sacrée*', the 'Sacred Way'.[72] By 1916 Pétain had come to understand modern industrialised war very well, and he set about building a logistical machine that could sustain it. A note from March 1916 describes Second Army's logistics as 'assured by motor convoys following an unchanging schedule' and describes a never-stopping system of road and rail transport; the logistical structure had a life of its own.[73] Part of this machine involved the regular rotation of units into and out of the front. Under Pétain, troops would not be asked to spend more than three or four days at the front before being relieved.[74] If during that time a given unit came under heavy attack it would be pulled out and allowed to rest as soon as humanly possible. Pétain deeply respected not only the physical but also the psychological trauma of industrialised war, and felt that the only reasonable response was to limit men's exposure to it as much as possible. Limiting the troops' exposure to casualties also helped to preserve the integrity of units, which in turn would allow them to integrate reinforcements more easily and maintain a higher standard of proficiency. The 'Noria' system (as it was called) would prove to be an essential advantage the French would build over their German counterparts, who instead left their units at the front for extended periods of time (this despite having an equitable number of reserve divisions compared with the French in early 1916).[75]

The 'Noria' system may have worked for Verdun, but it placed enormous strains on the French army's manpower reserve, which Joffre was anxious to preserve for the Somme. In his memoirs he wrote:

> the task I set myself as soon as the battle of Verdun entered into the distinct phase of a war of attrition was to give this defensive operation, so far as regarded our forces, its most economical form.... Verdun must become the cauldron in which the enemy reserves would be melted, while the decisive action would take place later on the Somme.[76]

This strategy placed Joffre and Pétain directly at odds, especially as the battle dragged on and the defences at Verdun became increasingly stretched. Pétain was understandably frustrated by Joffre's restricting the number of divisions he would send to Verdun, while also at the same time demanding that Pétain try to counter-attack and steal the initiative away from the Germans.[77] By early May, Pétain (recently promoted to commander of the Centre Army Group) was growing increasingly desperate not only for more reinforcements, but also for the Somme offensive to get underway and draw German attention away from Verdun.[78]

The French commitment to the Somme was being rapidly eaten up on the banks of the Meuse. The French contribution to the opening phases of the battle would be drastically cut back from 40 to just 12 divisions.[79] Foch, whose job it was to design the Somme battle, would be told to drastically scale down his plan by April, adding to the general's apprehension about the upcoming campaign.[80] The order from Joffre came at an awkward time for Foch, who was busy theorising a new approach to trench warfare: the 'scientific battle'. In a large document entitled '*La Bataille Offensive*' ('The Offensive Battle'), released on 20 April 1916, Foch laid the groundwork for the style of warfare that would ultimately prove so successful on the Somme.

In *La Bataille Offensive* Foch called above all else for a methodical approach to warfare, with battles being fought and won by the artillery, which he called 'the only [weapon] capable of destroying enemy [trenches]'.[81] Foch called for 'successive actions', each of which would only aim to take a narrow band of enemy trenches that had been meticulously prepared by artillery fire. Doing so, Foch wrote, would allow the French to advance with a minimum of casualties. The tactical precepts laid down are essentially the same that Foch had advocated as early as December 1914: move forward slowly, methodically, and by successive bounds (as opposed to singular 'general' offensives sending in successive 'waves' of infantry, one after the other). In a tactical sense the document echoes most of the basic precepts (the bypassing and encirclement of enemy strongpoints, use of a rolling barrage, etc.) laid down a year earlier in April 1915 in '*But et Conditions d'une Action Offensive d'Ensemble*'.[82] The similarities should not lessen the importance of Foch's writings in 1916; they are, after all, based on another year of experience and go into significantly more detail than earlier documents.

In the summer of 1915 Joffre complained bitterly that Foch and Pétain's vision of a materiel-intensive battle would be too costly, and would result in interminable delays that might never result in an actual attack taking place. One year later these two men would command two of the most important battles of the 20th century, and would apply their more cautious methodologies with great success. The cost, in both lives and munitions, would still be very high (millions of shells, and roughly 250,000 lives), but 1916 would ultimately send almost 100,000 fewer Frenchmen to their graves than did 1915. The death toll for the Germans, on the other hand, grew substantially. Over one million

Germans would be killed, captured or wounded on the Western Front in 1916 alone: 50 per cent more than the Germans had lost there in 1915.[83] Even the excessive expenditure of munitions would slowly begin to be addressed by commanders like Fayolle, who adopted a policy of suppression and 'neutralisation' rather than the outright destruction of trenches (a policy that ultimately relied on an increased use of poison gas shells).[84] Like it or not, the First World War had become the slow-paced, expensive war of position that Joffre had opposed for the first 16 months of the conflict.

Once the Battle of the Somme started on 1 July 1916 the influence of Joffre's strategy on tactics began to wane. The Entente's cards were on the table; it was then up to the executors to fight their battles as best they could. This is not, of course, to suggest that Joffre became suddenly passive. He still had to carefully balance the concurrent efforts on the Somme and the Meuse. Joffre's preference for the offensive meant that the Somme was generally given priority for men and munitions, so much so that from an initial contribution of just 12 divisions (at a time when over 30 were held on the Verdun front) the French army would eventually send more men to fight on the Somme than the British did over the course of its five months. Ultimately, however, the successes of the Somme operations and of Verdun were not enough to save Joffre. Fed up with the casualties and the lack of any clear end to the violent war, the French government replaced him with Robert Nivelle, a hero of Verdun, at the end of 1916. Ironically, the new commander-in-chief was far more offensive-minded than even Joffre, and would lead the French army to the brink of collapse in his ineptitude. Not until his replacement by Pétain in May 1917 would the French army's strategy and tactics work in harmony to produce a war-winning machine, rather than working at odds to engineer avoidable slaughter.

Notes

1. Niall Ferguson's *The Pity of War* is probably the most influential history book in this vein.
2. For more see Holger Afflerbach and David Stevenson, *An Improbable War? The Outbreak of World War I, and European Political Culture Before 1914* (Oxford: Berghahn Books, 2007), Annika Mombauer, *The Origins of the First World War: Controversies and Consensus* (London: Longman, 2002) and others.
3. Ian Ousby, *The Road to Verdun: France, Nationalism and the First World War* (London: Jonathan Cape, 2002), p. 38.
4. Ibid., p. 41.
5. Joseph Joffre (translated by Colonel T. Bentley Mott), *The Memoirs of Marshal Joffre: Volume Two* (London: Geoffrey Bles, 1932), p. 327.

6. Hew Strachan, *The First World War A New Illustrated History* (London: Pocket Books, 2006), pp. 13–14.
7. Austria and Italy had long been rivals, for example. The alliance between republican France and autocratic Russia was hardly less strange.
8. Annika Mombauer, *Helmuth Von Moltke and the Origins of the First World War* (Cambridge: Cambridge University Press, 2001), pp. 81–82.
9. Stone, Norman, 'Moltke-Conrad: Relations Between the Austro-Hungarian and German General Staffs, 1909–1914', *The Historical Journal*, Vol. IX, No. 2 (1966), p. 210.
10. A. Robert Doughty, 'French Strategy in 1914: Joffre's Own', *The Journal of Military History*, Vol. 67, No. 2 (2003), p. 429.
11. Warren Chin, 'Land Warfare From Machiavelli to Desert Storm', in Matthew Hughes and William Philpott (eds), *Palgrave Advances in Military History* (Houndmills: Palgrave Macmillan, 2006), p. 95.
12. Robert Doughty, *Pyrrhic Victory: French Strategy and Operations in the Great War* (Cambridge, Mass: Belknap Press of Harvard University Press, 2005), p. 28; William Philpott, *Bloody Victory: The Sacrifice on the Somme and the Making of the Twentieth Century* (London: Little, Brown, 2009), p. 21.
13. Michel Goya, *Le Processus d'Evolution Tactique de l'Armée Française de 1871 à 1918* (doctoral thesis for University of Paris IV, 2008), pp. 224–225.
14. Doughty, *Pyrrhic Victory*, p. 56.
15. Goya, *Le Processus d'Evolution Tactique de l'Armée Française*, p. 223.
16. Elizabeth Greenhalgh, *Foch in Command: The Forging of a First World War General* (Cambridge: Cambridge University Press, 2011), p. 92.
17. Joffre, *The Memoirs of Marshal Joffre: Volume Two*, p. 334.
18. Holger Herwig, *The First World War: Germany and Austria-Hungary 1914–1918* (London: Arnold, 1997), p. 181.
19. Robert T. Foley, *German Strategy and the Path to Verdun: Erich von Falkenhayn and the Development of Attrition, 1870–1916* (Cambridge: Cambridge University Press, 2005), p. 185.
20. John Bourne and Gary Sheffield, *Douglas Haig War Diaries and Letters 1914–1918* (London: Weidenfeld & Nicolson, 2005), pp. 213–214.
21. Quoted in General Sir James Marshall-Cornwall, *Foch as Military Commander* (London: Willmer Brothers Ltd., 1972), p. 150.
22. Jean-Baptiste Duroselle, *La Grande Guerre des Françaises: L'incomprehensible* (Paris: Perrin, 1994), p. 7; cited in Doughty, *Pyrrhic Victory*, p. 1; Greenhalgh, *Foch in Command*, p. 91.
23. The National Archives (UK), War Office 158/13, Untitled Letter from GQG, 7 March 1915.
24. Strachan, *The First World War*, pp.139–140.
25. Doughty, 'French Strategy in 1914', p. 434.
26. Elizabeth Greenhalgh, *Victory Through Coalition: Britain and France During the First World War* (Cambridge: Cambridge University Press), pp. 2–3.
27. Palat, *La grande guerre sur le front occidental*, p. 234 & *Service Historique de la Défense (SHD)*, 17N303 «Et[at] M[aj]or St Omer à G.Q.G. (Direction Arrière)» *30 Avril 1915*. These are just two instances of France providing guns and/or munitions for their allies. There are many other instances of similar requests being made for a range of necessary materials, sometimes paid for, sometimes not. This was one small component of what was an

enormously complicated economic relationship, especially regarding Great Britain.

28. Rémy Porte, «*La Mobilisation Industrielle: 'premier front' de la Grande Guerre?*» (Cahors: Soteca 14–18 Éditions, 2005), p. 173.

29. Doughty, *Pyrrhic Victory*, p. 205.

30. C. M. Andrew and A. S. Kanya-Forstner, 'The French Colonial Party and French Colonial War Aims, 1914-1918', *The Historical Journal*, Vol. 17, No. 1 (Mar., 1974), pp. 81-82

31. C.M. Andrew and A.S. Kanya-Forstner, 'France, Africa, and the First World War', *The Journal of African History*, Vol. 19, No. 1, World War I and Africa (1978), p. 13; For more on this Marc Michel's classic study of French Africa *Les Africains et la Grande Guerre: l'appel à l'Afrique (1914-1918)* (Paris: Éditions Karthala, 2014), as well as the work of Jacques Frémeaux, notably *Les Colonies dans la Grande Guerre: Combats et épreuves des peuples d'outre mer* (Soteca: 14-18 Éditions, 2006).

32. Louis Guiral, '*Je les grignote*'…*Champagne 1914–1915* (Paris: Hachette, 1965), p. X.

33. France, Ministère de la Guerre, Etat-Major de l'Armée, Service Historique, *Les Armées Françaises dans la Grande Guerre* [*AFGG*] Tome II (Paris: Imprimerie Nationale, 1923), p. 425.

34. Palat, *La grande guerre sur le front occidental*, p. 98.

35. SHD, 22N163, «*Rapport du Lieutenant Colonel Commandant le 102ᵉRgt d'Inf*»

36. SHD, 22N163, «*Le Général Dumas, Commandant le 17ᵉC.A. au Général Commandant le 33ᵉ Division*» 9 Mars 1915.

37. SHD, 25N87, '*Untitled Note*', «*L'opération dans les conditions où elle se présente ne semble pourtant pas pouvoir recevoir une organisation différente, et, son seul résultat me parait devoir être inéluctablement des pertes très élevées pour les effectifs engagés la destruction même des troupes qui y prennent part, sans qu'on puisse espérer conquérir un mètre terrain et on s'exposant même à perdre du terrain déjà conquis*»

38. SHD, 22N163, «*104ᵉRégiment d'Infanterie: Historique des faits du 12 au 28 février 1915*» 13 Mars 1915.

39. Liddell Hart Centre for Military Archives (LHCMA): Robertson 4/1.

40. François Cailleteau, *Gagner la Grande Guerre* (Paris: Economica, 2008), p. 102.

41. Joffre, *The Memoirs of Marshal Joffre: Volume Two*, p. 352.

42. Ibid.

43. Général M. Daille, *Histoire de la Guerre Mondial: Joffre et la guerre d'usure 1915–1916* (Paris: Payot, 1936), p. 112; SHD, 22N1832 «*Projet d'Attaque au Nord d'Arras*» 24 Mars 1915, GPN.

44. SHD, 22N1832; «*Projet d'Attaque au Nord d'Arras*»24 mars 1915, GPN.

45. Greenhalgh, *Foch in Command*, p. 113.

46. SHD, 22N1832; «*Compte-Rendu Sommaire des Opérations du 33ᵉ Corps d'Armée pendant les journées des 9, 10 et 11 Mai 1915*».

47. SHD, 19N735 «*But et conditions et d'une action offensive d'ensemble*» and Goya, *Le Processus d'évolution tactique de l'armée française de 1871 à 1918*, p. 271.

48. SHD, 22N1357; «*Résume des Opérations du 9 Mai au 18 Juin 1915*» 25 Juin 1915, 20 CA.

49. SHD, 16N1677; «*Premier enseignements à tirer des combats récents*» 20 Mai 1915; no. 3019.

50. *AFGG, Tome III* (1923), pp. 178–179.
51. Ibid., p. 181.
52. Ibid.
53. Palat, *La grande guerre sur le front occidental*, p. 431.
54. Greenhalgh, *Foch in Command*, p. 125.
55. Ibid., p. 127.
56. *AFGG, Tome III* (1923), p. 275.
57. Ibid., p. 563.
58. Greenhalgh, *Victory Through Coalition*, p. 9.
59. Philpott, *Bloody Victory*, p. 96.
60. Alexei Brusilov, *Mémoires du Général Broussilov: Guerre 1914–1918* (Paris: Librairie Hachette, 1929), pp. 227–231.
61. Philpott, *Bloody Victory*, p. 80.
62. New formations of volunteers raised at least partly at the insistence of Lord Kitchener (the British Secretary of State for War).
63. Joffre, *Memoirs of Marshal Joffre*, p. 462.
64. Bourne and Sheffield, *Douglas Haig War Diaries and Letters*, pp. 178–179.
65. Ibid., p. 180.
66. Maurice Genevoix, '1915 «Année Terrible»', *Revue Historique des Armées*, Vol. 21, No. 2 (1965), p. 5.
67. General Erich von Falkenhayn, *General Headquarters 1914–1916 and its Critical Decisions* (London: Hutchinson & Co., 1919), pp. 210–211.
68. Ousby, *The Road to Verdun*, p. 40.
69. Alain Denizot, *Verdun: 1914–1918* (Paris: Nouvelle Éditions Latines, 1996), p. 56.
70. Ibid.
71. Alistair Horne, *The Price of Glory: Verdun 1916* (London: Macmillan & Co. Ltd, 1962), p. 132.
72. Denizot, *Verdun 1914–1918*, p. 94.
73. AFGG, Tome IV (1927) Annexes 2, p. 1.
74. Horne, *Price of Glory*, p. 229.
75. Foley, *German Strategy and the Path to Verdun*, p. 183.
76. Joffre, *The Memoirs of Marshal Joffre, Volume Two*, pp. 465–466.
77. Denizot, *Verdun 1914–1918*, p. 96.
78. *SHD*, 1K188; 'Untitled letter'; 9 May 1916.
79. Strachan, *The First World War*, p. 184.
80. Philpott, *Bloody Victory*, p. 104.
81. *SHD*, 18N148; «La Bataille Offensive»
82. *SHD*, 19N735 «But et conditions et d'une action offensive d'ensemble»
83. François Cailleteau, *Gagner la Grande Guerre* (Paris: Economica, 2008), p. 102.
84. *SHD*, 16N2095; «Note sur le Préparation par l'Artillerie» 28 Septembre 1916; no. 18.

3
The Influence of Industry on the Use and Development of Artillery

Alex Bostrom

The First World War was the first truly industrial war. The home fronts were charged with providing truly vast quantities of men, munitions and materiel for their nations' armies. Nearly five years of continuous fighting made the economies of the belligerents crucial to success on the battlefield, as they strove to keep front lines supplied with the means to defend themselves and, occasionally, to attack. Due to the pivotal role of artillery in the conflict, the need to produce sufficient artillery munitions was especially important. In the First World War, artillery came to the fore as the most devastating weapon available, responsible for 67 per cent of deaths, compared with 15 per cent in the Franco-Prussian war of 1870–1871 and just 11 per cent in the Russo-Japanese war of 1904–1905.[1]

French high command had not expected such a protracted, static conflict, anticipating a relatively brief war, during which the army would rely on the munitions and materiel built up during peacetime. They did not foresee the large-scale industrial mobilisation that would be required to keep the army in the field. This chapter will focus on the consequences of these expectations and how the industrial mobilisation and development of the home front influenced events at the front lines. Ultimately, the decisions taken in the build-up to the war had significant negative effects on the French army's conduct of the war, resulting in munitions crises in the early months of the war, and severely hampering its ability to mount and maintain offensives. However, once mobilisation began, French industry underwent a dramatic transformation that facilitated the ability of the army at the front lines to fight effectively.

New warfare

Like all the belligerents, France was not ready for the style of fighting in the First World War.[2] The army based its tactical and strategic approach on lessons from 19th-century warfare, continuing to rely on mobility and the offensive. Increasingly modern and powerful weaponry was incorporated into this approach, rather than prompting the French general staff to question the foundations of their thinking.[3] This expectation of a mobile war was epitomised by the make-up of its artillery. France relied heavily on the 75 mm field gun, which was particularly suited to firing against advancing infantry over open ground and was relatively easy to manoeuvre across the battlefield. At the turn of the century, it had been the envy of armies across the world, but the faith placed in it by French high command would severely hamper the army once war broke out.[4]

The 75 mm was extremely quick-firing, but, because of its flat trajectory, it was unsuitable for the trench warfare that emerged following the Battle of the Marne in 1914. It lacked the destructive power and the steep angle of fire required to penetrate the defensive fortifications that would stretch from Switzerland to the English Channel. The battles of the First World War were suited to heavy artillery and howitzer cannons, capable of firing higher calibre shells at a steep trajectory. However, the French army went to war in 1914 with just over a hundred 155 mm Rimailho howitzers, compared with over 400 heavy artillery possessed by Germany.[5] Even with the reliance on the 75 mm cannon, the French artillery were outgunned and outranged.

Despite numerous debates among the French general staff on the merits of heavy artillery in the years before the war, and signs in the Russo-Japanese War and the Balkan Wars that heavy artillery was increasingly important in the 20th century, there remained a conservative body who were reluctant to devote the funds necessary to transform the army. They remained convinced of the versatility of the 75 mm field gun and the ability of the infantry to overcome even the strongest defences, remaining unwilling to incur the expense of a vast overhaul of the artillery.[6] The detractors of heavy artillery argued that, in trench warfare, it did not matter if one had a 10 kg shell or a 40 kg shell, because as long as it landed on the target then the damage would suffice. One would be far more likely to achieve this 'lucky shot' by firing ten smaller shells than one large shell, while firing ten large shells would merely exhaust the resources of industry: 'it was like using a club to kill a fly, with which you were much more likely to miss'.[7] The French believed in 'the predominance of manoeuvre over firepower', maintaining the emphasis on the infantry to dictate the outcome of battles, rather than the artillery.[8]

There had been some call before the war for an increase in heavy artillery from generals and observers aware of the increasing role it was playing in conflicts in Russia and in the Balkans. However, change was slow. In the months leading up to the outbreak of war, the state arsenals were already straining to provide a modest increase in the numbers possessed by the army. General Dubail, commander of the First Army, wrote of the desperate need for heavy artillery, while Colonel Carence was an early proponent of their use against defensive fortifications instead of sending infantry against 'the wall of steel...in vain'.[9] A bill was finally passed in the summer of 1913, and between October 1913 and April 1914 36 Schneider heavy cannons were ordered, along with 120 155 mm carriages for de Bange model guns.[10] Furthermore, 155 modern 75 mm cannons (1913 model) and 870 crates of munitions were also ordered, with the plan to order another 20 cannons, before they were interrupted by the war. At the outbreak of war, the second round of orders was too recent for it to be deemed useful to continue production.[11]

While some observers flagged potential problems with the French artillery, there was also recognition of the insufficiency of French industry and its ability to provide the munitions and materiel required by the army. In a report to the Minister of War from the then *Sous-Secrétaire d'Etat à la Guerre* on 30 March 1907, M. Henry Chéron noted that, whatever plans were drawn up to increase the state of their armaments,

> We have, at present, neither the necessary stocks, nor the necessary strength of production, nor the supplies of raw materials, nor even the measures in place at least to give us hope of procuring them in case of mobilisation. It is utterly unbelievable that our means of production do not match the stocks required as stipulated by the Ministry of War. All of this should be formulated into a methodical and precise program where all the production and consumption needs are coordinated, so that nothing is overlooked or left to chance.

The situation that was so critical in 1907 had not changed by 1914.[12]

Coupled with their misinterpretation of the style of warfare, French high command consequently possessed an outdated view of the role of artillery in a modern war. They saw the weapon as playing a primarily supporting role, with the infantry remaining the main protagonist in both the attack and defence. This misunderstanding is exemplified by the emphasis placed on shrapnel shells. France entered the war with 4.8 million 75 mm shells, of which 58 per cent were shrapnel, with just 42 per cent explosive shells.[13]

This is a clear indication of their perception of warfare, as shrapnel was of great use against exposed infantry, but largely useless against defensive fortifications. As a result, the French army was exposed in the early battles of the war, as artillery commanders continually neglected shrapnel, hastening the exhaustion of explosive shell supplies. Such was the state of the French munitions stocks that Joffre was required to promote the use of shrapnel, despite the fact that it was unsuited to trench warfare, lest a situation arise in which the stocks of explosive shells were exhausted completely. Joffre knowingly pressing for artillery commanders to prioritise less effective shells demonstrates the severity of the munitions situation that emerged in the first year of the war.[14]

There was also little recognition of the important link between artillery and infantry. Generals believed that the role of artillery was to support the infantry by destroying the obstacles in their way, but then its task was complete.[15] The idea of a large artillery bombardment in preparation for an attack did not exist before the war.[16] There was little coordination between infantry and artillery, with the former particularly unaware of the part that artillery was meant to play in its offensives.[17] This was primarily because in France control of the heavy artillery was given to the corps commander, whereas the Germans delegated it to the division, allowing infantry commanders on the ground to call up artillery support when required.[18] French soldiers were frequently exposed to the machine guns and artillery of the German army, receiving little protection from their own pieces, illustrating again the outdated perception of warfare held by the French army.[19]

Overall, on the eve of war, the French army's perception of warfare and the use of artillery meant that it was seriously unprepared for the fighting that would take place in northern France in the early months of the war. Although French high command would recognise their flaws relatively quickly, the extent to which pre-war expectations had influenced industry on the home front severely hampered the efforts to meet the demands of the army and to mobilise and produce the materiel and munitions needed for trench warfare.

Mobilisation

The industrial mobilisation strategy detailed in Plan XVII is the clearest indication of the mind-set of French high command and clarifies their expectations of the future war. Production orders in progress at the outbreak of war would be stopped, due to the recruitment of all capable manpower, and France would rely on the munitions and materiel that it had in its possession. The French started the war with initial stocks of 75 mm munitions of just 1,272 shells per piece; supplies of heavy munitions were even scarcer.[20] This was a clear indication that they anticipated a relatively brief war, and the consequences of such an approach would prove disastrous.

From day one of the outbreak of the war, the French mobilisation program, Plan XVII, foresaw that, during the first 40 days, 800,000 shells (554,000 shrapnel and 246,000 high explosive) would be produced, primarily making up completed shells from pre-made parts existing at the *réserve d'ateliers de montage de cartouches*. At the same time, 13,600 75 mm shells a day would be made up in the following manner: rear-charged shrapnel shells: 6,900; 1897 model shrapnel shells: 1,000; explosive shells: 5,700. This output would be achieved by the 60th day of mobilisation. For the other pieces of field artillery, no production of munitions was planned. For larger materiel, 10,000 155 mm shells would be produced, again formed from the parts existing already in the reserves. Nothing was foreseen for the other calibres. The flaws of this plan were swiftly highlighted by the high levels of consumption in the early battles of the war.[21]

The situation was further hampered by the perennial delays in agreeing on Plan XVII, which meant that, at the opening of hostilities, the reserves that were intended for resupplying the front lines in the early engagements were significantly depleted, as they had already been used to hasten the production of the stocks for mobilisation. As a result, when the war started, France and its industry were already on the back foot.[22]

The French general staff had originally asked at the end of 1909 that they be assured of 25,000 shells per day until the 50th day of mobilisation, while using the reserves of 800,000 shells supplied in advance, followed by 13,600 per day from then on. Later, in February 1913, they asked for 1,750,000 shells by the end of the second month of mobilisation. Production would need to increase to assure the necessary 950,000 shells in advance. It was not possible to achieve this measure before the outbreak of war, as all resources had been devoted to achieving the first supply of cannons stipulated in Plan XVII. This left the army in a particularly vulnerable position in the summer of 1914.

It is clear from the details laid out in Plan XVII that the French were not preparing for a vast consumption of munitions, or a long war. Although with hindsight it appears ludicrous that the French were so unprepared for what was to come, it must be remembered that it would have been impossible to foresee fighting on the scale that would occur between 1914 and 1918.[23]

This was admitted in a report published by the *Sous-Secrétariat d'Etat de l'Artillerie et des Munitions* in 1916, in which they conceded that, in drawing up Plan XVII, they had not foreseen that they would need to continue to produce new arms and munitions during the course of the campaign; still less that they would actually have to increase the strength of their artillery. They had felt that they could survive by simply producing munitions to keep them supplied from day to day. Their 'forecasts of munitions consumption were imprecise, even contradictory'.[24] This report is particularly interesting, as it reveals that a few months before the war, during army group exercises in the north of France, it was found that the theories and outlines for munitions consumption differed starkly from one army corps to another, even in largely comparable tactical situations. The bases on which they evaluated munitions consumption came from the interpretation of results from the most recent wars, in particular the campaign in Manchuria, but these interpretations varied greatly.

Industrial mobilisation – response to war's lessons

Following the outbreak of hostilities, the consequences of France's planning became apparent as it swiftly became clear to all observers that pre-war predictions needed to be drastically revised. Although the initial battles were relatively mobile, they involved a vast consumption of munitions, which drastically reduced the stocks of the General Reserve.[25] Furthermore, once the war settled into trench warfare following the battle of the Marne and the 'Race to the Sea', not only did munitions consumption remain extremely high, but also the style of fighting shifted dramatically to a type of siege warfare, which emphasised the need for high-powered modern quick-firing artillery capable of destroying the increasingly sophisticated network of defences on either side of No Man's Land. Although it remained unclear how long the war would last, it was evident that it would not be over swiftly, and that, to keep the armies in the field, they would require an enormous increase in materiel and munitions in order to sustain them against a much better-equipped enemy. If the French guns ran out of shells and stopped firing, the war would indeed be over very quickly.

During the 'Race to the Sea' between 28 September and 14 October, the French army fired 651,928 shells, at a rate of nearly 40,000 per day.[26]

Munitions stocks fell with alarming speed, with over half of the pre-existing stocks of 75 mm munitions expended by the end of the Battle of the Marne.[27] By 20 September 1914, shell supplies had deteriorated to such a level that Joffre was forced to tell the Minister of War that, if production did not increase considerably, 'we will no longer have the means to actively continue the war from 1 November.' He believed that the army required at least 50,000 shells per day, whereas, at the time he wrote, industry was producing only 12,000.[28]

Such was the need of the army that Joffre even demanded that the training shells used in artillery schools and any munitions available to the French army in Morocco, North Africa and its other colonies be sent to the front as quickly as possible.[29] By 27 September, the munitions crisis became so severe that the commander-in-chief imposed strict rationing, limiting the supplies of the army to just 300 75 mm shells per gun, with any surplus being held back to build up a reserve under his exclusive disposal. Armies would not receive any more munitions until 20 October, unless they were assigned a particular mission. Until further notice, commanders were to persist in stopping enemy attacks on their section of front and reinforce their defences in order to make them impenetrable.[30] From the start of the war, therefore, shell supply severely constrained the artillery's fighting potential, threatening the entire French army's survival.

Joffre quickly realised that saving munitions cost human lives, and lamented that, had munitions been available, 'important results could have been achieved'. Prolonging the situation would lead to increased losses, and 'would have a serious influence on the outcome of the war'.[31] This is further exemplified by the number of responses from commanders at the front claiming that, although they were attempting to save munitions, the need to respond to the actions of the enemy drove them to unavoidable levels of consumption.[32]

The problem was that, 'although consumption was frightening, it was, unfortunately, unavoidable' in order to hold back the German advance.[33] Millerand swiftly realised that 'no previsions had been made for what was now required' and that they 'had never believed that such consumption of munitions would ever have been possible or necessary'.[34] The front-line situation was, therefore, extremely perilous as a result of the lack of pre-war preparation. France required a rapid mobilisation of industry in order to meet the demands of the front line. If it did not mobilise sufficiently or quickly enough, Germany would overwhelm the French army with materiel and secure victory.

Industry

All nations had been caught off guard by the scale of warfare of the First World War.[35] However, French industry was in a particular state of disarray. The structure and general situation of the economy were not favourable towards France in 1914. French industry was in a state of decline in the build-up to the war, with its share of the production of the world's industrial goods dropping from 9 per cent in 1880 to 6 per cent in 1914. Its industrial sector was dwarfed by Germany's: France produced 3.3 million tons of steel per year compared with 13 million in Germany, while relying on imports for vital chemicals crucial to the manufacturing of explosives. Nevertheless, French private industry possessed a high level of technical proficiency, with firms such as Breguet and Renault having a strong tradition of excellence to draw upon when converted to mass production.[36]

However, not only was France unprepared for production on the scale required, but it also suffered serious losses due to the German invasion of northern France. The country lost 90 per cent of its iron ore, 75 per cent of its coke and 60 per cent of its coal, which translated to an industrial loss of 64 per cent of its cast iron output, 62 per cent of its steel output and half of its coal output.[37] This immediately put industry at a disadvantage, struggling to meet the factories' demands for raw materials. The most serious impact of these losses was on the availability of iron and steel, which were vital for the production of shell casings. Iron production in January 1915 was at just 25 per cent of pre-war levels, at around 1,100,000 tons.[38]

France's response to the crisis was hasty, rushed and ad hoc, as it sought to find both munitions and materiel to maintain a fighting force in the field at the front. It was necessary to turn to private industry to supplement the state arsenals, and mobilise all possibilities towards war production, departing starkly from the pre-war mobilisation plan laid out in Plan XVII. In the attempts to meet the front-line demands for quality, quantity and speed of delivery, many sacrifices were made. The haphazard nature of France's mobilisation meant that considerable problems emerged from the industrialists, in particular the shortage of raw materials, manpower and technical expertise.

Sacrificing quality for quantity also proved costly. Hasty attempts to increase output led to technical imperfections that had serious effects at the front lines, causing explosions in the barrel upon firing, and affecting accuracy and firepower. Furthermore, the reliance on private industry resulted in financial interests complicating the situation, as industrialists persisted in preserving their own profits, despite the needs of the country as a whole.[39]

Nevertheless, industry was able to recover from its initial problems, and, by 1917, was providing munitions on a sufficient scale to allow the army to conduct relatively unconstrained operations. It also advanced technically, aiding artillery commanders by providing increasingly advanced shells that were more effective in meeting their tactical demands.

French industry slowly overcame the lack of raw materials and the scarcity of manpower through the tireless work of Albert Thomas, the Undersecretary of State for Artillery and Munitions. Once the required technical and administrative structures were put in place, output improved rapidly, with the production of 75 mm shells increasing at a rate of around 175,000 shells per month to a peak of over 7,010,000 in May 1917.[40] By relying on the metallurgy union, the *Comité des Forges*, to aid with the recruitment and organisation of private industrialists, the Ministry of War was able to shift production away from the inadequate state arsenals. By April 1915, around half of 75 mm shells were being produced by firms new to munitions work. Furthermore, the workforce was strictly regulated, strikes were rare, and absenteeism even rarer.[41] Compared with Britain, France mobilised its industry much sooner and more effectively, motivated by the need to defend its territory. Furthermore, it was the collapse of the German home front that contributed to the armistice, demonstrating the pivotal importance of the interior to the war effort.[42]

On the technical side, development was smoother, with industry remaining open to new ideas and methods once it became clear not only that the war was likely to last a long time, but also that there was considerable profit to be made. The first main area of development was in the manufacturing of shell casings, in which there was a concerted effort to convert from traditional iron casings to cast iron and to steel, which had a far superior performance.[43] Ordinary iron shells contained a quarter of the explosive of a steel shell, and therefore caused minimal destruction, while steel shells needed to contain far more powder to be effective. Cast iron shells were developed that had a thinner wall and were as effective as steel shells despite containing around half the amount of powder.[44] This allowed savings of raw materials, while not compromising the offensive capabilities. Furthermore, during the course of 1915, production shifted from manufacturing by drilling to the process of pressing. This had the advantage of producing more uniform shells, providing greater consistency when firing. Although it took time to introduce changes, ultimately they resulted in cheaper, more efficient production, and had important tactical implications at the front lines, improving range, destructive power and accuracy.[45]

Overall, munitions production increased at a considerable rate. By the end of November 1914, production of 75 mm shells had reached 22,000 shells per day, and rose to 33,000 in December, and 42,000 in January 1915.[46] This continued to increase to 96,000 by November 1915 and passed 100,000 in February 1916.[47] Although production always fell short of achieving the high targets demanded by the army, French high command was able to motivate both the Ministry of War and the munitions industry to make all efforts possible to increase production by setting the bar high. By the summer of 1916, output began to exceed consumption, and from then on 'anxiety could be banished, the difficult period was over'.[48] France increased its production to such a level that it no longer constrained tactics on the front lines, and actually facilitated the mounting of large offensives without having to worry about compromising future stocks. French industry was even able to provide considerable quantities of munitions to its allies, while also furnishing the newly arriving American army in 1918.[49]

Industry facilitating tactics

The expansion in industrial output allowed the army at the front lines to act with greater freedom and flexibility, utilising new tactics in an attempt to break the deadlock of trench warfare. We have already touched on the improvements in accuracy offered by more uniform methods of shell production; however, the increase in stocks of shells available at the front had a more important effect on the density of artillery bombardments. It was only following the Nivelle Offensive in April 1917 and the subsequent appointment of Philippe Pétain as commander-in-chief that the French army really began to recognise the importance of density of fire, rather than simply firing large numbers of shells on a broad front. This transition was also prompted by the mutinies in the spring of 1917, which resulted in greater demands being placed on the artillery to ensure the destruction of enemy defences to take the strain off the infantry.[50] The key issue was the number of shells fired per kilometre of front, and the depth to which they were fired, as it was the weight of fire per square metre of ground that truly revealed the destruction effected by a bombardment. This was already under consideration by the German army before the war and employed to great effect at the Battle of Verdun in February 1916.[51]

The clearest illustration of this transition is the difference between the Champagne Offensive of September 1915 and the Battle of Malmaison in October 1917. At Champagne, the French army fired 1,390,000 75 mm shells over the course of five days, equating to a weight of fire of 320 tonnes of 75 mm shells per kilometre of front. However, at the Battle of Malmaison, Philippe Pétain, the new commander-in-chief, who had campaigned since 1915 for increased emphasis on artillery preparation, limited both the depth and the width of the offensive, and therefore, on the six days preceding the attack, on a front of 11 kilometres, 'an unprecedented concentration of guns' fired 1,750 tonnes of shells per kilometre of front.[52] By 1918, the density of artillery per section of front had increased even further, with the ability to place one 75 mm battery per hundred metres of front, whereas at the outbreak of the war one would have been, at best, every 800 metres.[53] The ability to do so relied entirely on industry, not just to produce the required materiel, but also to produce sufficient munitions. By September 1918, the munitions industry was producing 5,635,000 shells, almost twice its output in January 1916, and enormous compared with the 790,000 shells manufactured in August 1914.[54] The munitions industry, therefore, facilitated the employment of new tactics, as by this stage of the war it was able to provide enough shells to allow increased density of fire. It was crucial to the French success at Malmaison, and at subsequent battles throughout late 1917 and 1918.

The increasing abundance of 'special shells', developed by industry, also enabled a more subtle approach to the use of artillery. Prompted by the German use of gas on the Western Front in early 1915, the French began experimenting with their own shells charged with a mixture of phosphorus and carbon disulphide, delivering 50,000 to the army at the end of May 1915. Ultimately, two sorts of 'special shells' were developed: asphyxiating shells charged with either fumigérite and chlorosulfite or phosgene (1,500 to 12,000 produced daily, depending on the model) and incendiary shells, charged with phosphorus (6,000 75 mm shells per day, 1,000 heavy shells per day).[55] These proved vital for 'neutralisation fire', which was key to the restoration of the element of surprise to the attack.

Until late 1916, the focus had been on using artillery to achieve 'total destruction' of the enemy defences and personnel.[56] The focus on 'destruction' had an inevitable effect on shell supply.[57] Generals attempted to calculate the number of shells that were required to achieve 'the total destruction of the enemy defences, trenches, interior, flanks and batteries', while stressing that it was impossible to reduce this number without risking exposing the infantry to almost certain failure.[58] One of the major flaws of this approach was that it rendered French attacks very inflexible, restricted by the need to fire a huge quantity of shells. However, from late 1916, a more subtle tactic was gradually adopted.

'Special shells' offered new opportunities for more advanced use of artillery. They facilitated the emergence of the idea of 'neutralisation' rather than 'total destruction', which merely required that enemy trenches and batteries be incapacitated at the moment of the attack for long enough to allow the infantry to advance. This tactic was employed in the assault on Fort Douaumont on 24 October 1916 with considerable success, with Colonel Wisse subsequently declaring: 'the production of special shells of all calibre appears indispensable'.[59] Following the failure of the initial offensive on the Somme, the emphasis of the generals shifted, with the phrase 'destruction *or* neutralisation' increasingly present in artillery documents from then on.[60] A synergy of the two methods emerges, with destruction of the key defensive points carried out during the preparation stage, while, at the moment of attack, neutralising fire 'completes the job that could not be carried out by destruction fire'.[61]

French high command assigned great importance to the role of neutralisation fire in an offensive, with the Instructions of 31 October 1917 stating that 'the chances of success...reside above all in the surprise and in the actions of neutralisation at the moment of the attack, rather than in seeking complete destruction'.[62] The development of 'special shells' was crucial to this. They represented 'the most effective method of neutralisation' and could, if fired in sufficient quantity, even cause enemy casualties.[63] Grand Quartier Général (GQG) recognised that surprise could be restored, and the length of preparations reduced, 'through intensive use of neutralisation fire, with a very large use of special shells', which would nullify the defences that had not been destroyed.[64] The triumph of neutralisation by 'special shells' was demonstrated at the Battle of Malmaison. Although preceded by a relatively short but extremely powerful preparation, the gas shells fired at the moment of attack were very effective at neutralising the enemy batteries, with the French soldiers advancing over six kilometres, one of the largest gains of the war to that point.[65] One of the interesting conclusions drawn from this attack was that neutralisation by gas shells, rather than through explosive shells, was more economical in terms of the number of shells that needed to be fired to achieve success. Even in late 1917, considerations of shell supply were still prevalent, with gas shells also allowing a significant reduction in the length of the preparatory bombardment, further preserving shell stocks.[66] The role of industry was crucial to the development of 'neutralisation' tactics, as it was able to supply 'special shells' in sufficient quantity for the artillery to exploit them for tactical success.

Increasing shell supply also enabled the introduction of the 'rolling barrage', a tactic designed to support the infantry by tying down the enemy while they advanced. It required a high concentration of artillery, firing a density of eight shells per hundred metres of front, with the bombardment advancing in bounds of approximately 150 metres every three minutes, depending on the terrain.[67] The infantry followed behind the wall of shells at a distance of between 50 and 100 metres.[68] The rolling barrage was conducted by the 75 mm field gun, firing both shrapnel and explosive shells.[69] Ahead of this was a barrage of high-calibre shells that advanced in much larger bounds of 500–1,000 metres and focused on the important tactical points such as trenches and concrete defences.[70] This approach needed much greater coordination between the infantry and artillery divisions than had been previously seen.[71] As it consumed a vast quantity of munitions, Colonel Roger remained sceptical about the merits of devoting so many shells to this tactic.[72] Although the rolling barrage was first seen in basic forms in 1915, and was employed more frequently from 1916 onwards, the state of munitions production meant that the artillery lacked the shells for it to be truly effective.[73] However, by late 1917, shell supply had increased to allow an unconstrained adoption of the rolling barrage. Again, at Malmaison, the tactics were employed with great success, with German soldiers surprised at the arrival of the French infantry so close behind the artillery.[74] Without the improved industrial output of shells, the implementation of this important tactic, which proved so successful in gaining territory, would not have been possible.

Finally, one of the key areas in which the influence of shell production is clearest is in the return of the element of surprise to offensives. Although GQG recognised early on that surprise was important for tactical success, it was seemingly a necessary casualty of prolonged preparatory bombardments.[75] During the middle years of the war, a lengthy artillery preparation was viewed as 'one of the most certain guarantees of success'.[76] Surprise was sacrificed, as it was impossible to hide an imminent attack due to the extensive transportation of munitions and materiel to the front lines, the length of a bombardment, and increased levels of aviation activity.[77] The French army failed to recognise that artillery and surprise could work together, as demonstrated by the German army at Verdun in February 1916.[78]

By 1918, however, with the wealth of resources finally available to the French army, surprise became increasingly viable. General Foch now regarded it as 'indispensable to success'.[79] Surprise could now be achieved through a rapid and intense bombardment, significantly reducing the length of the preparation, and therefore limiting the enemy's ability to call up reserves.[80] The arrival of sufficient modern rapid-fire artillery, coupled with the fact that, according to Lt-Colonel Picot, 'munitions now existed in sufficient quantities', enabled large numbers of shells to be fired in a very limited space of time.[81] The ability to neutralise enemy defences was pivotal, as it removed the need for lengthy destruction fire.[82] Furthermore, accompanying fire, in particular the rolling barrage, was able to support the infantry as it advanced, hindering the ability of the enemy to man their defences and install their machine guns. While surprise was restored to the agenda through the Instructions of 31 October 1917, it was crystallised fully in *Directive No. 5*, issued on 12 July 1918.[83] This detailed the need to limit reconnaissance fire almost completely, relying, if necessary, on a very short preparation in which the artillery commanders could fine-tune their calculations. The attack would subsequently be unleashed following a very brief and very violent bombardment, often supported by tanks to maximise the element of surprise.

Overall, in the early years of the war, the French army was significantly hampered by the pre-war expectations of high command and the lack of preparation for the industrial requirements of a modern conflict. As a result, the army remained vulnerable until 1916, with shell crises threatening the ability of the artillery to continue to fight and engage the enemy, and hastily constructed, poor-quality shells compromising its effectiveness. Although, before the war, the general staff had been confident in their tactical approach, and particularly their reliance on field guns instead of heavy artillery, the lack of larger-calibre guns persistently hampered both offensive and counter-battery fire.

Once industrial production began to increase, however, following the strenuous efforts of Albert Thomas, the problems and restrictions at the front lines began to ease, and the artillery was able to play a more productive and decisive role in offensives. Constraints were removed and new tactics were facilitated, and, although it took time before outdated practices were abandoned, by late 1917 the combination of neutralisation fire, special shells and rolling barrages proved increasingly effective. Such developments would not have been possible without the rapid improvement of French industry, which was, by 1918, able to supply artillery and munitions in enormous quantities not just to the French army but also to the newly arriving American army and its allies in the east. This should be viewed as a considerable achievement in a war in which asserting materiel superiority was so crucial to success.

Notes

1. Guy Pedroncini, *Pétain, Général en chef, 1917–1918* (Paris: Presses universitaires de France, 1974), p. 41.
2. R.J.Q. (Ralph James Q.) Adams, *Arms and the Wizard: Lloyd George and the Ministry of Munitions, 1915–1916* (College Station: Texas A&M University Press, 1978), p. 2.
3. Dimitry Quéloz, *De la manoeuvre napoléonienne à l'offensive à outrance: la tactique générale de l'armée française, 1871–1914*, Vol. 1, Bibliothèque stratégique (Paris: Institut de stratégie comparée Économica, 2009).
4. David G Herrmann, *The Arming of Europe and the Making of the First World War* (Princeton, NJ: Princeton University Press, 1996), p. 80.
5. Ibid., p. 203.
6. Ibid.
7. Frédéric Georges Herr, *L'artillerie: ce qu'elle a eté, ce qu'elle est, ce qu'elle doit être avec 4 croquis dans le texte* (Paris: Berger-Levrault, 1923), p. 34.
8. Ibid., p. 1; Douglas Porch, *The March to the Marne: the French Army, 1871–1914* (Cambridge: Cambridge University Press, 1981), p. 232.
9. Porch, *The March to the Marne*, p. 235; Jean de Pierrefeu, *G.Q.G. Secteur 1. Trois ans au Grand quartier général par le rédacteur de 'communique'* (Paris: L'Édition française illustrée, 1920), p. 34.
10. Bruce I Gudmundsson, 'Learning from the Front?: Tactical Innovation in France and Flanders, 1914–1918', Thesis D.Phil. (University of Oxford, 2009, 2007), p. 276.
11. AN 94 AP 84, n.d., Archives Nationales, Resumé des mésures prises par le Service de l'Artillerie depuis l'ouverture des hostilités, 11 December 1914, p. 7.
12. SHAT 6 N 16, n.d., Service Historique de l'Armée de Terre, Vincennes, Note: Commission de l'Armée. Réponse au Rapport Gervais sur les Munitions, 22 April 1915, p. 22.
13. Joseph Jacques Césaire Joffre, *Mémoires Du Maréchal Joffre (1910–1917)* (Paris: Plon, 1932), Vol. 2, p. 24.
14. Service Historique de l'Armée de Terre, *Les Armées françaises dans la Grande Guerre* (Paris: Imprimerie Nationale, 1922), pp. 9, 21.
15. Colonel Lucas, *Colonel Lucas. L'Evolution des idées tactiques en France et en Allemagne pendant la guerre de 1914–1918* (Paris, impr.-édit. Berger-Levrault, 5, rue Auguste-Comte, 1932), p. 13.
16. Général Maitre, 'Des Idées Sur L'emploi de L'artillerie Pendant La Guerre', *Revue Militaire Francaise*, Vol. 11 (1924), p. 206.
17. Douglas Porch, 'The Marne and After: A Reappraisal of French Strategy in the First World War', *The Journal of Military History*, Vol. 53, No. 4 (1 October 1989), p. 378, doi: 10.2307/1986106.

18. Allan Reed Millett and Williamson Murray (eds), *Military Effectiveness*, Mershon Center Series on International Security and Foreign Policy (Boston: Unwin Hyman, 1988), p. 221.
19. Lucas, *Colonel Lucas. L'Evolution des idées tactiques en France et en Allemagne pendant la guerre de 1914–1918*, p. 36.
20. Service Historique de l'Armée de Terre, *Les Armées françaises dans la Grande Guerre*, pp. 61–62.
21. Gerd Hardach, 'La Mobilisation Industrielle En 1914–1918: Production, Planification et Idéologie,' in Patrick Fridenson (ed.), *1914–1918: L'autre Front* (Paris: Editions ouvrières, 1977), p. 82.
22. AN 94 AP 84, Résumé des mésures prises par le Service de l'Artillerie depuis l'ouverture des hostilités. 11 December 1914, p. 4.
23. SHAT 6 N 16, Note: Commission de l'Armée, 22 April 1915, Réponse au Rapport Gervais sur les Munitions, p. 2.
24. AN 94 AP 84, Sous-Secrétariat d'Etat de l'Artillerie et des Munitions. Résumé des travaux depuis le début de la guerre. 1916. Not dated.
25. Hardach, 'La Mobilisation Industrielle En 1914–1918: Production, Planification et Idéologie,' 82; Arthur Fontaine, *French Industry During the War* (New Haven, Conn: Yale University Press; London, 1926), p. 282.
26. Service Historique de l'Armée de Terre, *Les Armées françaises dans la Grande Guerre*, pp. 14, 555.
27. Robert A Doughty, *Pyrrhic Victory: French Strategy and Operations in the Great War* (Cambridge, Mass: Belknap Press of Harvard University Press, 2005), p. 116.
28. Service Historique de l'Armée de Terre, *Les Armées françaises dans la Grande Guerre*, tome 2, volume 1, annex no. 19, p. 11. Le Général Commandant en Chef a monsier le ministre de la guerre, 20 September 1914.
29. Ibid., tome 2, volume 1, annexes volume 11, annex no. 239, p. 27. Télégramme chiffré, Général Commandant en Chef a ministre Guerre, no. 7837, 28 September 1914.
30. Ibid., pp. 14, 394. GQG Note, no. 7503, 27 September 1914.
31. Ibid., pp. 211–265, 45. Télégramme chiffré, Général Commandant en Chef a Guerre (cabinet), no. 2813, 13 October 1914.
32. 16 N 696, n.d., Service Historique de l'Armée de Terre, Vincennes, Note: Le Général de Division Dubail, Commandant la 1ere Armée, a M. le Général Commandant en Chef, no. 221/5, 2 December 1914.18; 18 N 293, n.d., Service Historique de l'Armée de Terre, Vincennes, Le Général de Division de Villaret, Commandant la 7e Armée, a Monsieur le Général Commandant la GAE, no. 2909/3.S.OP, 5 February 1916.
33. Émile Emmanuel Herbillon, *Colonel Herbillon. Souvenirs d'un officier de liaison pendant la guerre mondiale. Du général en chef au gouvernement* (Lagny, impr. E. Grevin Paris: éditions Jules Tallandier, 1930), p. 41.
34. Ibid., p. 56.
35. Adams, *Arms and the Wizard* (1978), p. 2.
36. Millett and Murray, *Military Effectiveness*, pp. 195–196.
37. Gaston Jèze, *The War Finance of France: The War Expenditure of France* (London, New Haven: Yale University Press, 1927), p. 189.
38. Jean-Claude Mauffre, *Un Aspect de La Mobilisation Industrielle Au Cours de La Première Guerre Mondiale: La Fabrication Des Obus En France* (Paris: U.E.R., 1970), p. 45.

39. Hardach, 'La Mobilisation Industrielle En 1914–1918: Production, Planification et Idéologie'; Rémy Porte, *La mobilisation industrielle: 'premier front' de la Grande Guerre?* (Saint-Cloud: 14–18 éditions, 2005).
40. Frédéric Reboul, *Mobilisation industrielle: des fabrications de guerre en France de 1914 à 1918* (Paris: Berger-Levrault, 1925), p. 28.
41. Elizabeth Greenhalgh, 'Errors and Omissions in Franco–British Co-operation over Munitions Production, 1914–1918', *War in History*, Vol. 14, No. 2 (1 April 2007), p. 188, doi: 10.1177/0968344507075876.
42. Ibid.; Hardach, 'La Mobilisation Industrielle En 1914–1918: Production, Planification et Idéologie', pp. 103–104.
43. Joffre, *Mémoires Du Maréchal Joffre (1910–1917)*, p. 28.
44. Louis Baquet, *Souvenirs d'un directeur de l'Artillerie* (Paris: H. Charles-Lavauzelle, 1921), p. 100. http://gallica.bnf.fr/ark:/12148/bpt6k551594., 5 September 2014.
45. SHAT 10 N 29, n.d., Service Historique de l'Armée de Terre, Vincennes, Note: Réunion des chefs de groupes pour la fabrication des obus 75, 26 June 1915; SHAT 10 N 49, n.d., Service Historique de l'Armée de Terre, Vincennes, Note sur la substitution des obus forges aux obus forés.
46. Ibid., pp. 21, 69.
47. Ibid., pp. 3, 618.
48. Ibid., pp. 42, 413.
49. Millett and Murray, *Military Effectiveness*, p. 195.
50. Pedroncini, *Pétain, Général en chef, 1917–1918*, p. 44.
51. Bruce I. Gudmundsson, *On Artillery* (Westport, Conn: Praeger, 1993), p. 23.
52. Pierrefeu, *G.Q.G. Secteur 1. Trois ans au Grand quartier général par le rédacteur de 'communique'*, 186; Reboul, *Mobilisation industrielle*, p. 30.
53. Reboul, *Mobilisation industrielle*, p. 38.
54. Ibid., p. 28.
55. Service Historique de l'Armée de Terre, *Les Armées françaises dans la Grande Guerre*, pp. 111, 215.
56. 475 AP 194, n.d., Archives Nationales, Nivelle, Note pour M. le Ministre de la Marine, not dated, probably late 1916.
57. SHAT 16 N 1995, n.d., Service Historique de l'Armée de Terre, Vincennes, Note sur l'emploi de l'artillerie en liaison avec l'infanterie dans le combat de rupture, no. 5.1357, 7 August 1917, p. 1.
58. SHAT 18 N 272, n.d., Service Historique de l'Armée de Terre, Vincennes, Colonel Mouchon, De l'Offensive, September 1916, p. 18.
59. Ibid., Centre d'Etudes d'Artillerie – Emploi de l'artillerie dans l'attaque du 24 octobre sur la rive droite de la Meuse, 20 January 1917.
60. Service Historique de l'Armée de Terre, *Les Armées françaises dans la Grande Guerre*, pp. 431–540, 748, Note sur les contre-batteries, no. 9503, 20 September 1916; Letter from Pétain to Painlevé, 28 May 1917, in Pedroncini, *Pétain, Général en chef, 1917–1918*, p. 41; Lucas, *Colonel Lucas. L'Evolution des idées tactiques en France et en Allemagne pendant la guerre de 1914–1918*, p. 147.
61. SHAT 16 N 1995, Instruction sur l'action offensive des grandes unites dans la bataille, 31 December 1917, p. 26.
62. Maitre, 'Des idées sur l'emploi de l'artillerie pendant la guerre,' p. 337.

63. SHAT 16 N 1995, Instruction sur l'action offensive des grandes unites dans la bataille, 31 December 1917, p. 165.
64. GQG Note, 6 February 1918, in Maitre, 'Des idées sur l'emploi de l'artillerie pendant la guerre', p. 337.
65. Doughty, *Pyrrhic Victory*, p. 389.
66. Service Historique de l'Armée de Terre, *Les Armées françaises dans la Grande Guerre*, pp. 52, 1107.
67. SHAT 16 N 1995 Note sur l'emploi de l'artillerie en liaison avec l'infanterie dans le combat de rupture, no. 5.1357, 7 August 1917, p. 28.
68. Service Historique de l'Armée de Terre, *Les Armées françaises dans la Grande Guerre*, 431–612, p. 856, Note por les armées, no. 1805, 24 September 1916.
69. Ibid., pp. 43, 346.
70. SHAT 16 N 1995, Rapport du Goumoens de la mission en France du 22 août au 9 September 1917, no. T.4227, p. 94.
71. Herr, *L'artillerie*, p. 154.
72. Colonel Roger, 'Les Méthodes D'appui de L'attaque Par L'artillerie Au Cours de La Guerre', *Revue Militaire Francaise* 10, no. Octobre–Decembre (1921), 342.
73. Doughty, *Pyrrhic Victory*, p. 306; Lucas, *Colonel Lucas. L'Evolution des idées tactiques en France et en Allemagne pendant la guerre de 1914–1918*, p. 146.
74. Ibid., p. 308.
75. Service Historique de l'Armée de Terre, *Les Armées françaises dans la Grande Guerre*, pp. 52, 67.
76. GQG Instructions de 31e Octobre 1917 in Lucas, *Colonel Lucas. L'Evolution des idées tactiques en France et en Allemagne pendant la guerre de 1914–1918*, p. 196.
77. Service Historique de l'Armée de Terre, *Les Armées françaises dans la Grande Guerre*, pp. 52, 67.
78. Lucas, *Colonel Lucas. L'Evolution des idées tactiques en France et en Allemagne pendant la guerre de 1914–1918*, p. 142.
79. Ferdinand Foch, *Mémoires pour servir à l'histoire de la guerre de 1914–1918* (Paris: Plon, 1931), p. 166.
80. SHAT 16 N 1995, Instruction sur l'action offensive des grandes unites dans la bataille, 31 October 1917, p. 3.
81. Ibid., Instruction sur l'action offensive des grandes unites dans la bataille, 31 October 1917, 166; SHAT 16 N 2096, n.d., Service Historique de l'Armée de Terre, Vincennes, Lt-Colonel Picot, Compte-rendu de mission à la IIIe Armée, 28 March 1918.
82. SHAT 16 N 1995, Instruction sur l'action offensive des grandes unites dans la bataille, 31 October 1917, pp. 6–7.
83. Ibid., Instruction sur l'action offensive des grandes unites dans la bataille, 31 October 1917, p. 29.

4
Missed Opportunity? The French Tanks in the Nivelle Offensive

Tim Gale

Writers of military history have often been keen to highlight missed opportunities in the campaigns and battles that they discuss. Indeed, there is a whole genre of military history books devoted to showing how campaigns and battles could have been much better conducted. Unfortunately, these works usually fail to acknowledge adequately the great benefit of hindsight and will often ignore many confounding factors in the original scenario. Perhaps no war has had so many alleged missed opportunities as the First World War. This chapter will consider whether there were any missed opportunities connected with the first combat engagement of the French tanks on 16 April 1917, including a consideration of a number of criticisms made about the engagement by Heinz Guderian, the German armour expert.[1] The tank engagement was widely seen as a failure at the time and afterwards; for example, Guderian argues in his 1937 book *Achtung Panzer* that the French tanks should have given a much better showing on 16 April 1917. To claim this engagement was a missed opportunity, as Guderian does, is to strongly imply that there was a failure of vision, but this case study will show that it was not any lack of imagination in the tank officers' plans but the hard reality of immature technology and a misjudged approach by the French commander-in-chief General Robert Nivelle to the offensive in general that caused the tank attack to fail. In addition, this study of the French tanks in the Nivelle Offensive will demonstrate that failure in the short term can be a spur leading to long-term success.

By 1917, the French and British had already missed a major opportunity by failing to co-operate at the outset in their tank programmes. It is very telling about the Anglo-French relationship in the first half of the war that neither side informed the other about its tank programme until they were both well underway. As soon as the French

were informed about the British programme in June 1916, the commander of the French Tank Corps (the *Artillerie Spéciale – AS*), Colonel (later
General) Jean Baptiste Estienne, was despatched to Lincoln to see what
the British had achieved.[2] Although Estienne was most impressed with
the British tank and recommended immediate co-operation, it was difficult at this late stage because the British and French tank designs were
so different.

As far as the French were concerned, the British missed a major opportunity by using tanks for the first time during the final stages of the
Battle of the Somme in 1916. This had in one fell swoop removed
the surprise element of the tanks and forced the French to completely
reconsider their tactical approach. Estienne's initial ideas on tactics had
centred on the tanks being used in a surprise attack across a wide front,
without an accompanying artillery barrage. For the attack, the tanks
would leave the French front line before the infantry, who would only
advance to the first enemy trench when the tanks had taken it. Several
hundred metres behind the tanks conducting the assault would be tanks
towing sledges carrying infantry for exploiting the attack.[3] Such was
French concern that the French government contacted E.S. Montague,
the British Minister of Munitions, and asked him to stop the British
tanks being used until the spring of 1917, when the French tanks would
be ready. Montague discussed this with Haig in September 1916 but the
latter, although sympathetic, was not prepared to change his plans at
such a late stage.[4]

Although the French were furious that the British were not prepared
to delay the introduction into combat of the tank, they were certainly
asking a lot if they expected the British in the second half of 1916 to wait
until enough French tanks were available for a large-scale attack, as this
was at least six months away. The British knew about the serious delays
in the French tank programme and could thus be reasonably certain
that their tanks would not see action for a lengthy period if they waited
for the French to be ready.[5] On the other hand, this appeared to be
an opportunity for the French to gain important information from the
British experience. Unfortunately, as was typical in the Great War, it was
difficult to discern which parts of the British experience were generally
applicable and which were particular to that engagement. For example,
the commander of the French military mission to GHQ, General Pierre
des Vallières, made an initial report on the British tanks which suggested
that direct artillery fire would not be a problem for the tanks. This
was highly misleading, as the French were to find out.[6] On the other
hand, J.L. Breton (an early enthusiast for tanks in the French Armaments

Ministry) wrote that, although the British use of tanks had been premature, it had helped convince even the 'most sceptical' in France of the utility of tanks.[7] Regardless of the merits of the arguments about British first use, the French had to develop a new tactical approach and the tanks were now tasked with being a form of artillery support for the infantry.

The French tanks were to have their first engagement in the Nivelle Offensive in April 1917. The new commander-in-chief of the French army, General Robert Nivelle, had been promoted in order to replicate the widely acclaimed success he had enjoyed as commander of the Verdun front in October and December 1916 but on a much larger scale. In a large-scale offensive that was expected to finish the war for all intents and purposes, Nivelle planned to pin the German army in place at the Noyon salient, while a strong attack broke through the German lines elsewhere. This was to be accomplished by means of the new artillery methods developed at Verdun and a strong manoeuvre force, comprising of a newly formed army group, *Groupe d'armées de reserve* (Reserve Army Group – GAR), under the experienced but undistinguished General Joseph-Alfred Micheler.[8] Micheler's force consisted of three armies: Tenth Army was to be the reserve while Fifth and Sixth Armies were to 'completely rupture' the enemy front.[9] In essence, the Nivelle plan relied on using artillery to smash a corridor for the French infantry through the first two German lines. Within the first three hours of the attack, these German positions would be taken and the French infantry would be ready to attack the third German position, which was expected to be largely untouched by the French artillery preparation. This is the point at which the French tanks would come into action.[10] As there were a limited number of tanks available, they were only to be used on Fifth Army's front, much to the disgust of Sixth Army's commander Charles Mangin, who bombarded GQG with requests for tanks for his front. Two tank *groupements* (battalions) were attached to Fifth Army, to fight in the Juvincourt and Berry-au-Bac area. As the tank units were raised through the artillery, they were organised like the artillery into batteries of three or four tanks, *groupes* of three batteries and *groupements* consisting of three *groupes*.

In 1917, the French had two tank designs available for use: the Schneider and the St Chamond. The St Chamonds were unavailable on 16 April and the *AS* entered its first combat engagement with its Schneider tanks. The latter tank design was 13.5 tonnes in weight and armed with two machine guns and a short-barrelled 75 mm cannon, with a very limited field of fire. It was chronically underpowered by a crude internal combustion engine, typical of the time, limiting its speed to little more than walking pace, with armour sufficient to repel rifle bullets and pieces of shrapnel but little else.

French Fifth Army would be attacking well-thought-out and prepared German defences that were seven kilometres in depth, consisting of three positions, separated from each other by two to three kilometres. There was a fourth position nine kilometres back. The first position consisted of three lines, there being several trenches in each line. The second position had three parallel trench lines, while the third had only one line of trenches.[11] Most of the German artillery was employed between the second and third positions, with a number of advance batteries further forward. Anti-tank defence was consigned to indirect-fire batteries and several isolated field guns (for direct fire), placed at the rear of the second position.[12] The ground over which the tanks would advance rose gradually up to the German positions and offered no specific problems of manoeuvre for them. Most crucially, the area the tanks would be fighting in was overlooked by high ground north-east of Berry-au-Bac and the Californie plateau to the north-west, both of which were heavily populated by German artillery observers.

One very effective but simple measure that the Germans had taken in response to the first British tank attack was to widen their trenches significantly, which immediately prevented the French tanks from operating independently of the infantry.[13] There was clearly no way for the French to modify the existing tank designs to enable them to cross such wide trenches, and making a way over the trenches for the tanks became a vital task for the supporting infantry, as the tank crews clearly could not do this for themselves. Therefore, the German defences were significantly stronger than had been envisaged in Estienne's original tactical ideas.

The official tank tactics for the battle were as set out in *AS Ordre général No.1*, 1 January 1917 and an annexe of 20 February 1917.[14] In combat, each tank would have a frontage of 50 metres, with the battery having a front of 200 metres (with the battery commander second in line from the right) and the *groupe* having a front of around 1,000 metres.[15] There was one section of the infantry attached to each battery, with three or four men with each tank and the rest of the section close behind it.[16] Jean Perré points out that, in real battle conditions, the consequences of such tight frontages were 'fatal', particularly for the supporting infantry. However, it is important to note that the German artillery was expected to be almost entirely suppressed on 16 April, and thus the tanks and their supporting infantry were not expected to be subjected to heavy artillery fire.[17]

General Olivier Mazel, commander of Fifth Army, set out the plan of attack for the tanks in March, each tank *groupement* being attached to a corps. The tanks were to be employed to support the infantry in the attack on the third and, possibly, the fourth German positions, which were expected to be relatively undamaged by the lengthy French artillery preparation. *Groupement Bossut*, commanded by *Chef d'escadron* Bossut with 82 Schneider tanks, was attached to XXXII Corps d'Armée (CA – infantry corps), *Groupement Chaubès*, commanded by *Chef de bataillon* Chaubès with 50 Schneider tanks, to V CA.[18] The tanks with XXXII CA were obliged to approach the battlefield in a long road column (due to the size of the road) and to cross a very narrow bridge before advancing over the first German position. Once past this, the *groupement* would then have to cross the second German position before deploying into a battle line to attack the third German position. The other *groupement* (with V CA) had an apparently easier and shorter route to the first German position, which would be crossed prior to advancing over the second position to attack the third German position, north of Juvincourt. The tanks were expected to give the attacking infantry considerable support in taking the last enemy positions and thereby prolong the latter's attack. The infantry were given strict orders not to wait for the tanks or get distracted by them.[19] Thus, the tanks were here to be used as support for the infantry; they were not seen as an indispensable or separate part of the attack. As the tanks were to support the second phase of the division's attack, they were to go forward of the attacking infantry three and a half hours after the main attack started.[20]

However, Jean Perré mentions that this note and the instruction that the tanks would comply with infantry attack was not enough, in the event, to counter-balance the aggressive spirit of the tank officers, derived from the influence of the numerous cavalry officers within the AS.[21] The cavalry element within the AS was certainly dominant when Lieutenant Fourier arrived for initial training in November 1916, and he leaves no doubt that the cavalry officers set the tone for tactical thinking in the early AS.[22] One of the *groupement* commanders, Louis Bossut, was a decorated cavalryman, and his conception of tank combat was that of a cavalry-like surprise charge, an idea that was already prevalent when he arrived at Champlieu (the main AS base). However, the dominance of cavalry ideas was not really a matter of numbers; it reflected a continuance of the pre-war status of the different arms. An examination of the casualty lists for 16 April shows that, of 34 AS officers, 13 came from the cavalry, 11 from the infantry and nine from the artillery, so the *AS* was clearly not staffed primarily by the cavalry.[23] It is also worth noting that the other *groupement* commander on 16 April, Louis Chaubès, was an artillery officer.

Bossut was very pessimistic on the eve of the attack, as he was aware that the Germans knew of the French tanks and where they would be used; the appalling weather only added to his anxiety.[24] He told his brother (also serving in the *AS*) on the evening of 15 April: 'despite all that I've been able to do, our attack will be in very bad conditions'.[25]

Bossut believed that it was essential for the *groupement*'s morale for him to lead it from the front, but Estienne initially ordered him to command his unit from a command post near the infantry commander. After lively correspondence, Estienne relented, largely because Bossut persuaded him that the *groupement* would be in effect impossible to command once it passed the French lines, which proved to be the case during the battle. Bossut placed his second in command, Captain de Gouyon, in charge of the *groupement* and de Gouyon was stationed with the infantry staff, following the second infantry wave. De Gouyon had very limited resources to communicate with the *groupement*: a small group of runners and one flag.

Both tank *groupements* were moved into Fifth Army's area by 13 April 1917. The assembly position was chosen as the village of Cuiry-lès-Chaudardes, north of the Aisne. *Groupements Bossut* and *Chaubès* left Champlieu on 11 April and disembarked at Courlandon station on the morning of 12 April. *Groupement Bossut* arrived at Cuiry-lès-Chaudardes that evening, after a difficult nine-kilometre march in driving rain on a very dark evening, with *Groupement Chaubès* arriving the following night.[26] As the attack was again delayed, the *groupements* took the opportunity to make further checks and preparations.[27]

On 16 April, the tanks set off in the early morning from their deployment positions. *Groupement Bossut* was fortunate that its long drive to the French front line in a two-kilometre column was ignored by the German artillery. However, as it reached the narrow bridge over the Miette River it began to receive heavy artillery fire, which continued as the tanks crossed over the French front line. Major Bossut was killed when his tank was hit by an artillery shell just after the tanks had crossed the first German positions. Although a tragedy, this had no impact on the course of his *groupement*'s battle. As the ground was more broken up in front of the second German line, the tanks had greater difficulty crossing it and, for example, one *groupe* lost half its tanks to breakdowns there.[28] One *groupe* (AS 9) got 11 tanks to the third German line, but they were forced by the state of the ground to form into a column to cross the first trench and were then subjected to heavy and accurate German artillery fire, which either immobilised or destroyed all the tanks bar one.[29] Some of the *groupement*'s tanks got past the third German line, but, as there was no infantry in support, the *groupement* was forced to return in *groupes* to the French lines by late afternoon. The *groupement* had penetrated the German lines considerably further than the infantry but had been unable to exploit this success.

Groupement Chaubès had an even worse time. It left its assembly position at 06.20 in a column more than a kilometre long. Almost as soon as the first *groupe* came out of the cover of some woods, the tanks were spotted by German aeroplanes and subjected to immediate artillery fire. As the individual *groupes* moved towards the first German position, they were taken under fire from the flank by German positions untouched by the French artillery preparation and, more seriously, by German heavy artillery being directed by observatories on the Craonne plateau. As the *groupes* moved successively to the German trenches, German artillerymen had the opportunity to carefully adjust their fire, and the last tank *groupes* were subjected to very accurate fire. When the tanks arrived at the first German trench, it was considerably wider than expected and they had to wait for the supporting infantry to come and help them across. The supporting infantry, however, had been subjected to similar artillery fire in their advance, and insufficient numbers were able to get to the German trenches to assist the tanks. The *groupement* ended bunched up just in front of the German positions and was gradually shot to pieces, until it was clear to the *groupe* commanders that their position was untenable and they retired back to the French lines. It was probably fortunate that eight tanks of the last *groupe* (AS 8) had broken down in marshy ground on the way to the jump-off position and were unable to enter the battle.[30]

The failure of the French artillery preparation had doomed Nivelle's plans for a breakthrough; the French infantry took such heavy casualties that their advance quickly slowed to a halt. The tanks had somewhat more success, but this was only relative. Although *Groupement Chaubès* had really not got into combat at all, V Corps reported that the tanks of *Groupement Bossut* had been a great help to its infantry, even though exploitation of their success was prevented by the weight of German artillery and long-range machine-gun fire.[31] Fifth Army's report was less enthusiastic. It noted that the tanks had 'arrived too late' to help the infantry and that it appeared that they could make no headway under artillery fire.[32] However, it also reported that all had admired the 'heroic and stoic effort' of the *AS* in the 'horrible conditions' of that day.[33] The Army Group report on the operation concluded that there had been no way to exploit the tanks' success, as the infantry were unable to follow them and had largely been stuck on the first German position. Nevertheless, it reported that the tanks had made a useful contribution to the operation, particularly by inflicting losses on German counter-attacks, thus enabling the French infantry to consolidate the positions conquered by the tanks.[34]

These modest successes had been bought at a considerable human and material cost; the *AS* had lost 34 killed, 37 missing and 109 wounded, the casualties including a large number of officers.[35] The loss of equipment was equally high: 31 tanks from *Groupement Bossut* and 26 tanks from *Groupement Chaubès* had been destroyed by German artillery, out of a total of 132 tanks deployed.[36] The situation appeared to be so bad that it was rumoured within the *AS* that it was to be disbanded and the men returned to their regiments.[37]

Fortunately, one tank *groupement* had not been committed in the April attack and was therefore still available. The second combat outing of the *AS*, only two weeks after the first, was executed in a very different manner, demonstrating that the *AS* was capable of initiating rapid and effective innovations, making sure that the tough experience of 16 April was not in vain.

Groupement Lefebvre consisted of three *groupes*: two with Schneider tanks and one with St Chamond tanks. *17ᵉBataillon de Chasseurs à Pied* (17 BCP), an elite chasseur battalion, which had been training under the direction of Estienne with the tanks since 3 January, was attached to the *groupement*.[38] The *groupement's* attack on 17 April had been called off at the last minute due to the failure of the infantry attack it was supporting.

This would be the first engagement of the St Chamond tank. The St Chamond was a design initiated by the vehicle department (*Service Auto-mobile*) of the Ministry of Armaments. This tank weighed 23 tonnes and was armed with a full-size 75 mm gun and four machine guns, being powered with an ambitious petrol–electric engine that was beyond the capabilities of the French engineers to make reliable until very late in the war. The tank was plagued with both mechanical failures and ditching problems throughout its use. On the plus side, it was surprisingly fast on level ground and very manoeuvrable because of its independently driven tracks. By comparison to the Schneider, the interior was spacious and electrically lit and exterior observation was good.

On 25 April, the *groupement* was placed under Sixth Army command for an attack east of Laffaux. Although there were awkward approach routes and a deep zone of large shell-holes, the going for the tanks was generally good and the assembly areas were hidden from German observation.

The *AS* officers had taken the opportunity to analyse the 16 April attacks and make sure that mistakes were not repeated. This time, the *groupes* were placed close to the French lines in order that they could advance at the same time as the infantry, not after them. Each battery had specific tasks and objectives, with one battery held in reserve under the *groupe* commander.[39] The tanks were better integrated with the infantry by having the command post of the *groupe* attached to that of the infantry division. The *groupe* commanders now had some tactical flexibility by virtue of having a reserve component. Rather than moving in a line of *groupes*, as in April, the *groupements* were echeloned in depth. There was an aircraft attached to each *groupement* to keep the tank commander informed and to direct artillery fire onto enemy anti-tank batteries. Fighters were dedicated to protect this plane and chase off any enemy artillery-observation planes. Each tank was equipped to call down smoke shells from the artillery to mask its movement.[40] Another innovation was to leave part of the accompanying infantry under the direct control of the *groupe* technical officer, thus ensuring they would better support the tanks.[41]

On 5 May, the Schneider *groupe* moved into action. The tanks arrived at the German lines within half an hour, without losses, despite being under continuous artillery fire. Here they met the first wave of the infantry that had been stalled by machine-gun fire. The tanks freed them up and destroyed numerous machine guns; one tank used cannon fire to trap a group of over 20 Germans in their trenches until they surrendered. The tanks then helped the infantry capture Laffaux Mill. They saw off an immediate German counter-attack, and two tanks even advanced as far as a ravine three kilometres from their jump-off point, before the lack of infantry support caused them to retire.

The attack of the St Chamond *groupe* (AS31) was not so successful. Unsurprisingly, the St Chamonds had considerable difficulty in just getting to the assembly area and the *groupe* lost four tanks to breakdowns on the way.[42] Once in action, the tanks broke down one after another. For example, the left battery entered combat with only two tanks, as the other two were out of action before even reaching the jump-off position. One of the former then broke down and the sole remaining tank was forced to return since the supporting infantry was trapped by machine-gun fire. However, the St Chamonds were not totally useless; two attacked a blockhouse that had halted the French infantry, killing 50 German defenders and causing another 30 to surrender. In another action, one tank opened fire at 200 metres on a large German counter-attack and drove it off.[43]

On 5 May, the *groupement* had losses of 13 officers and 42 men, with the accompanying infantry losing 32 men.[44] Tank losses had been low; only one tank had been destroyed (out of 31 deployed), and thus the results were appreciably better than those of 16 April.[45]

This success was due to a number of factors. The well-prepared routes allowed the tanks to move rapidly and the French air force had mastery of the skies. Unlike on 16 April, French counter-battery fire had effectively suppressed the German artillery and its observation positions, notably reducing the risk to the tanks. The close proximity of the French and German trench lines also meant that the tanks got to the German lines too quickly for the latter's artillery to respond. In sum, this was not a successful attack, but the tanks contributed much of what success there was and their performance was significantly improved from that at Juvincourt.

From the point of view of Estienne and the *AS*, the Nivelle Offensive operations had exposed the deficiencies of both the tanks themselves and the tactical approach taken during these engagements. In relation to tactics, it was clear that the main danger to the French tanks would be from the German artillery. For example, German 111th Field Artillery Regiment, based around Craonne, had knocked out 17 of *Groupement Chaubès'* tanks with under 300 shells of various calibres at a range of three to six kilometres.[46] It had been expected that the tanks would be vulnerable to direct fire from artillery, but the substantial losses to indirect fire had been an unwelcome surprise.

However, the tanks had not been designed to take direct artillery fire, as this was simply beyond the technology of the time. Most of their armour was completely proof against ordinary bullets and resisted the German SmK armour-piercing rifle rounds very well. The Schneider's weaker rear armour was a cause for concern, as it had proven not to be bulletproof on 16 April and there had also been instances when German aircraft fire penetrated the roofs.[47] However, the single artillery casualty on 5 May demonstrated that the tanks could survive artillery fire quite effectively, provided that they kept moving. The main danger remained the vulnerable tracks, which were easily broken by explosions that left the rest of the tank undamaged. Once stationary, the tanks were nearly always destroyed.[48] However, specifically because of the danger from artillery, Estienne had always advised using the tanks at dusk, rather than in broad daylight as they were on 16 April.[49] He also recommended that they should never be left under German artillery fire for more than an hour.[50]

A number of questions arise about this engagement. In particular, should the French have undertaken a limited-size first attack, as the British had done in September 1916? It is clearly impossible to appreciate in advance all aspects when deploying a completely new weapon into an existing tactical situation. The dilemma then becomes a difficult choice about how to introduce the new equipment. Small-scale actions can give useful intelligence while limiting risk, but they can also give considerable information to the enemy about the new weapon, without making a decisive contribution to the engagement, which is what happened to the British at Flers. Surprise had been lost to the French, and thus it seemed logical to experiment with a large-scale employment.[51] As the Nivelle Offensive was planned to be the most decisive battle since the Marne, there was no military reason to hold back a potentially effective weapon.

Other faults in the *AS* planning can be attributed to a lack of combat experience with the tanks. For example, the time it would take to move the tanks into their deployment positions was considerably underestimated, resulting in the *groupements* arriving late, although it is clear that an earlier arrival would not have altered the course of the battle. It has been seen that the liaison between the *AS* and the other arms was either poor or non-existent. This was largely due to the infantry support being improvised over too short a period, with the infantry officers being insufficiently trained on how to work with the tanks. However, the main obstruction for effective infantry–tank liaison was the amount of German artillery and machine-gun fire on the battlefield.[52] The regimental history of 17 BCP notes the unwelcome fact for the accompanying infantry that tanks attracted enemy fire, particularly that of machine guns, to which the tanks were immune, unlike the infantry.[53] Most of the supporting infantry on 16 April and 5 May were unable to help their tanks, due to being pinned down by such fire.[54] Once again, this was a fault of the offensive in general rather than the *AS*, and it is difficult to see how better liaison would have altered the outcome of the battle. Indeed, despite considerable effort put into this area, liaison remained a problem throughout the war because of the limited battlefield communications available in this era. Guderian suggests that engineers, rather than infantry, should have been attached to the tanks, but, although they might have made a quicker passage over the

German trenches, they would have been just as vulnerable to fire as the infantry.[55]

It is an easy assumption that Bossut and the prevailing cavalry ethos in the early *AS* should shoulder much of the blame for 16 April, but this would be unfounded. Certainly, there were some mistakes in Bossut's plans, but these are not particularly attributable to his cavalry background. For example, Bossut had correctly predicted that there would be no command and control of the *groupements* once they got past the French lines. The last XXXII CA HQ heard from Bossut was a message sent via a pigeon that arrived around 10.00, saying that he was sorry but that the tanks were running behind schedule.[56] De Gouyon, in nominal command of *Groupement Bossut*, exercised no discernible influence on the battle and the *groupe* commanders had difficulties even communicating with each other. Fifth Army's report pointed out that the loss of Bossut and his two assistants left Captain Forsanz (commander AS 4) in charge but out of effective communication because the *groupement* was so spread out, which left Forsanz in command in name only as he was unable to issue new orders.[57] Although Commandant Chaubès remained throughout the battle at the infantry command post, as Estienne had wanted Bossut to be, he exercised no more control over his *groupement* than Bossut had.

It has been subsequently argued that the operation was as carefully planned as it could have been; the *AS* had been planning the attack since February and there had been many liaison meetings between the *AS* and the senior infantry commanders before the battle.[58] Indeed, Bossut had spent four days at Fifth Army HQ, planning the attack in consultation with generals Micheler and Gamelin. Moving the *groupements* in large columns across the battlefield proved catastrophic on 16 April. However, it needs to be emphasised that the entire success of the Nivelle Offensive was predicated on both destroying the first two German positions and silencing the German artillery. Since neither of these events occurred, the tanks were considerably more exposed to artillery fire than could have been reasonably foreseen by the *AS* staff. However, if the *groupes* had attacked simultaneously, rather than separately, the German artillery would not have been able to concentrate its fire on each *groupe* in turn, and this was clearly a mistake in the plan. Estienne recognised this as an error and admitted that the tanks should not have been moved into combat on a fixed time-scale but only after the German observation posts had been taken.[59]

What should have been predicted was the heavy traffic on the roads during the offensive, which would have produced delays even if the weather had been good. However, the danger of moving the tanks in large columns was immediately rectified for the attacks on 5 May, when the tanks were moved by battery into their starting positions. Heinz Guderian argued that the tanks should have been committed earlier in order to keep pace with the infantry, before the latter were exhausted, but it is difficult to see how this would this have made any substantive difference on the day.[60] The tanks got over two kilometres further than the infantry anyway; if they had been committed earlier they probably would have become even more isolated, and without effective infantry support there was no possibility for the tanks to succeed.

The mistakes made in the planning of the Nivelle Offensive were only one set of problems for the *AS*; the others concerned the tanks themselves. The Schneiders were shown to have a number of deficiencies. So high was the interior temperature after running the engine for more than 30 minutes, Estienne advised that the tanks would have to be limited to short actions in the future, due to the crews suffering heat exhaustion within four or five hours.[61] There was a suggestion by some Schneider crews that their petrol tanks had caught fire spontaneously, having heated to a critical temperature over the long advance on 16 April, although this seems unlikely as there is no evidence that this ever happened on any other occasion. Just as worrying, the Schneider clutches were prone to breaking when traversing difficult terrain for any length of time.[62]

Another unwelcome surprise to the *AS* was how easily their tanks caught fire. The experience of the Nivelle Offensive suggested that, once artillery had breached the tank armour, they were very likely to catch fire if hit again. In addition, neither the Schneider nor the St Chamond had armour on the underside of their hulls, which meant that high-explosive shells could set the tanks on fire from underneath.[63] For example, *AS* Lieutenant Fourier was badly burned when a shell exploded just under his St Chamond on 5 May, the explosion blowing his 23-tonne tank off the ground and filling it with a 'column of fire'.[64] The Schneiders were difficult to get out of quickly because of their cramped interiors and the fact that the entire crew could only leave through the two small rear doors. The St Chamond had more exits but more crew too, and when a St Chamond caught fire the interior lights usually failed, which created further difficulties in evacuation.[65] In battle conditions, this meant that, with both designs, once their tank was on fire, most of the crews got trapped and were burned alive.[66] For those Schneider crews on 16 April that had placed additional petrol containers on the outside of their tanks, next to the rear doors, getting out in a hurry proved fatally impossible.[67] Léon Dutil describes this practice as 'criminal' and it was quickly forbidden.[68] However, this does not account for the considerable number of tanks that caught fire, as this inadvisable practice was by no means universal on 16 April. Tests demonstrated that the Schneiders did not catch fire when hit by an artillery shell, but artillery fire often punctured the petrol tank, which sprayed petrol around the hot interior and then caught fire.[69] The internal petrol tank of the Schneiders was to be moved in due course to the rear, but the dangers of fire for both designs remained throughout the war.

The St Chamond design was also subject to extensive modifications; Estienne reported that it was primarily the tanks' inadequate tracks that had caused the numerous breakdowns.[70] An increase in the width of the tracks had been asked for since Estienne saw the first prototype in 1916, but only 15 tanks out of 75 had the new wider tracks by 16 June 1917. Various other faults included the fragility of the petrol tanks, which frequently detached themselves from their mountings due to vibration within the tanks.[71] The *AS* also asked for the petrol tank to be armoured, because of the vulnerability to explosions under the tank. There was so much vocal criticism from within the *AS* about the St Chamonds' reliability that the factory's *Directeur général*, Thomas Leurent, was forced to write to the tank programme's oversight committee, the *Comité consultatif de l'artillerie d'assaut*, to defend the design.[72]

The primitive technology available continued to cause problems throughout the war. Notably, on 16 November 1917, only nine Schneider *groupes*, out of 16, were immediately ready for action due to mechanical problems.[73] Although a great effort was made to rectify the medium tanks' faults, they remained prone to breakdowns and ditching until the end of the war.[74]

However, there was to be an unexpected bonus to the Allies from the mixed results of their first tank offensive; the Germans were seriously misled by their success against the tanks. The Germans assumed that the performance of the tanks on 16 April was typical and thus failed to develop precautions against them or develop their own tanks. This was to have serious long-term consequences, as the failure to act in 1916–1917 was to leave the German infantry without any effective means to counter the French tanks in 1918. Only at the very end of the war was the German army seeking effective infantry anti-tank weapons, which was, of course, too late. For example, the German anti-tank rifle, introduced in the spring of 1918, seems to have put only one French tank out of action during the entire war, and the anti-tank mines used by the Germans were not much more effective.[75]

Despite the terrible casualties and the significant loss of material, the *AS* action at Juvincourt had thus unexpectedly provided some distinct advantages to the French. The Nivelle Offensive gave the *AS* the (unwelcome at the time) advantage of exposing all the main faults of the tanks in one operation, thus giving them a good platform for adaptation. This enabled them to make a rapid improvement in battlefield performance just two weeks after the battle of Juvincourt at Laffaux (5 May 1917), an improvement that is impressive in both its scale and speed of implementation.

There was also the need to initiate a series of urgent improvements to the tank designs. The changes made after 16 April may not have entirely made up for the tanks' initial design deficiencies, but the tanks were markedly improved in performance and protection as a result of this experience. However, no amount of enthusiasm for the tanks from the military could compensate for the primitive equipment that had to be worked with. The experience at Juvincourt also had another long-term benefit, as it persuaded Estienne that the medium tanks were not going to be the success he had hoped for, and this directed his attention to the development of the Renault light tanks, which were to prove the most successful tanks of the Great War. Characteristically, Pétain was quick to recognise the value of the *AS*; it was to receive his full support and the tanks became an important component of the French army for the rest of the war.

To sum up, the French made sure that their medium tanks' debut was not a missed opportunity by carefully analysing the engagement and making sure that lessons were learned and changes rapidly implemented. As has been discussed, the operation was actually more promising than it seemed to be at the time and it is also difficult to see how it could have been better planned, given the lack of battlefield experience the French tanks and their crews had. Even with the various operational mistakes made, the tanks in some areas advanced over two kilometres further than the infantry and were able to pass the second German position. Guderian's most extravagant claim in *Achtung Panzer* is that a complete breakthrough would have been possible on 16 April if the tanks had been deployed more effectively, but this seems improbable for all the reasons discussed above.[76] Quite simply, the Nivelle Offensive failed because of an inadequate artillery preparation for the results desired. This should not obscure the significant performance of the *AS* on 16 April and 5 May 1917, particularly considering how difficult the conditions for tank combat were.

Notes

1. Heinz Guderian, *Achtung Panzer,* reprint, translated by Christopher Duffy (London: Cassell, 1937).
2. Estienne, *Compte-rendu d'une mission en Angleterre les 25 et 26 Juin 1916,* 26 June 1916, 16N2121.
3. GQG – *Emploi tactique des cuirassés terrestres,* derived from a conversation with Estienne on 12 December 1915, 18 August 1916, *AFGG IV/2,* Annexes 3, no. 2958; see Jean Perré, *Batailles et Combats des Chars français. L'Année d'Apprentissage 1917* (Paris: Lavauzelle, 1937), p. 29.
4. Albert Stern, *Notebook 1914–1918,* pp. 87–90. Stern Papers – GB0099, *Liddell Hart Centre for Military Archives.*
5. or example, see *Le sous-secrétaire d'État de la Guerre (Artillerie) à M. Le général commandant en chef,* AFGG 4/2, annexes 3, p. 2507.
6. French military mission to GHQ, *Note sur l'emploi des CT le 15 Septembre,* 17 September 1916, AFGG 4/3, annexes 1, p. 463.
7. Quoted in Stern, *Notebook,* p. 89.
8. AFGG 5/1, p. 161.
9. GAR, *Ordre général pour les Ve et VIe armées,* 5 February 1917, AFGG 5/1, annexes 1, p. 603.
10. See Robert Allan Doughty, *Pyrrhic Victory: French Strategy and Operations in the Great War* (London: Harvard University Press, 2005), pp. 318–345.
11. Jean Perré, *Batailles et Combats des Chars français,* p. 21.
12. Ibid., p. 22.
13. *1 AS* Brigade, *Emploi de l'artillerie d'assaut dans la bataille,* 30 August 1918, 16N2156.
14. GQG, *Ordre General No 1: Bases Générales de l'organisation de l'AS,* 1 January 1917, 16N2142.
15. Although in practice the frontages were somewhat wider; see Charles-Maurice Chenu, *Du Kepi Rouge aux Chars d'Assaut* (Paris: Albin-Michel, 1932), p. 232.
16. Estienne, *Rapport au sujet de la participation aux opérations de la V Armée des groupements Bossut et Chaubès de l'artillerie d'assaut,* 23 April 1917, 16N2120, p. 7.
17. Perré, *Batailles et Combats des Chars français,* p. 33.
18. V Armée, *Instruction particulière concernant l'emploi des chars d'assaut,* 23 March 1917. AFGG 5/1, annexes 2, p. 1007.
19. Ibid.
20. Estienne, *Rapport,* p. 8.
21. Perré, *Batailles et Combats des Chars français,* p. 33.
22. Marcel Fourier and Maurice Gagneur, *Avec les chars d'assaut* (Paris: Hachette, 1919), p. 4.
23. Artillerie d'assaut, *Liste nominative donnant les pertes en officiers,* 5 May 1917, 16N2149.
24. Perré, *Batailles et Combats des Chars français,* p. 34.
25. Quoted in Colonel E Ramspacher, *Le General Estienne: Père des Chars* (Paris: Editions Lavauzelle, 1983), p. 61.
26. Estienne, *Rapport,* p. 1.
27. Ibid., p. 2.

28. Ibid., p. 4.
29. Ibid., p. 6.
30. Estienne, *Rapport*, p. 9.
31. *Compte rendu sur l'emploi des chars d'assaut, le 16 avril 1917, 5 CA*, 24 April 1917, AFGG 5/1, annexes 2, p. 1661.
32. V*ᵉ* Armée, *3 Bureau Rapport*, undated, p. 5, 16N2120.
33. Ibid., p. 6.
34. GAN, *Emploi des chars d'assaut à la bataille de l'Aisne*, 30 June 1917. AFGG 5/1, annexes 2, p. 1943.
35. GQG de AFE, *Chars Blindées, no 24.387, Tableau rectifie des pertes en Chars et personnel, par engagement, au cours de la campagne*, 9 September 1919, 16N2120.
36. Estienne, *Rapport, Tableau no. 2*.
37. Chenu, *Képi Rouge*, p. 248.
38. *Historique du 17ᵉ Bataillon de Chasseurs à Pied pendant la Guerre de 1914–1918*, (Paris: Berger-Levrault, undated), pp. 11–12.
39. Léon Dutil, *Les Chars d'Assaut. Leur Création et leur Rôle pendant la Guerre (1915–1918)* (Paris: Berger-Levrault, 1919), p. 50.
40. Perré, *Batailles et Combats des Chars français*, p. 93.
41. AFGG V/1, annexes 2, no. 1935.
42. Ibid.
43. Ibid.
44. Ibid.
45. Ibid.
46. III Régiment d'artillerie de campagne, 116/17, *Dans quelle mesure le régiment de combat L'a contribue à repousser l'attaque de tanks dirigée le 16 Avril 1917 contre le front de la division d'Ersatz Bavaroise*, 8 June 1917, p. 1, 16N2120.
47. Estienne, *Rapport*, p. 12.
48. AFGG 5/1, annexes 2, 1661.
49. Estienne, *Rapport*, p. 14.
50. Ibid.
51. A point made by Pétain; see *Le Général commandant en chef à Monsieur le ministre de l'armement et des fabrications de guerre*, 4 July 1918, 16N2120.
52. Estienne, *Rapport*, p. 13.
53. Anonymous, *Historique du 17ᵉ Bataillon de Chasseurs à Pied* (Paris: Berger-Levrault, undated, circa 1920), p. 12.
54. Estienne, *Rapport*, p. 7.
55. Guderian, *Achtung Panzer*, p. 66.
56. V*ᵉ* Armée, *3 Bureau Rapport*, p. 1.
57. Ibid., p. 5.
58. Dutil, *Les Chars*, pp. 48–49.
59. Estienne, *Rapport*, p. 14.
60. Guderian, *Achtung Panzer*, p. 67.
61. Estienne, *Rapport au sujet de la participation du groupement Lefebvre et du 17ᵉ BCP aux opérations de la VIᵉ armée, les 5 et 6 Mai 1917*, 18 May 1917, 16N2120.
62. Estienne, *Rapport 18 Mai*.
63. This also made the crews vulnerable to injury from fragments of grenades that exploded under their tanks. See Estienne, *Rapport 18 Mai*.
64. Fourier, *Les Chars*, p. 108.

65. However, note that at this time neither the Schneider nor any of the British tanks had interior lighting.
66. Stern Notebook.
67. GAN, *Le Général Commandant en Chef à Monsieur le Ministre de l'Armement et des Fabrication de Guerre*, 4 July 1917, 16N2120.
68. Dutil, *Les Chars*, p. 46.
69. *Le Général commandant en chef*, 4 July 1917.
70. Estienne, *Rapport 18 Mai*.
71. Ibid.
72. *L'Administrateur directeur général de la cie. à Monsieur le ministre*, 14 June 1917, 16N2120.
73. GAN, *Artillerie d'Assaut, Situation des groupes d'AS au point de vue disponibilité à la date du 15 Novembre 1917*, 16 November 1917, 16N2120.
74. See Tim Gale, *The French Army's Tank Force and Armoured Warfare in the Great War* (Farnham: Ashgate, 2013), pp. 62–65.
75. See Gale, *French Army's Tank Force*, Table A.1, p. 245.
76. Guderian, *Achtung Panzer*, p. 67.

5
Applying Colonial Lessons to European War: The British Expeditionary Force 1902–1914

Spencer Jones

Introduction

The British Expeditionary Force (BEF) occupied a unique place among the great European armies that went to war in August 1914. It was an all-volunteer force whose composition stood in contrast to the conscripted militaries of the continent. This form of service was much in keeping with the ideals of British parliamentary democracy and enhanced individual tactical training, but these advantages came at the expense of numbers. Voluntary recruitment seriously limited the army's pool of manpower and the BEF consisted of just six infantry divisions and a single cavalry division at the outbreak of war. In numerical terms it was only fractionally stronger than the small Belgian army and was dwarfed by the forces of France and Germany.[1] However, its small size belied its fighting qualities, and the BEF established an impressive reputation as a result of its battlefield performance in 1914.[2]

Both the size and skill of the BEF owed a great deal to its colonial background. The protective shield of the Royal Navy meant that Britain had little fear of direct invasion and consequently had neither the need nor the desire to maintain a large army of continental proportions. With the Royal Navy ensuring home defence, the primary combat duty of the army was to provide imperial security, expanding British influence and protecting her interests around the empire.[3] The variety of potential trouble spots and the weak logistical network on many imperial frontiers meant that it was desirable to maintain a small and flexible army that was capable of rapid deployment and swift operations. The small, all-volunteer British army was well suited to this role. John Bourne has aptly described the army of the pre-war era as 'a colonial police force' and noted that its outlook and values were shaped by its imperial experience.[4] However, some historians have viewed the colonial experience of the BEF as a source of weakness. The meaning of the phrase 'colonial army' has become obscured and a casual assumption has developed that such a force could not possibly be prepared for modern warfare on the continent.[5]

This chapter will explore the concept of the BEF as a 'colonial army' and reach an informed conclusion on the value of the British army's imperial background in the context of the fighting of 1914. The chapter will examine the army's experiences of colonial warfare and highlight the complexities of this type of combat, demonstrating that frontier campaigns were often complex and dangerous. Particular attention will be paid to the Anglo-Boer War (1899–1902), which was the largest and bloodiest colonial campaign fought by the British army in the years before the First World War. The second part of the chapter will consider how colonial warfare influenced the outlook of the army towards tactics, training, equipment and doctrine, showing how the wealth of recent combat experience possessed by officers at all levels of the BEF shaped its development in the early 20th century. Finally, the chapter will assess the combat performance of the BEF in 1914. Ultimately, this work will demonstrate how the colonial experience of the BEF was a foundation of strength rather than a source of weakness. The BEF certainly possessed vulnerabilities and suffered from certain idiosyncrasies that proved detrimental in 1914, but, taken as a whole, it proved an effective fighting force. The development of the army was profoundly shaped by imperial warfare, especially the Anglo-Boer War, and these tactical lessons were of considerable value in 1914.

Colonial warfare

The reign of Queen Victoria (1837–1901) was marked by a staggering number of colonial wars. The British army was involved in at least one operation in every year of her 64-year reign, fighting a total of 230 wars in the period.[6] Of these, only the Crimean War (1854–1856) was fought against a European opponent. The remainder were colonial wars fought to either expand or defend the empire. These wars were waged in an enormous variety of geographical and climatic conditions, from the deserts of Egypt and Sudan, to the mountains of the North West Frontier, to the jungles of Burma or the forests of New Zealand.[7] The variety of terrain was matched by the varied nature of Britain's enemies, from the Egyptian and Sikh armies, trained and organised on European lines, to the primitively armed but highly disciplined Zulus, to the fanatical and reckless Mahdists. The intensity of the conflicts varied widely, ranging from tiny operations such as the Anglo-Zanzibar War of 1896, which lasted just 40 minutes, to major struggles such as the suppression of the Indian Mutiny (1857–1858) and the Anglo-Boer War (1899–1902).[8]

Popular imagination often views colonial warfare as a series of hopeless mismatches between soldiers armed with modern weapons and poorly equipped natives. However, as contemporary army reformer Leo Amery observed, 'These wars against savages were by no means the child's play that foreign critics have often asserted'.[9] Although technology provided a critical and often decisive advantage to European forces, it was not a universal panacea to the problems of frontier warfare. Intelligence, logistics, morale and leadership were all crucial factors.[10] In the absence of these strengths, even technologically advanced armies could come to grief. Notorious battlefield defeats at Isandlwana (1879), Maiwand (1880) and Majuba Hill (1881) were all partially a result of poor British command and leadership. Elsewhere, the Italian disaster at the Battle of Adwa (1896) served as a stark warning of the risks of arrogance and incompetence.

Despite the dangers, colonial warfare served as a means for young British officers to test themselves in battle and establish a reputation within the army. Colonial warfare was an unforgiving school. Rudyard Kipling's poem 'The Young British Soldier' advised wounded soldiers in Afghanistan to commit suicide rather than fall into enemy hands, and the fear of capture by merciless enemies was a very real one for both officers and men.[11] Several prominent officers of the BEF in 1914 carried scars from wounds suffered in earlier colonial wars. Major-General Henry Wilson had a severe facial scar suffered in hand-to-hand combat in Burma that had earned him the cruel nickname 'Ugly Wilson'.[12] Major-General Sir William Robertson had been seriously injured when he was betrayed and attacked by a guide on the North West Frontier in 1895.[13] Lieutenant-General Sir Archibald Murray had been shot in the stomach in the Anglo-Boer War and was still troubled by the effects of the wound in 1914.[14] The most famous colonial survivor was General Sir Horace Smith-Dorrien, who, although unwounded, had been one of just five British officers who escaped the disaster at Isandlwana in 1879.[15]

Colonial warfare was a dangerous environment, but it did have the important advantage of providing officers with practical combat experience.[16] However, integrating the lessons of imperial warfare into tactics and training proved difficult. The sheer variety of the campaigns fought by the British army made composing a universal approach impractical and, for many officers, undesirable. However, military setbacks in the 1880s resulted in the introduction of some doctrinal guidance for colonial warfare in the 1890s. The 1893 edition of *Infantry Drill* contained a short section on 'Savage Warfare', which advised on the use of the square formation but offered few further directions.[17] In 1896 this was followed by Charles Callwell's famous treatise *Small Wars*, a sizeable semi-official publication which offered a combination of historical example and practical advice for fighting a variety of foes.

In the absence of official guidance, individual officers and battalions drew their own lessons from combat. For example, General Sir Ian Hamilton based much of his early tactical thinking on his experiences as a lieutenant at the Battle of Majuba Hill.[18] However, because experience was inconsistently spread across the army, direct learning could prove patchy. In the aftermath of defeat at Majuba Hill, the officers of the Northamptonshire Regiment were said to have taken an oath that they would not rest until their unit had improved its standard of shooting.[19] This resulted in a marked improvement in the battalion's marksmanship, but this change was not mirrored elsewhere in the army. Some experienced units even chose to guard their own hard-earned knowledge, to the detriment of the army as a whole.[20] Unfortunately, the result of this parochial approach was an army with much useful combat experience but an uneven approach to tactics and training.

The weaknesses in British tactics were exposed in the Anglo-Boer War (1899–1902). The Boers were determined foes equipped with modern magazine-loading rifles and small quantities of the latest artillery. They also possessed unusual fighting characteristics, with an emphasis on mobility and firepower, which made them a uniquely dangerous opponent.[21] Indeed, Callwell considered that the military style of the Boers meant that they had more in common with a European opponent than with Britain's usual colonial enemies.[22] The conflict would prove to be the bloodiest of all the 'small wars' fought by the British army in the era.[23]

The defining feature of the Anglo-Boer War was the use of smokeless magazine rifles. Although previous colonial opponents had occasionally made use of small numbers of modern weapons, this was the first time the British army had encountered magazine firepower on a large scale. The range, accuracy and rapidity of Boer marksmanship came as a grave shock to inexperienced British battalions.[24] The crucible of rifle fire revealed three major problems with British army tactics. First, the intensity of Boer firepower necessitated the adoption of widely extended infantry formations. Lord Roberts recommended between six and eight yards per man, but in practice extension frequently exceeded this distance. At the Battle of Diamond Hill (11–12 June 1900) some battalions advanced extended to 30 yards per man.[25] Widely extended on the battlefield and often beyond the direct control of higher command, both junior officers and men found themselves required to exercise a great deal of personal initiative. Peacetime training had not anticipated this feature of modern war, which in turn led to men becoming paralysed in action. This could lead to desultory long-distance firing in the place of a determined attack or fundamental mistakes in the defence, best expressed by the misfortunes of the hapless 'Backsight Forethought' in Ernest Swinton's classic tactical study *The Defence of Duffers Drift*.[26] At worst, it could result in panic and defeat.[27]

A second, related problem was that the fieldcraft of the average British soldier was poor. Troops drilled in a system that emphasised strict discipline struggled to adapt to fluid fighting conditions. One brigade commander noted: 'At first officers and men were very stupid about finding cover.'[28] Similarly, soldiers struggled to conduct a firefight without direct orders and frequently proved to be no match for the skilful individual marksmen of the Boers.[29] Leo Amery offered a scathing assessment of the average soldier, stating: 'They were indifferent shots, careless of cover, slow to comprehend what was taking place, or to grasp the whereabouts of the enemy, always getting surprised or lost, helpless without their officers.'[30]

The third problem that confronted the British army was the need for much greater firepower at all levels. Infantry discovered that their volley-based musketry training was inadequate for modern warfare. It was also found that firefights were longer and more intense than anticipated, requiring considerable ammunition and incurring significant casualties.[31] For the cavalry, it was found that the standard-issue carbine was all but useless against an enemy armed with a rifle that had an effective range more than double that of the cavalry's firearm. The equipping of horsemen with infantry rifles provided a short-term but cumbersome solution; nevertheless, they were a necessary requirement in a war where the cavalry carried out most of its fighting dismounted.[32] Finally, the Royal Artillery had the embarrassment of being outranged by Boer 'Long Toms' – 155 mm siege guns that had been deployed in the field – and were forced to turn to the Royal Navy to provide a hastily improvised heavy artillery piece in the form of the 4.7 inch gun.[33]

Overall, the unforgiving nature of warfare on the *veld* ruthlessly exposed outdated tactics and inefficient officers, revealing that much pre-war training had been misguided. However, after initial defeats, the army demonstrated its flexibility and devised new approaches that often stood in direct opposition to those recommended by the drill book.[34] The effectiveness of Boer firepower necessitated a profound reconsideration of assault tactics, with a fresh emphasis on dispersed attack formations, prolonged artillery support and flanking movements. In early 1900, Lord Roberts made the adaptations official through the issue of a series of memorandums entitled 'Notes for Guidance in South African Warfare'.[35] This new in-theatre doctrine emphasised firepower and manoeuvre, while highlighting the importance of practicality.

Although South Africa was the graveyard of many officers and even more army careers, it was also a brutally effective proving ground for the best leaders in the field. While the success of the venerable Lord Roberts proved that age was not necessarily a barrier to success, many of the officers who saw their reputation enhanced during the war were of a younger generation and thus perhaps less hidebound and more adaptable. A common thread linking many of the senior officers of the BEF in 1914 was that they had succeeded in South Africa.[36] John French had commanded cavalry forces in the early months of the war and been promoted to lead the Cavalry Division in 1900, a duty which he performed with distinction. French was ably assisted by his chief of staff, Douglas Haig, who distinguished himself with his forceful leadership in the guerrilla phase of the conflict. Edmund Allenby had served in the Cavalry Division as a junior officer and was later promoted to command his own mobile column. Horace Smith-Dorrien had commanded an infantry brigade and later an all-arms mobile column, and had seen first-hand the effects of modern rifle fire on attacking troops. Successful staff officers also saw their reputations enhanced. Archibald Murray, Henry Wilson and David Henderson all performed well in their respective roles, which in turn saw their careers enhanced in the years of peace that followed.

The war brought a new generation of combat-experienced officers to the forefront of the British army and became a starting point for introspection, debate and reform. Unlike earlier colonial campaigns, which were small-scale and thus rarely had any influence beyond the officers and units involved, the majority of the army had fought in South Africa. This provided a shared base of experience from which future lessons would be distilled. When considering the colonial background of the BEF of 1914, it is important to remember that the Anglo-Boer War was the defining element.

Integrating colonial experience

The duration and intensity of the Anglo-Boer War left a deep mark on the psyche of the British army. The conflict had featured many of the key elements of modern warfare. The British army had witnessed the effectiveness of modern rifles, long-range artillery, defensive entrenchments and even wire entanglements. Required to fight on the offensive for the majority of the war, the British had experienced first-hand some of the difficulties inherent in attacking a well-armed and deeply entrenched foe. The solution had been a combination of greater mobility, superior leadership, close artillery support, improved infantry tactics and an element of sheer attrition.[37]

The war had clearly shown the importance of firepower. Magazine-loading infantry rifles were longer-ranged, faster-firing and more accurate than ever before. In response, both sides sought to minimise casualties through the employment of extended formations, use of cover, and the construction of trenches and other man-made defensive positions. However, as the burden of the attack lay on the British, the army was forced to accept the fact that casualties could not be entirely avoided in an advance against a well-armed enemy. Veteran officers soon realised that the key to a successful attack was suppression of enemy fire. The best way to achieve this effect was through maximising friendly firepower and making the most of modern rifles, machine guns and supporting artillery.

The keynote of British tactical reform prior to the First World War was the imperative to harness firepower. The most striking change was the reform of British infantry fire tactics. Before the Anglo-Boer War, the army had reduced the battlefield potential of magazine rifles by employing them in a rigid and unrealistic system of volley fire.[38] This had proved inadequate in combat and had been replaced with a system of officer-directed independent fire, but the weakness of individual British marksmanship had been a persistent problem.[39] Lord Robert summed the issue up:

> [The British soldier] was the exact opposite of the Boer, especially in his want of knowledge of the ground and how to utilise it, and in his defective powers of observation. His shooting cannot be described as good...there was no real marksmanship...The shooting at short ranges...was ineffective, and at long ranges the distance was seldom accurately estimated.[40]

Announcing a reform of musketry training in 1902, Roberts stated that the first object in the training of a soldier was 'to make him a good shot'.[41] To this end, the old system of volley firing was abandoned and was replaced with exercises that aimed to make each soldier an effective individual marksman. In 1903 it was agreed to provide a minimum of 300 rounds of practice ammunition to each man per year, and, although this was reduced to 250 rounds due to budget restrictions in 1906, the figure was substantially greater than the practice ammunition allocation on the continent.[42]

Musketry training comprised a variety of exercises inspired by the hard apprenticeship the army had served on the *veld*. In contrast to pre-war training, all firing exercises took place with the soldier kneeling or prone, and many were carried out under a strict time limit. The objective of this work was to develop the 'snap shooting' skills that had given the Boers such an advantage in close-range fire-fights. The most famous exercise of all was the 'Mad Minute'. In this drill the soldier was required to fire 15 rounds within 60 seconds against a target 300 yards away. To increase the difficulty, the rifleman started with five rounds in his weapon and was only allowed to reload in five-round increments, thus ensuring he would need to change magazine twice.[43] Completing this challenging exercise was considered the true test of the soldier, and a great deal of individual and regimental pride was attached to scoring highly. In addition, coveted marksmanship badges and extra pay were awarded to those who reached a high standard in rifle training.[44]

Infantry training was further enhanced by the procurement of a new rifle in the form of the Short Magazine Lee-Enfield (SMLE). Designed with the experience of South Africa in mind, the SMLE was shortened to make it easier to handle when fighting from behind cover, yet retained the accuracy of a longer-barrelled weapon. The bolt action was designed so as not to interrupt the aim of the soldier, which enabled a skilled marksman to fire rapidly and accurately.[45] The SMLE was also designed so that it could serve as a universal rifle for infantry and cavalry. The experience of inadequate carbines had convinced the mounted arm of the need for a superior weapon, and the SMLE was an ideal replacement. Its comparatively small size and admirable accuracy made it the perfect weapon for the cavalry to employ in dismounted action.

The cavalry took advantage of the new weapons by training their troopers on the same musketry course as the infantry, including completion of the 'Mad Minute' exercise. However, although the Anglo-Boer War had demonstrated the need for a fresh emphasis on shooting and dismounted work, the conflict had also shown the value of shock action, with the successful charge at the Battle of Elandslaagte (21 October 1899) and the mounted breakthrough at Klip Drift (15 February 1899) proving that traditional tactics were far from obsolete.[46] How best to integrate a combination of dismounted firepower and mounted shock action was a problem that taxed the army for a number of years. The resulting tactical debate was long and often controversial.[47] However, by 1912 the cavalry had settled on a hybrid approach to tactics that emphasised a combination of both fighting styles.[48]

An equally fierce debate gripped the Royal Artillery in the aftermath of the South African war. The conflict had marked the first time in decades that the gunners had faced an opponent armed to a comparable standard; in some cases Boer equipment had actually been superior.[49] A great deal had gone wrong for the Royal Artillery in the early months of the war. Setbacks had included the destruction of Colonel Charles Long's batteries at the Battle of Colenso (15 December 1899) and the prolonged but ineffective preliminary bombardment at the Battle of Magersfontein (11 December 1899). However, by the time of the Battle of the Tugela Heights (14–27 February 1900) the gunners had improved their tactics and coordination with the infantry to the point that the long arm played a decisive role.[50]

In the aftermath of the war the artillery pondered the implications of its experiences. In 1902 the Royal Artillery Institution invited officers to produce an essay in answer to the question 'Has the experience of war in South Africa shown that any change is necessary in the system of field artillery fire tactics (in the attack as well as the defence) in European warfare?'[51] The question drew numerous detailed replies. The respondents varied in their interpretations but were virtually unanimous on the fact that the war had great relevance for European fighting. The key themes that emerged were the need for improved weapons, the importance of concealment from enemy fire and the thorny issue of co-operation with the infantry.

This resulted in the procurement of new weapons for all branches of the artillery. Field artillery received the 18-pounder, horse artillery the 13-pounder, and the new heavy artillery branch was equipped with 60-pounder guns. These weapons owed much of their design to the experience of South Africa. The 18-pounder was the heaviest field gun in its class, with officers arguing that the war had shown that heavy shells were essential to suppress enemy trenches.[52] Similarly, the 60-pounder was a gun designed with the Boer 'Long Toms' firmly in mind.[53] The new procurement policy resulted in efficient, practical weapons. However, the small size of the army and its colonial duties, where there was little call for massed artillery, meant that actual numbers of guns were comparatively low. Each British infantry division of 1914 was supported by a total of 76 artillery pieces, of which four were 60-pounders. By curious coincidence, this was exactly the same number of guns that had been assembled for the Battle of Pieter's Hill (27 February 1900), which was notable for being the most sophisticated artillery bombardment of the Anglo-Boer War.[54]

In the absence of overwhelming strength in numbers, the Royal Artillery was forced to consider the value of concealing its weapons. The war had shown that concealed artillery was difficult to locate and almost impossible to silence permanently.[55] However, concealment of guns was a contentious point for the Royal Artillery. The idea of hiding behind hills and in earthworks ran contrary to the prized fighting spirit of the gunners. Furthermore, it also required complex firing procedures, as targets would often be engaged without being in direct line of sight.[56] Yet, conversely, deploying guns in the open was likely to bring swift destruction from the fire of the enemy. This was a serious danger when considering the possibility of war against a European foe, such as Germany or Russia, which would have a preponderance of artillery. The Royal Artillery struggled with the best policy to adopt and ultimately compromised by suggesting the final decision was best left to the 'man on the spot'.[57] In 1914 most gunners chose the concealed route, although the unusual circumstances of the Battle of Le Cateau (26 August 1914) led to some guns deploying in the open and suffering severely as a consequence.

One of the difficulties inherent in the concealed versus open position debate was whether a hidden battery could properly support the infantry. The lessons of South Africa had shown that modern rifle fire made unsupported infantry attacks futile. Instead, careful artillery preparation and then support throughout the attack were paramount. Some officers argued that guns thrust into the firing line were the solution to infantry support, whereas others argued that calm and accurate fire from concealed positions was the best policy.[58] Artillery–infantry co-operation was one of the essential features of modern warfare, and, although the British army was aware of the importance of the issue, it had not found a definitive solution by the eve of the First World War.[59]

In the absence of rigid doctrinal guidance on precise tactics, the army trusted to the initiative of its officers and, to a lesser extent, its men. This had been a startling lesson of the South African war and one that was seized upon in the years that followed. The 1902 edition of *Combined Training* stated: 'Success in war cannot be expected unless all ranks have been trained in peace to use their wits' and decried 'the paralyzing habit of an unreasoning and mechanical adherence to the letter of orders and routine'.[60] At the 1906 General Staff Conference, cavalry officer Brigadier-General Michael Rimington stated: 'The keynote of our training is always the same: *Develop the individual initiative of every officer, non-commissioned officer and man.*'[61] In 1909 the authority of the man on the spot was codified in *Field Service Regulations*.

However, the developing spirit of initiative came at the cost of a degree of conformity. Although the keynote of British tactics was the need to harness firepower, the army's strategic role remained the defence of the empire. An overly rigid adherence to a particular tactical approach could lead to defeat if the army was called upon to fight in a colonial struggle where the conditions were inappropriate. As such, both the General Staff and the Army Council were reluctant to enforce operational or tactical conformity on the military.[62] While this guaranteed flexibility, it weakened the ability of the army to coordinate effectively on large-scale deployments. This was a particular problem as training in the operational level of war was limited by considerations of time, cost and available space. Aldershot Command, consisting of 1st and 2nd Divisions, was best served in this respect and was rightly regarded as the elite of the army. The remaining infantry divisions were left to train individually unless brought together for army manoeuvres. Unfortunately, this meant that the divisions had little experience of working alongside one another, and inter-divisional staff co-operation was particularly poor. The Army Council rather casually assumed that the commander-in-chief would ensure unity of action through the force of his personality.[63]

Nevertheless, although a certain weakness remained, the British army underwent a considerable tactical improvement between 1899 and 1914. These changes began in the Anglo-Boer War and the army swiftly recognised that they had universal value. The tactical overhaul that followed was based on the experience of facing modern firepower, and, within the budgetary constraints of the day, sought to improve the fighting strength of the three British 'teeth' arms through improved equipment and training. These skills were to prove of great value when the colonial army deployed to the continent in 1914. At the outbreak of war, Captain Richard Meinertzhagen commented in his diary:

> Our Expeditionary Force is terribly small, but a mighty weapon, for every soldier can shoot and every man is determined to fight. The Germans will soon find that out. We are not the soldiers of the South Africa War, but, man for man, a great deal more efficient, better trained, better armed and better led than the German.[64]

The colonial army in 1914

British official historian James Edmonds famously described the BEF of 1914 as 'incomparably the best trained, best organised, and best equipped British army which ever went forth to war'.[65] However, Edmonds also recognised that the army possessed certain weaknesses, particularly its small size.[66] The other fundamental problem was the lack of operational synergy. Commander-in-chief Sir John French was hampered by a dysfunctional GHQ and proved unable to impose his authority on his subordinate formations. As a result, the BEF became fragmented during the trials of the Great Retreat. Haig's I Corps and Smith-Dorrien's II Corps retreated on diverging lines after the Battle of Mons and then essentially fought their own campaigns until reunited in early September. Similarly, the pressures of the retreat caused Allenby's oversized Cavalry Division to splinter into its component brigades. The disorganised BEF was pursued by the full weight of Alexander von Kluck's First Army and was only able to break away after the risky stand at the Battle of Le Cateau (26 August). The situation was dangerous; the mauling of the 1st Cheshires at Audrienges (24 August) and the destruction of the 2nd Munster Fusiliers at Etreux (27 August) demonstrated the grave risks of the retreat. Nevertheless, the BEF ultimately eluded German pursuit with comparatively few casualties and was in a position to play an important role at the Battle of the Marne in early September. However, operational problems would continue to dog the army for the remainder of the campaign, particularly at the Battle of the Aisne (13–15 September).

The ability of the BEF to overcome its operational vulnerabilities and perform well on the battlefields of 1914 owed a great deal to its colonial background. Leo Amery had commented of the Anglo-Boer War that a less experienced force than the British army would have failed utterly; the same comparison can be made for the BEF's campaign in 1914.[67] Given the lack of leadership from the top of the army, much of the fighting of 1914 was characterised by 'soldier's battles' in which a great deal of responsibility fell onto the shoulders of relatively junior officers. Fortunately, the colonial experience of the British army and its approach to training ensured it was well equipped for this type of combat. It could find expression in relatively minor incidents, such as Major Tom Bridges' famous improvisation of a marching band, using instruments acquired from a nearby toy shop, to rally exhausted soldiers at St Quentin.[68] More importantly, the spirit of initiative also informed crucial battlefield decisions. Smith-Dorrien's resolution to turn and fight at the Battle of Le Cateau went against Sir John French's orders, but the decision was entirely in keeping with the ethos espoused by *Field Service Regulations*. The decision proved to be correct and the battle resulted in II Corps breaking away from German pursuit. At the Battle of Ypres (19 October–22 November), the pace and intensity of the fighting meant that brigadiers and battalion commanders were best placed to make key decisions. During the fighting for Gheluvelt on 31 October, the quick thinking of Brigadier-General Charles FitzClarence in organising an immediate counter-attack and the determination of Major Edward Hankey in carrying out the orders saved the BEF from disaster. FitzClarence had no formal authority over Hankey's battalion, which belonged to a different brigade, but the spirit of initiative that permeated the army ensured their fruitful co-operation.

The value of colonial experience was further demonstrated in tactical combat, as the reforms of the post-Boer War period were put to the acid test in August 1914. The legend that attacking German infantry mistook British rifle fire for machine guns may be doubted, but the overall effectiveness of the BEF's musketry was high.[69] To take a single example, during rearguard fighting at Frameries (24 August), British rifle fire took a severe toll on attacking German regiments, annihilating six assault companies of the 24th (Bradenburg) Regiment and inflicting over 25 per cent casualties on the supporting 64th Infantry Regiment.[70] Smith-Dorrien was so impressed by 'the shooting power of our infantry' at the Battle of Mons (23 August) that it influenced his decision to turn and fight at Le Cateau three days later.[71]

The quality of British musketry was particularly important, as a number of factors diminished the level of support that the Royal Artillery could provide. The pace of the campaign and the nature of many rearguard actions prevented the gunners from deploying more than a handful of guns. When the long arm did find opportunity to deploy on a larger scale, as it did at the Battle of Le Cateau and the Aisne, it found itself outnumbered and outgunned by German artillery.[72] The numerical advantage enjoyed by the Germans became even more pronounced at the Battle of Ypres, where the Royal Artillery was further limited by severe shortages of ammunition. In these circumstances, while the heroism and self-sacrifice demonstrated at Le Cateau had its place, the gunners immediately recognised the importance of concealment.[73] Even though outgunned, the performance of the Royal Artillery at the Battle of Ypres was particularly effective. The British gunners were capable of inflicting severe damage on attacking enemy infantry while remaining concealed from German counter-battery fire.[74]

Arguably, the arm which benefited most from the Anglo-Boer War was the cavalry. The acrimonious debate on cavalry tactics had ultimately produced the best-trained horsemen in Europe by 1914.[75] The cavalry proved itself more than a match for its German rivals. Clashes between the two mounted arms on the Great Retreat saw the British prove their dominance. The action at Cerizy (28 August) represented a textbook combination of fire and cold steel, while the affair at Nery (1 September) was a victory based on superior firepower. The bruising encounters with British cavalry left the German horsemen reluctant to engage.[76] Ruminating on the superior performance of British cavalry in 1914, a veteran German cavalry officer noted: 'Owing to the advantage of long term service, as well as to the lesson learned in the South African War, the British cavalry were indisputably far better trained for dismounted action than their Continental fellow horsemen.'[77] The British cavalry's ability to fight dismounted would prove particularly valuable when they were deployed in a holding role at the Battle of Ypres.

The experience of 1914 proved that the lessons of the Anglo-Boer War had been essentially correct. Inevitably, there were surprises in store. The weight and power of German artillery came as an unpleasant shock and necessitated a revision of British entrenchment methods, while the effectiveness of machine guns was illustrated beyond doubt. However, the fundamental tactics that the British had derived from colonial warfare, namely, the need for initiative, fieldcraft, concealment and firepower, all proved their worth in 1914.

It is significant to note that the Germans saw the BEF's colonial background as a source of strength. A surviving veteran recalled: 'Every effort had been put into our training, but it was completely inadequate preparation for such a serious assault on battle hardened, long service colonial soldiers.'[78] A German semi-official account of the Battle of Ypres published in 1917 commented: 'Many of our gallant men were killed, and the officers, who were first to rise in an assault, were special target of the enemy's sharpshooters, well trained in long colonial wars.' The same account referred to the tenacity of British defensive lines and attributed their effectiveness to the experience gained in 'a colonial war against the most cunning of enemies in equally difficult country'.[79] The German source assumed that most of the BEF's soldiers were combat veterans of the Anglo-Boer War. This was incorrect, but the lessons of the conflict had defined the army's tactical approach in the inter-war years and clearly proved their value in 1914.

Conclusions

When assessing the importance of the reforms inspired by the Anglo-Boer War, it is important to note that the army attempted to integrate lessons that had universal value. The BEF was a true expeditionary force that could be required to fight on colonial frontiers or against a European opponent on the continent. As a result, theatre-specific lessons from the Anglo-Boer War, such as the use of large quantities of mounted infantry and the employment of pom-pom guns in an infantry support role, were abandoned by the time of the First World War. Instead, the focus was placed upon tactics that were appropriate for fighting the most formidable opponents the British were likely to encounter. In terms of colonial deployments, this was taken to mean either a third conflict with the Boers of South Africa or a major operation on the North West Frontier. If a continental deployment was required, then this would mean a clash with Germany or possibly Russia.

The army's ability to prepare for a variety of deployments marked an improvement on the ethos of the military in the Victorian era. In the late Victorian army there had been a distinct intellectual line between the 'continentalists', who favoured the adoption of European tactics, particularly those practised in Germany, and the 'colonialists', who argued that the British army should take its own path by focusing on tactics suitable for 'small wars'.[80] In the army of the Edwardian era this distinction had all but disappeared. Although there remained vigorous tactical debate, the discussions were framed in terms of what would make the army most effective against an enemy equipped with modern weapons. The root of this change lay with the Anglo-Boer War. The size, ethos and duties of the British army meant that it could not easily follow continental examples and instead had to learn within its own framework.

The value of colonial experience was proven in 1914. Thrust into a confused and hard-fought campaign, the BEF emerged victorious in large part due to its tactical skills and tenacity. The contrast between the opening moves of the Anglo-Boer War and the initial months of the First World War is striking. In the earlier conflict, the army lumbered into action and was outmanoeuvred and embarrassed by a force of citizen militia. In 1914, the small BEF frequently outfought its larger German opponent and established a reputation for military skill that has endured for a century. It is difficult not to agree with the assessment given by one First World War veteran in 1921, who stated: 'Paul Krueger [president of the Transvaal who had declared war in 1899] was the best friend the British Army ever had.'[81]

Notes

1. James Edmonds, *Official History of the Great War: Military Operations France and Belgium 1914*, Vol. 1 (London: MacMillan, 1922), p. 10.
2. For a useful summary of the historiography of the BEF of 1914, see Fred R. Van Hartesveldt, *The Battles of the British Expeditionary Forces, 1914–1915: Historiography and Annotated Bibliography* (Westport: Praeger, 2005), pp. 4–14.
3. The National Archives UK [hereafter TNA], WO 33/48, Paper 148A: Military Requirements of the Country, 1888.
4. John Bourne, 'The British Working Man in Arms', in Hugh Cecil and Peter Liddle (eds.), *Facing Armageddon* (London: Leo Cooper, 1996), p. 337.
5. For negative views on the value of colonial warfare, see G.R. Searle, *The Quest for National Efficiency: A Study in British Politics and Political Thought 1899–1914* (Oxford: Blackwell, 1971), p. 50; John Ellis, *The Social History of the Machine Gun* (London: Pimlico, 1993), p. 102; Robin Neillands, *The Old Contemptibles: The British Expeditionary Force 1914* (London: John Murray, 2005), pp. 100, 136, 138.
6. Byron Farwell, *Queen Victoria's Little Wars* (Barnsley: Pen & Sword, 2009), p. 1.
7. Edward Spiers, *Late Victorian Army 1868–1902* (Manchester: University of Manchester Press, 1992), pp. 275–276.
8. Ian Hernon, *The Savage Empire: Forgotten Wars of the 19th Century* (Stroud: Sutton Publishing, 2000), p. 6.
9. Leo Amery, *The Times History of the War in South Africa*, Vol. 2 (London: Sampson Low, Marston & Company, 1904), p. 26.
10. C.E. Callwell, *Small Wars: Their Principles and Practice*, Third Edition, (London: War Office, 1906), pp. 43, 57, 71.
11. Rudyard Kipling, 'The Young British Soldier'. http://www.kipling.org.uk/poems_youngbrit.htm, accessed 5 June 2013.
12. Brian Curragh, 'Henry Wilson's War', in Spencer Jones (ed.), *Stemming the Tide: Officers and Leadership in the British Expeditionary Force 1914* (Solihull: Helion & Co., 2013), p. 69.
13. John Spencer, 'The Big Brain in the Army': Sir William Robertson as Quartermaster General', in Jones (ed.), *Stemming the Tide*, p. 89.
14. John Bourne, 'Major-General Sir Archibald Murray' in Jones (ed.), *Stemming the Tide*, p. 50.
15. C.R. Ballard, *Smith-Dorrien* (London: Constable & Company, 1931), pp. 9–18.
16. Amery, *Times History*, Vol. 2, p. 26.
17. *Infantry Drill* (London: HMSO, 1893) pp. 109–110.
18. Ian Hamilton, *The Fighting of the Future* (London: K. Paul, Trench & Co., 1885).
19. John Dunlop, *The Development of the British Army 1899–1914* (London: Methuen, 1938), p. 37.
20. Quoted in Tim Moreman, 'The British and Indian Armies and North West Frontier Warfare 1849–1914', *Journal of Imperial and Commonwealth History*, Vol. 20, No. 1, (1992), p. 43.
21. Spencer Jones, *From Boer War to World War: Tactical Reform of the British Army 1902–1914* (Norman: University of Oklahoma Press, 2012), pp. 22–24.
22. Callwell, *Small Wars*, p. 31.

23. Jones, *Boer War to World War*, p. 34.
24. 'Not by a Staff Officer', 'Some Remarks on Recent Changes', *United Service Magazine*, October 1904, p. 47.
25. *Report of His Majesty's Commissioners Appointed to Inquire Into the Military Preparations and Other Matters Connected with the War in South Africa*, 4 Vols. (London: HMSO, 1903), Cmd No.1789–1792, Vol.2, Q13247, p. 66 [Hereafter *Elgin Commission*].
26. E.D. Swinton, *The Defence of Duffer's Drift* (Boulder: Paladin Press, 2008 [Original 1904]).
27. 'Beedos', 'Military Training', *United Service Magazine*, October 1904, p. 78.
28. *Elgin Commission*, Vol. 2, Q 16974, p. 286.
29. On this topic, see Spencer Jones, ' "The Shooting of the Boers was Extraordinary": British Views of Boer Marksmanship in the Second Anglo-Boer War, 1899–1902', in Karen Jones, Giacomo Macola and David Welch (eds), *A Cultural History of Firearms in the Age of Empire* (Aldershot: Ashgate, 2013), pp. 251–267.
30. Amery, *Times History*, Vol. 2, pp. 34–35.
31. *Elgin Commission*, Vol. 2, Q16772, p. 272.
32. TNA WO 105/29, Lord Roberts Papers, 'Opinions as to arming the Cavalry with the long rifle'.
33. TNA WO 108/266, Reports on Artillery Equipment in South Africa: Heavy Artillery, p. 21.
34. G.F.R. Henderson, *The Science of War* (London: Longmans, Green & Co., 1905), p. 372.
35. TNA WO 105/45, Lord Roberts Papers, 'Notes for Guidance in South African Warfare', 26 January 1900.
36. Three divisional commanders of 1914 had not served in the Anglo-Boer War. These were Samuel Lomax (1st Division), Thomas Snow (4th Division) and Charles Fergusson (5th Division). However, all had seen action in other colonial conflicts.
37. Jones, *Boer War to World War*, pp. 34–36.
38. *Elgin Commission*, Vol. 2, Q13941, p. 107.
39. Ibid., Vol. 1, Q 173, p. 7.
40. Ibid., Vol. 2, Q 10442, p. 440.
41. Quoted in 'K.', 'Suggestions for the Improvement of the Annual Course of Musketry', *United Service Magazine*, June 1904, p. 300.
42. Jones, *From Boer War to World War*, p. 93. I am grateful to Dr Simon House for providing comparative statistics for the French army.
43. *Musketry Regulations Part I, 1909* (London: War Office, 1909), p. 260.
44. Jones, *From Boer War to World War*, p. 94.
45. Ian Hogg and John Weeks, *Military Small Arms of the 20th Century*, Sixth Edition (London: Cassel, 1992), p. 101.
46. Stephen Badsey, *Doctrine and Reform in the British Cavalry 1880–1918* (Aldershot: Ashgate, 2008), pp. 103–104.
47. For detailed discussion of the debate, see Stephen Badsey, 'The Boer War (1899–1902) and British Cavalry Doctrine: A Re-evaluation', *Journal of Military History*, Vol. 71, No. 1 (2007), p. 76; Gervase Phillips, 'The Obsolescence of the *Arme Blanche* and Technological Determinism in British Military History', *War and Society*, Vol. 9, No. 1 (2002), pp. 39–41; Gervase Phillips,

'Scapegoat Arm: Twentieth Century Cavalry in Anglophone Historiography', *Journal of Military History*, Vol. 71, No. 1 (2007), p. 38.

48. *Cavalry Training 1912* (London: War Office, 1912), pp. 98–104.
49. Jones, *Boer War to World War*, pp. 114–116.
50. Ken Gillings, *The Battle of the Thukela Heights: 12–28 February 1900* (Randburg: Ravan Press, 1999), pp. 52–56; Jones, *Boer War to World War*, pp. 148–149.
51. The numerous responses were published in the *Minutes of the Proceedings of the Royal Artillery Institution*, Vol. 29 (1902–1903).
52. TNA WO 108/184, Notes by Colonel J.M. Grierson RA on Return from South Africa.
53. John Headlam, *History of the Royal Artillery From the Indian Mutiny to the Great War*, Vol. 2 (London: Royal Artillery Institute, 1937), p. 82.
54. Jones, *Boer War to World War*, pp. 148–149.
55. TNA WO 108/184, Notes by Colonel J.M. Grierson.
56. *Elgin Commission*, Vol. 2, Q13247, p. 66; Q13941, p. 111; Q15850, p. 233.
57. TNA 163/14, Inspector General of Forces [IGF] Report for 1908, pp. 159–160.
58. Jones, *Boer War to World War*, p. 151.
59. Mark Connelly and Tim Bowman, *The Edwardian Army: Recruiting, Training and Deploying the British Army 1902–1914* (Oxford: University of Oxford Press, 2012), pp. 82–87.
60. *Combined Training 1902* (London: War Office, 1902), p. 4.
61. Joint Services Command and Staff College Library, 'Report on a Conference of General Staff Officers at the Staff College, 2–12 January 1906', p. 32. Emphasis in the original.
62. TNA WO 163/13, IGF Report for 1907, pp. 6–7.
63. TNA WO 163/18, Army Council Minutes, p. 567.
64. Richard Meinertzhagen, *Army Diary 1899–1926* (Edinburgh: Oliver & Boyd, 1960), p. 80.
65. Edmonds, *Official History*, Vol. 1, p. 11.
66. Ibid., p. 10.
67. Amery, *Times History*, p. 26.
68. Richard Holmes, *Riding the Retreat: Mons to Marne 1914 Revisited* (London: Pimlico, 2007), pp. 206–208.
69. Jones, *Boer War to World War*, pp. 99–101.
70. John Mason Sneddon, *The Devil's Carnival: 1st Battalion Northumberland Fusiliers, August–December 1914* (Brighton: Reveille Press, 2012), p. 91.
71. Quoted in Ian F.W. Beckett, *The Judgement of History: Sir Horace Smith-Dorrien, Lord French and 1914* (London: Tom Donovan, 1993), p. 34.
72. Martin Farndale, *History of the Royal Regiment of Artillery 1914–1918* (Woolwich: Royal Artillery Institution, 1986), pp. 60–82.
73. Ibid., pp. 67–82.
74. Ibid., pp. 79–81.
75. Spencer Jones, 'Scouting for Soldiers: Reconnaissance and the British Cavalry 1899–1914', *War in History*, Vol. 18, No. 4 (2011), pp. 511–513.
76. Ibid., p. 512.
77. Lieutenant-Colonel A.G. Martin, 'Cavalry in the Great War: A Brief Retrospect', *Cavalry Journal*, Vol. 24 (1934), p. 447.

78. Jack Sheldon, *The German Army at Ypres 1914* (Barnsley: Pen & Sword, 2010), p. 105.
79. G.C.W. [Graeme Chamley Wynne], *Ypres 1914: An Official Account Published by Order of the German General Staff* (London: Constable & Company, 1919), p. 45.
80. Howard Bailes, 'Patterns of Thought in the Late Victorian Army', *Journal of Strategic Studies*, Vol. 4, No. 1 (1981), pp. 39–45.
81. Quoted in Nicholas Evans, 'From Drill to Doctrine: Forging the British Army's Tactics 1897–1909', PhD Thesis (London: King's College), p. 94.

6
Jan Smuts, Paul von Lettow-Vorbeck and the Great War in German East Africa

Stuart Mitchell

The East African Front in the Great War is no longer a forgotten the-atre.[1] In recent years works by Hew Strachan, Ross Anderson and Edward Paice have promoted a more sophisticated understanding of the Great War in East Africa.[2] It is questionable whether it was ever truly 'forgot-ten'. The dynamic exploits of the German field commander Paul von Lettow-Vorbeck captured the imagination of the German public at the time and have loomed over the historiography since the war's closure in November 1918. Fêted as an expert in guerrilla warfare and the man who evaded the might of the British Empire until 23 November 1918, 12 days after the Armistice, the legend of Lettow has periodically stoked the fires of interest in the campaign.[3] Leading a force overwhelmingly com-posed of regionally recruited 'native *askari*', the German commander fought a campaign that is remarkable for its improvisation and coor-dination. Nevertheless, as Hew Strachan has recognised, it is one that has largely rested on the false premises that Lettow's achievements were unique and that his conduct was consistently rooted in the practices of guerrilla warfare.[4] Conversely, the British conduct has been portrayed as blundering, hamstrung and ill-conceived. This is not a position without merit; indeed, many of the battles were defined by a lack of organisa-tion, poor preparatory measures and strategy. Yet the context is often downplayed: the British and South African generals were operating with significant administrative and political impediments that Lettow did not have to contend with to the same degree. In the first two years of the war British resources were stretched and the strategy remained firmly naval-focused. It was only with the arrival of significant numbers of South African troops in early 1916 that the War Office was finally able to consider concerted offensive action against German East Africa. This article will assess the conduct and context of command on the East African Front in 1916, comparing the South African commander J.C. Smuts's tenure as commander-in-chief of the Imperial British Forces and Paul von Lettow-Vorbeck's as commander of the *Schutztruppe*.

This article is not intended to be a straightforward narrative account of the campaign to bring von Lettow-Vorbeck to heel; this has been covered in considerable detail elsewhere.[5] It will instead begin to emulate the work that historians of the British army of the Western Front have done over the last 30 years in bringing a greater degree of operational analysis to well-known events. This work will not overturn decades of scholarship, nor does it set out to do such a thing, but it will contribute to the growing body of literature that is now looking in greater detail at the contextual environment both the British and German forces were fighting in.

The most serious and decisive fighting in East Africa occurred in 1916, and, while Lettow's campaign spluttered on until after the war's official conclusion, the bulk of the colony had been occupied by the British and Belgian forces by the year's end. This will therefore form the focus for the article and allow a greater analysis of the background, administrative environment and operational conceptions of the two key commanders.[6] To understand the difficulty of General Smuts's position, it is important to establish the political and administrative pressures he was subjected to as well as understanding the context of the wider army at the time. Conversely, the reputation of Lettow-Vorbeck as a guerrilla fighter *par excellence* has led many to overlook the organisational systems that he established in collaboration with the civilian colonial governor Heinrich Schnee. At the start of the year the Germans were in possession of territory in British East Africa; they were significant in number and well organised. Vorbeck's forces also held important operational advantages, such as control of the two key railways, the Usambara line and the Central line, which facilitated defence along interior lines. By the end of the year they had been pushed into the very south of the colony on the banks of the Rufiji River and had suffered from a campaign which left much of the colony devastated.[7]

Paul von Lettow-Vorbeck

Paul von Lettow-Vorbeck was born 20 March 1870 in the Saarland, Prussia.[8] He served in both the Boxer rebellion and later the subjugation of the Herero and Nama peoples in German South-West Africa between 1904 and 1906. He was an experienced colonial campaigner and had lost the sight in his left eye during the genocidal pacification of the African colony.[9] During the subjugation Lettow acted as adjutant to Lothar von Trotha, commander of the German forces in South-West Africa and later a company commander in the field. Here Lettow was exposed to the command and control practices of the *Schutztruppe*, which were based upon small, mobile field companies led by Europeans, but overwhelmingly comprised of *askari*. After the injury to his eye in 1906 Lettow returned to Germany, where he filled further staff roles and commanded the Second *Seebataillon* in Wilhelmshaven between 1909 and 1913. In late 1913 he was ordered to East Africa, where, upon arrival in January 1914, he proceeded to reconnoitre the ground he would be defending upon the outbreak of war.[10] This included an inspection of the Kilimanjaro and Meru Mountains region in the north of the colony. Cutting through this fertile area was the vital Usambara railway, which ran from the coastal port of Tanga 200 miles north-west to the town of Moshi, which lies in the shadow of Kilimanjaro. This line would prove to be pivotal in moving companies of *Schutztruppe* to meet the British invasion force at Tanga in 1914. Lettow's tour took him to Arusha, north-west of Moshi, and Kondoa Irangi to the south. The journey's route gave the commander an insight into the geography of the region and indicated the areas where mobile forces would suffer health issues. He understood that tsetse flies were more prevalent in the southern areas and would thus be problematic for mounted troops and livestock.[11] It also provided a secondary benefit. In travelling the colony Lettow inspected first-hand the military forces at his disposal. In some regions these also included private volunteer organisations which consented in a time of war to fall in under the orders of the *Schutztruppe*, thus providing the commander with an immediate method of expansion and further recruitment.[12]

At this stage it was unclear to Lettow who the enemy would be; thus, his companies were dispersed and his methods had to be applicable in both situations:

> According to my view, the force had the double duty of preparing to meet an enemy from outside with modern armament, as well as a native enemy within our borders; their training for battle had therefore to take account of two distinct sets of conditions.[13]

Lettow's focus for training remained rooted to certain European principles. He strove to improve the marksmanship of his *askari* with little success, while also integrating proficient use of machine guns among the European officers and NCOs. Musketry among native contingents remained poor. One British officer described the quality of shooting among both the *askari* and their British equivalents, the King's African Rifles: 'He [African troops] cannot shoot, as a rule, and when you are opposed to him the safest place is usually in the firing-line.'[14] Despite the limited utility of machine guns in the early skirmishing, it would not take long before improvements were noted by the British forces. A substantial body of testimony arose depicting the damage the rapidly improving German machine gunners could inflict.[15] Discipline in the *Schutztruppe* was firm and unforgiving, but generally respectful of customs.[16] Importantly, Lettow's conception of warfare remained wedded to the Prussian ideals of concentration and encirclement.[17] Under his short tenure prior to the outbreak of war Lettow did not radically overhaul the *Schutztruppe*, but his increased emphasis on firepower modernised the force.[18] It was not a revolutionary guerrilla force. It was well trained in 'bush' warfare, a kind of conflict that placed a great emphasis upon short, sharp engagements at close quarters that took the enemy by surprise. As Charles Miller observed, this had more to do with the pre-war doctrine the *Schutztruppe* adhered to.[19] Despite this, in the early engagements the British native forces – the King's African Rifles (KAR) – proved to be equally effective as their German counterparts.[20] Nevertheless, almost two years of neglect and stagnation followed, until 1916 when the KAR were progressively increased from three under-strength and dispersed battalions, comprising 21 companies, to 22 battalions 'bearing the whole brunt of the fighting during 1918'.[21]

While the two native contingents may have started out on an equal qualitative footing, their respective usages would differ markedly. Lettow saw that his role as commander of a subsidiary theatre was to ensure he drew in as many enemy forces and resources as possible.[22] This required an offensive disposition:

> My view was that we would best protect our colony by threatening the enemy in his own territory. We could very effectively tackle him at a sensitive point, the Uganda Railway, and one might almost say that the numerous German settlers in the country traversed by our Northern Railway (Tanga-Moshi) were already deployed for this object.[23]

Lettow's reconnaissance of the country had demonstrated that the fertile north-eastern region around Kilimanjaro would be the easiest area to defend and would also provide an important jumping-off point from which to launch attacks into British East Africa. Furthermore, the Usambara railway allowed the rapid shuttling of forces to threatened coastal areas. For two years this policy proved effective: the Ugandan railway was repeatedly disrupted; the town of Taveta, in British East Africa, was captured; and a number of efforts to strike back were repelled. Lettow's greatest victory came on 3–4 November 1914, when the Indian Expeditionary Force B attempted to land and capture the port of Tanga, a terminus at the end of the Usambara line. Having sailed non-stop from India, the tired IEF B made a landing and attempted to make in-roads into the town. After a haphazard and ill-coordinated advance the British attack was first repulsed and later subjected to counter-attack, which forced the demoralised and disorganised forces to re-embark, leaving a large quantity of materiel in the hands of the *Schutztruppe*.[24] Lettow had concentrated his forces rapidly using the railway and won an important victory. While question marks hung over the decisions taken by the British commander Major-General A.E. Aitken and the quality of his troops, the defeat strengthened Lettow's convictions and emboldened him to encroach further into British territory.[25] Tactically Lettow had outmanoeuvred his opponents, but the basis of his future successes cannot be attributed to his tactical methods alone.

At the outbreak of war Lettow faced a debate with the colonial governor Heinrich Schnee over what strategic course German East Africa would follow. As colonial governor, Schnee should have had final executive authority within German East Africa, yet the privileged place of the military within German society made this an unrealistic prospect. Principally Schnee favoured diplomatic negotiation of neutrality of the colony's ports along existing treaty lines and a defensive posture inland, which might preserve the economic development he had brought to the region.[26] Yet, his actions in attempting to supply the German cruiser *Konigsberg*, mobilisation of troops through Dar es Salaam and the continuing existence of the high-powered wireless in the port, all forbidden by neutrality agreements, belie his claims that the 'war was started [in East Africa] by British attacks on the coast'.[27] Lettow, on the other hand, preferred an active defence, in line with his idea that the responsibility of colonial authorities was to draw as many resources as possible into the theatre of operations. In the opening weeks Lettow showed himself willing to wilfully disregard Schnee's ongoing neutrality negotiations and defy his authority. He seized the British post at Taveta on 15 August, and later, on 24 August, launched a short sharp incursion into Portuguese East Africa, killing one Portuguese medical Non-Commissioned Officer (NCO) and six *askari*.[28] The relationship between the two men would remain fractious, but as the military imperatives became more obvious after the seizure of Taveta and the Battle of Tanga Lettow's influence correspondingly grew. That the broken relationship between two key figures in German East Africa even occurred provides an indication of how intermittent communication with Germany had become.[29] This provided both Schnee and Lettow with a significant level of autonomy, allowing them greater freedom to organise their forces and manage their internal organisation. In comparison, the British were riven by administrative and bureaucratic problems that hamstrung the coordination of efforts.

The argument between Schnee and Lettow has come to overshadow much of the excellent administrative work that underpinned the continuing successes. Without the work of 'cunning' colonial governors like Schnee in the colonies it is doubtful whether Lettow would have been as successful in expanding, supplying, moving and treating the *Schutztruppe*.[30] The victory at Tanga secured the subordination of civilian authority to military control, and during 1915 measures were taken to ensure the *Schutztruppe* were as self-sufficient as possible. The two main railways provided a pivotal lifeline, moving troops and supplies, while the Amani Biological Institute in Usambara provided scientific expertise that would prove vital in maintaining the health of the force. Furthermore, plantations grew resources that would do much to make German East Africa self-sufficient. Cotton plantations supplied the raw materials, looms were built in missions and workshops, leather from cattle and game went to make shoes, dyes were gathered from the Ndaa tree for uniforms, rubber was vulcanised using sulphur, and an ersatz motor fuel was produced using coconut palm.[31] In a parallel manner to the European experience, the colony was gearing its economy towards war. The production of munitions remained virtually impossible, but a large-scale refitting of wet cartridges salvaged from the *Rubens*, which had broken the blockade and run aground in Mansa bay in April 1915, provided a significant stockpile. The overhaul could not have been possible without significant internal coordination and the pre-war foundations of industry to build upon. Lettow recognised that the cornerstone of improvisation was developing the existing means of production: 'All the small beginnings of food-stuff production that had already existed on the plantations in time of peace were galvanized into more extensive activity by the war, and by the need of subsisting large masses.'[32]

One economic effect of this lurch towards self-sufficiency was a rapid depletion of currency. It fell to Schnee to rectify the problem; the solution was the minting of a German East African currency. Paper notes were first tried, but British counterfeiting and poor durability led to a lack of faith in this method of exchange. In response, a coinage system was implemented, which proved much more effective.[33] The currency reforms led to discussions taking place between the British colonial administrative staff and managers of the National Bank of India and the Standard Bank of South Africa to decide a suitable exchange mechanism and which currencies would be accepted.[34] The interim currencies were banned; nonetheless, they proved durable enough to persist as a method of payment in Portuguese East Africa.[35]

Generalship and the fighting quality of the *Schutztruppe* may get the majority of the historical plaudits, but its capacity to resist in 1916 rested upon sound organisation, rapid improvisation and effective modes of supply. While the *Schutztruppe* were organised in a way that facilitated living off the land to a certain degree, they still required a long supply chain of porters drawn from the local populace. To meet this need a relay system of native carriers was established along permanent supply routes, which reduced the hardships wrought upon the indigenous people called upon to fill this role. Hygiene and discipline were firmly maintained, and facilities were available for accommodating Europeans passing through. By quartering porters permanently along the main supply routes their health and welfare could be more easily maintained. Once Smuts launched his attack on the colony in spring 1916 these measures increasingly became dislocated by the rapidity of movement, and the porters on both sides were again subjected to appalling marches with heavy loads over unforgiving terrain.[36]

Lettow was a product of the Prussian system, a military autocrat with an eye for organisation. He was well-versed in 'bush fighting' but, as scholars have pointed out, he was no revolutionary guerrilla.[37] In the *Schutztruppe* he inherited an effective fighting force with the capacity for expansion and a well-established doctrine which Lettow integrated with a greater emphasis on firepower, and the machine gun in particular. By the virtue of circumstance, Lettow had limited political oversight from Berlin. Consequently, only a select number of individuals could act as a check on his authority, most notably the former captain of the *Konigsberg*, Max Looff, and the colonial governor Heinrich Schnee.[38] Schnee's role in the defence of the colony is often overlooked, but he should share the plaudits for overseeing the mobilisation of the colony's economy and many of the improvised structures that underpinned Lettow's success in 1916. It was under his tenure that German East Africa was able to establish effective supply chains, expand production and stabilise a rapidly ailing economy under incredibly trying circumstances. Without these improvements there could not have been any expansion in the *Schutztruppe*, porters could not have been paid or food procured. The absence of national oversight enabled Schnee and Lettow to make unilateral decisions according to necessity. Smuts would have no such freedom.

Jan Christiaan Smuts

Smuts is a difficult general to judge. His territorial achievements out-stripped the three commanders-in-chief who came before him, yet the campaign was typified by hunger, disease and an inability to pin down his opponent. Ross Anderson has echoed the balanced tone and approach of Charles Fendall in observing that 'Smuts's operational aims were reasonable, but he failed to reconcile them with the reality on the ground, be it terrain or supply.'[39] Fendall, not one to shy away from administrative criticism, was more forgiving, choosing instead to blame the 'want of enterprise...on the part of his mounted brigade commanders'.[40] To reach an adequate conclusion regarding the suc-cess of Smuts's campaign in East Africa it is necessary to understand the context and pressures he was under. Unlike Lettow, Smuts was beholden to two major political forces: the War Office in Britain and the government of the Union of South Africa, in which he was sec-ond in influence only to Prime Minister Louis Botha. Furthermore, there were a number of administrative bodies with their own ways of doing things that Smuts, or at least the officers under Smuts, had to contend with. The force he presided over was largely South African to start out with, but this steadily became more heterogeneous as troops from West Africa, India and the KAR were brought in to make good losses. 1916 marked a sea-change in the manner in which Britain and her army waged war: where ad hoc-ism and 'business as usual' had previously typified British efforts, they were rapidly being replaced by more thor-ough and sophisticated approaches.[41] Despite its peripheral character, the East African Front was not hermetically sealed from this shift. The requirements and expectations of politics, administration and transfor-mation sculpted the campaign Smuts could wage. These restrictions and general systemic trends should not absolve him of his errors, but a con-textual understanding is important if a reasonable conclusion is to be reached.

Born on 24 May 1870 at Bovenplaats in the Malmesbury district of Cape Colony, Jan Smuts grew up with 'Afrikaans at home, heard Dutch in church and ... had his school and university education in South Africa entirely through the medium of English'.[42] He was educated at Victoria

College in Stellenbosch, where he met his future wife Isie Krige. In 1891 he entered Christ's College, Cambridge, where he read law. Upon graduation he entered the Middle Temple of the Inns of Court, successfully passing the examination in 1895. This education set him in good stead for his return to South Africa, where he became an influential figure in the nationalist movement. This culminated in his active role fighting for the Boer Republic in the Second South African War 1899–1902. During the conflict Smuts demonstrated his tactical awareness and a genuine aptitude for guerrilla warfare. His invasion of the Cape on 1 August 1901 covered over 1,000 miles and caused considerable loss to the British forces. Moreover, as his successes mounted he rallied support to his banner, forming a force of over 2,000 men. By the end of the campaign Smuts's force had traversed the Cape and lay in the north-west close to the border with South-West Africa, although he failed in his primary goal of paving the way for the establishment of a Cape Afrikaner government.[43] Although tactically his campaign had been a success, instability and uprisings, coupled with the vicious incarceration of the Afrikaner people by the British, forced the nationalists to the peace table. Unlike Lettow, Smuts had conducted a genuine guerrilla campaign which relied upon mobility, striking at the British weak points and rallying support to a nationalist cause. His legal background and generalship during the war earned him a privileged place in peace negotiations alongside Louis Botha and his future political rival James Barry Munnik Hertzog. In the years that followed, Smuts established himself as a leading figure in politics, first within the Cape Colony and, after 1910, in the Union of South Africa.

The outbreak of the First World War coincided with a period of intense civil unrest within the Union. Smuts had advocated for reconciliation between the British and Afrikaner in the wake of the Second South African War. Once union had been achieved, a gulf grew between those who sought a united South Africa within the Empire and nationalists who demanded an Afrikaner republic. The First World War polarised these divisions, driving republicans towards armed insurrection against the ruling unionists. Against the backdrop of the South African commitment to occupy German South-West Africa, S.G. Maritz launched a disorganised coup to topple the Botha government. Through negotiation and swift military action the 'armed protest' was put down and the ringleaders scattered, killed or captured.[44] This backdrop was important for Smuts in two fundamental ways. As both a political and a military leader, he had to consider the ramifications of his campaigning on the lives of those he presided over at home, and he was never truly away from the politics of the Union. The First World War was expanding the support for senior commanders in the form of more specialised staff officers, yet in Smuts the curiosities of politics had thrown up a general whose concerns were more akin to an early-modern monarch than his Western Front contemporaries.[45] Letters from John X. Merriman, Henry Burton and Louis Botha during Smuts's 1916 campaign provided the commander-in-chief with a constant link to the domestic political situation. It was impossible for such an influential individual to divorce himself from domestic politics. On 5 June, John Merriman wrote to Smuts from the House of Assembly in Cape Town, decrying

> Those miserable Nationalists! Incompetence leading Ignorance! Have [sic] done and are doing an infinity of harm. Their despicable jealousy of Botha, and yourself have obsessed them to such an extent that they see everything awry. How different it would have been if, as a united folk, we had been able to send our united light cavalry to Mesopotamia to turn the scale on that field![46]

Graver tidings came from the Finance Minister Henry Burton on 12 September 1916:

> You have heard, of course, about the so-called 'second rebellion', a stupid movement engineered by fellows like Schonken, and van der Merwe (not Jakhals), and a few others with the secret oath business and so forth.[47]

The second rebellion never got off the ground, and was stopped in its tracks by Christiaan de Wet, a conspirator in the first rebellion, who refused to go along with the scheme. The rest of Burton's letter was filled with discussion of various acts passing through the House of Assembly, including a discussion regarding suggestions made by Lord Sydney Buxton, Governor-General of South Africa, for a commission reassessing 'trade-after-the-war'.[48] On 6 August 1916, the day after Smuts reopened the offensive operations that would clear the Central Railway and push Lettow across the Rufiji River, Louis Botha wrote to Smuts:

> I enclose a letter from Buxton. Please return it to me with your comments. I have already discussed the appointment of a commission to make some recommendations as to what kind of industries we should now deal with and how. Possible one Commission can be appointed for both.[49]

Much of the political contents of letters to Smuts can be readily dismissed as updates given to an interested and well-connected man, but this was a case of Smuts influencing domestic and imperial policy from his command in East Africa. Moreover, the territorial interests of the Union were never far from Smuts's mind; he and Merriman had discussed East Africa as a potential destination for South African troops in August 1915 and the territorial potential that brought with it: 'we could probably effect an exchange with Mozambique and so consolidate our territories south of the Zambesi and Kunune.'[50] These ambitions would prompt Smuts to greet Portuguese entry into the war with apprehension lest they occupy territory that might otherwise prove a useful bargaining chip.[51] The upshot of such political machinations was a fractious relationship between allies in a campaign that required the utmost co-operation.

The coordination of supply, and the sickness brought about as a consequence, has cast a long shadow over Smuts's operational performance in East Africa. The huge territorial gains were bought at the cost of his dysentery and malaria-ravaged troops. Between 1914 and 1918 the British, including imperial troops, lost 3,445 men killed in action, while nearly double that figure, 6,100, died of disease.[52] One serving officer noted the severity of the problem in summer 1916: 'The camps along the [central] railway were full of sick and worn-out men. There were five thousand white men in hospital and several thousand more who well might have been there.'[53] The situation was worse for horses, which also had to contend with the tsetse fly; the attrition rate was close to 100 per cent between March 1916 and January 1917.[54] But how much of this can be attributed to Smuts's supply arrangements and his operational decisions? Byron Farwell concluded: 'Smuts appears not to have fully realized the importance of supplies.'[55] The supply system came perilously close to collapse during the two rainy seasons of 1916. Soldiers suffered periodically for lack of food. As was the case throughout the campaign, the native porters were even worse off and were often forced to resort to scavenging off the land. Nevertheless, certain mitigating factors have to be considered. The heads of the various supply and staff branches had limited experience of campaigning in the demanding environment of East Africa, while the supporting staff of junior officers overseeing administration were insufficient for a region this large.[56] Despite their best efforts, they were, like many of their Western Front equivalents, operating in an ad hoc fashion.[57] Senior officers such as the head of Administrative Services, the Deputy Adjutant & Quartermaster General (DA&QMG) R.H. Ewart, struggled to juggle the competing demands of supply and administration while formations were separated by huge distances and floundered in the field. They had first to deal with infrastructure which had either been intentionally ravaged by Lettow's *Schutztruppe* as they retreated or was rendered utterly impassable by the ferocity of the downpours. The effects of such weather were vividly depicted in Whittall's account of Smuts's campaign commanding Royal Naval Armoured Cars:

> The rain continued with unabated violence day and night, and it was hopeless even to think about trying to move any of the cars until it should have ceased. The main source of worry as to that was whether the cars would not disappear altogether in the sea of liquid mud which had once been a 'road'.[58]

To circumvent the problems of mobility, supplies required stockpiling and more localised distribution over shorter distances. For Brigadier-General Jacob (Jaap) van Deventer's 2nd Division, which had been boldly pushed forward to Kondoa Irangi at the end of the first phase of operations, this proved impossible, and the supply line stretched over 60 miles from Lol Kissale and 100 miles from Arusha.[59]

It was not simply the distance and terrain that posed a problem; senior officers had little faith that fighting formations possessed officers capable of handling supply issues. When the idea of delegating control of supplies to 2nd Division was mooted by Charles Dobbs, the assistant quartermaster general (AQMG), Ewart recognised the issue of adding inexperience to a strained situation: 'we have to accept the fact that the Staffs of the 2nd Division are not all Imperial officers and have not had the training of the latter'.[60] His point was reaffirmed in a note sent from the director of supply and transport's (DST) office: 'All store Depots in L of C [Lines of Communication] have to submit fortnightly return for audit. This is never done by Divisional units who have not the personnel to do so.'[61] They had a point; almost exactly a month earlier ammunition had been requested by the Brigadier-General Royal Artillery, J.H.V. Crowe, across a wide variety of calibres taking up valuable space and ultimately going unused. This arose 'from nothing more than a nervous desire to have ammunition of all natures as far forward as possible'.[62] Although the request came from a senior officer, there was certainly some validity in Ewart's and his subordinate's apprehensions. Nonetheless, Ewart recognised that any criticism needed to be couched very carefully and recommended to the AQMG: 'if similar wholesale orders for amn. [ammunition] are given I think you should talk the matter over with BGGS and if necessary insist on the demands being restricted to quantities which may reasonably be expected to be needed'.[63] Despite its improvement in 1917, the supply system still fundamentally rested on coordination between front and rear, as well as between the different administrative branches. Ordnance, supply and transport, and medical services all had to work effectively together to establish needs and a realistic time-frame for supply. At the head of the columns commanders had to ensure their pace did not outstrip their porters, and they marshalled their resources as well as the conditions permitted. This was not always possible; eager troops moved days beyond their supply and the standard of horsemanship slipped among South African units spearheading the attack.[64] Co-ordination of these elements relied upon the inter-personal relations between the heads and deputies of the various branches, and there was still very much an ad hoc approach, which responded to problems rather than predicting and planning for them. In part this was due to the incredibly difficult geography and the size of the task in hand, but, as Fendall noticed, there was still an 'irregular' air about the staff.[65]

There is no shortage of evidence for Smuts's involvement in supply matters. His interventions testify to the value he placed in it. He drove his staff to concentrate efforts on opening up the Central Railway and pushed for prompt resupply from Europe.[66] This was not always productive; he passed on remarks via his Brigadier-General, General Staff (BGGS), J. J. Collyer, that he was disappointed in the quality of the bridging in two places on the Central Railway. Ewart evidently felt this to be unfair in light of the long working hours and the size of the task.[67] Both the prioritisation of the railway at the expense of roads and the ordering of supplies were cause for remark from Ewart. The latter was simply described as 'rather depressing'.[68] Yet at other times Smuts was too withdrawn from certain decisions. In discussing the issue of importing trolleys from South Africa for light rail transport, the DA & QMG wrote in one of his letters to AQMG: 'I hope the Chief will soon give some definite decision as [illegible name] has been receiving conflicting instructions + I want to put the matter straight!'[69] Privately, the realities of warfare in the tropics troubled Smuts. He wrote a frank letter to his wife in exasperation: 'Colonel Piet Botha of Brits's division tells me that 700 of Brits's men are down with fever at Kissaki! What am I to do? It is really amazing how people are getting fever.' Later in the same missive his attention turned more specifically to supply in the Rufiji area during the rainy season: 'How am I to pursue the enemy thither? And if I do so and the rain comes, how do we get food and what will become of us, cut off from the world on the Rufiji? But everything will come right, and I shall make other plans.'[70] It is unfair to cast Smuts as ignorant or uncaring of matters of supply; he was involved in the decision-making process, and it was a factor in his operational thinking. Yet he was too inconsistent: veering from overbearing to withdrawn. He understood the importance of supply and recognised that he was setting his officers a mountainous task. Even before the war had ended, he wrote:

> It may be said that I expected too much of my men, and that I imposed too hard a task on them under the awful conditions of this tropical campaigning. I do not think so. I am sure it was not possible to conduct this campaign successfully in any other way.[71]

This was perhaps a well-rehearsed *post facto* rationalisation, but it at least gained a degree of acceptance in both South Africa and Britain.[72] There was also a degree of truth in the claim that the conditions themselves made disease and sickness an inevitability: disease rates among animals remained high after Smuts's departure despite improved conditions.[73] Nonetheless, during 1916 these problems were exacerbated by the deeper systemic failure of supply, and Smuts, with his divided attention and 'unorthodox style', was not the right man to fix it.[74]

The heterogeneous character of Smuts's force added further complication to matters of administration and cohesion. The imperial and colonial troops of the British Empire all fell under different administrative authorities. This was more marked in the early stages of the war, with the Colonial Office, Indian administration and the War Office in London splitting responsibilities. As South Africans began bolstering the forces in the theatre, administrative arrangements were further complicated. At no point were operations conducted under a single unified authority. The post-war analysis of the lessons from the theatre recognised the absurdity of the situation in 1917: 'two British columns, working in close co-operation in the field, were organized, paid and supplied by different authorities.' It went on to conclude: 'This system – or lack of system – was inevitably wasteful in supplies, in clerical staffs, and in all the rearward services, and is stated to have affected adversely the efficiency of the fighting troops.'[75] This was certainly an impediment and contrasted sharply with Lettow's and Schnee's isolation.

Smuts was a general who had to operate at the strategic and operational levels of war. This made him appealing to both the Colonial Office, who preferred to see the territory gained occupied by British forces, and the unionist political elite in South Africa, who held out hope of territorial gains at the conclusion of the war. This came at the expense of relations with his allied forces in the Belgians and Portuguese. On a more practical level, Smuts had to contend with more jobs than a commander-in-chief might otherwise expect. He was never fully removed from the political process in South Africa and so had to contend with both military and political exigencies. It would not be unreasonable to expect that this limited the degree to which he could engage with issues of supply. Yet Smuts made a number of robust interventions, and was at least clear about his intentions, even if these were not always well received. He presided over an administratively divided force which lacked expertise throughout its ranks. A formal structure existed between these officers, but success was largely dependent on the relationships between the men. The size of the logistics task in German East Africa was immense, while the resources were comparatively few. Had Smuts perfected the art of supply, it is unlikely the campaign could have gone on without significant difficulty arising; the terrain was simply too inhospitable and the systemic flaws too insurmountable. Lettow's destruction of infrastructure during the retreat hampered the lines of communications and stacked more jobs to an already overworked administrative branch, all the while leading the allied forces through the worst areas for disease. The actions of the enemy served to further exacerbate the problems faced by Smuts and his forces.

Operational conceptions

In the case of both Smuts and Lettow, context and capability shaped their operational conceptions. Smuts brought with him a way of warfare that focused on rapid movement, encirclement and decisive battle. Despite his unorthodox, guerrilla origins, these were principles of attack that were entirely aligned with those promoted in the British *Field Service Regulations Part I*.[76] Smuts's operational conception was fundamentally correct, given the circumstances and past defeats inflicted upon the British in German East Africa. Lettow's operational plans shifted as the circumstances changed. His early thoughts drifted towards a decisive battle in the Handeni region in the north of the colony, but as the campaign evolved and British troops pushed into the northern territories in force he prosecuted an operational plan which combined a retreat into the interior with the land equivalent of a fleet-in-being strategy. It was imperative that Lettow keep his army-in-being.

Smuts executed a territorial war in line with the political objectives and, according to Strachan, 'behaved as a politician rather than a general'.[77] There is a degree of truth in this appraisal, but it should not be the final word. Every facet of Smuts's prior military experience had stressed the importance of acting rapidly with mounted troops. Throughout the Second South African War, hit-and-run tactics using fast-moving mounted troops was his *modus operandi.*[78] The experiences during the German South-West African campaign did little to alter his conceptions, and were reinforced by Louis Botha's plan of action, which was fundamentally cavalry based.[79] The adoption of a policy of movement was also promoted by the actions of previous generals. Major-General Michael Tighe, on 12 February 1916, had attacked entrenched *Schutztruppe* on Salaita Hill, an imposing rise with trenches and stone breastworks both at the foot and along the slopes. The attempted bombardment ignored the trenches at the foot of the hill, which in turn took a heavy toll on the attacking troops, which included a significant contingent of newly arrived South Africans. The attack ended in failure for the British and Smuts was fully aware of the implications. Botha wrote to him in late February:

> A list of killed, wounded and missing was published here – 172, of which 133 were Union men. This, without any information, has created a rather painful situation, Smartt and I had to use all our influence to keep it out of the House. Tighe must have got a good drubbing, but in any case, now that you are there, everything feels easier.[80]

It was not just imperial ambition, but political costs that influenced Smuts's operational method. The conclusion, driven by the later knowledge of the incredible rates of sickness, that Smuts might have been better engaging in an 'early battle, a frontal assault when lines of communication were short', would simply have been continuing a policy that had already proven costly in terms of lives and political capital.[81] Both British and South Africans alike understood that a new approach had to be adopted if Lettow was to be overcome. The fundamentals of a two-pronged attack flanking German positions in the north-east of the country was shared by General Sir Horace Smith-Dorrien, the original general penned-in to command the East African Force in 1916.[82] The continuation of this policy set in train a game of cat-and-mouse that would see both Lettow and Smuts jockeying for a favourable situation in which a decisive action could take place. In a country as inhospitable as German East Africa, the Germans initially held a distinct advantage with their local knowledge and organisational preparations. It had been suggested by one British veteran of the campaign that Smuts's plan was hamstrung by the lack of vigour shown by his subordinate commanders.[83] Given the operational difficulties, rugged terrain, issues with disease and enduring supply problems, this seems overly harsh. Smuts's approach to the campaign was dictated both by his previous experiences in warfare and by the political circumstances, which required territorial gains with limited expenditure in lives to provide the Entente war effort with some much-needed succour from the hardships being incurred in other theatres. In this much he was successful.[84] That it would ultimately fail to pin down Lettow was due more to difficulties in conducting operations and the skill of his opponent than to any flaw in his operational planning.

Lettow's operational conception initially revolved around forcing a decisive encounter with one of Smuts's advancing columns. By concentrating his forces he could inflict significant damage on one of his opponents, yet he was unwilling to do this on his enemy's terms. Tactically, Lettow favoured the defensive to lure the enemy into an attack from whence he could employ his reserves in the flank to cause significant damage to the disorganised attackers. This plan relied upon strong defensive locales, and thus a significant portion of the fighting during 1916 took place in the hills and mountainous regions of the colony. This operational conception required Lettow to perform a risk assessment, judging the possibility of a favourable decisive engagement against the potential losses that would occur to himself.[85] As the campaign in 1916 went on and the possibility of a decisive action diminished, the imperative became to inflict losses on isolated detachments while maintaining the integrity of his own forces. In this were the seeds of his reputation as a guerrilla specialist, and he was particularly successful.[86] On 7 September 1916 Lettow's forces landed a blow on Major-General Coen Brits's columns commanded by Brigadier-Generals Beves and Enslin near Kissaki, south of the Central Railway. The following day another British detachment under Nussey fell upon the alert German defenders, compounding the loss of the previous day.[87] These actions were enough to provide Lettow with enough time to withdraw his forces across the Rufiji River.[88] Lettow's retreat to the interior preserved his forces for a significant duration, and, despite Smuts's growing optimism in December 1916, he recognised that his opponent was 'a tough fellow, determined to hold out to the very end and even to retire into the Portuguese territory rather than surrender'.[89] Lettow's modified approach reflected the centrality of his aim to always occupy as many British forces as he could. Decisive battle was his preferred plan of operations, but Smuts's movements, the terrain and his numerical inferiority made this difficult to execute. By retiring to strong defensive positions he constantly held up converging British forces, but neither he nor his opponent could lure one another into a fight that might bring some sort of resolution to this theatre. In some respects this suited both men: the territorial aims of Smuts were fulfilled while Lettow's fighting force remained intact.

Lettow was an exceptional practitioner of 'bush warfare'. He manoeuvred his troops impeccably and his flanking counter-attacks swung the tide of battle on a number of occasions. His success rested on a foundation of strong administrative and organisational cohesion within German East Africa, while his reputation as a guerrilla fighter greatly overlooks the classic Prussian methods of convergence and decisive battle that he so desired. Smuts was operating in a more restrictive context: there were political pressures in terms of both territorial expectations and economy in lives. His plans reflected these limitations, but they were also bolstered by his own military background. His experience in the Cape Colony during the Second South African War and the attack on German South-West Africa both encouraged his penchant for sweeping cavalry movements. Ultimately it was more than operational conceptions which hamstrung the British attempts at defeating Lettow: systemic supply issues, terrain conditions and the brilliance of his enemy were as much to blame.

Notes

1. Ross Anderson, *The Forgotten Front: The East African Campaign 1914–1918* (Stroud: Tempus, 2004) *passim*; David Stevenson, *1914–1918 The History of the First World War* (London: Allen Lane, 2004), p. 124.
2. Hew Strachan, *The First World War Volume One: To Arms* (Oxford: Oxford University Press, 2001); Ross Anderson, *The Forgotten Front: The Battle of Tanga 1914* (Stroud: Tempus, 2002); Edward Paice, *Tip and Run: The Untold Tragedy of the Great War in Africa* (London: Weidenfeld & Nicolson, 2007).
3. J.R. Sibley, *Tanganyikan Guerrilla: The East African Campaign 1914–1918* (London: Pan/Ballantine,1973); Gary Sheffield, *Forgotten Victory: The First World War: Myths and Realities* (London: Headline, 2001), p. 325; David M. Keithly, 'Khaki Foxes: The East Afrika Korps', *Small Wars and Insurgencies*, Vol. 12, No. 1 (2001), pp. 166–185.
4. Hew Strachan, *The First World War Volume One*, p. 570; this chapter has also been published separately under the title *The First World War in Africa* (Oxford: Oxford University Press, 2004). The original has been used in this piece.
5. The best accounts are Anderson, *The Forgotten Front: The East African Campaign 1914–1918*; Strachan, *The First World War Volume One*, pp. 599–643; Edward Paice, *Tip and Run*; Anne Samson, *World War One in Africa: The Forgotten Conflict Among the European Powers* (London: IB Tauris, 2013); Charles

Miller, *Battle for the Bundu* (London: Macmillan, 1974); Charles Hordern, *Military Operations in East Africa Volume One: August 1914–September 1916* [*Official History*] (London: HMSO, 1941).

6. For a similar comparative approach see Samson, *World War One in Africa*, pp. 132–141.
7. Populations were displaced, farmland was damaged, and local stores were raided and requisitioned by soldiers on both sides. Byron Farwell was particularly scathing of Lettow's strategy; see *The Great War in Africa 1914–1918* (New York: Viking, 1987), p. 355.
8. The von Lettow-Vorbecks were originally landed aristocracy from Pomerania.
9. Paice, *Tip and Run*, p. 17.
10. Paul von Lettow-Vorbeck, *My Reminiscences of East Africa* (London: Hurst and Blackett, 1920), p. 4.
11. Ibid., p. 11.
12. Ibid., pp. 6–8.
13. Ibid., p. 9.
14. Lt. Col. W. Whittall, *With Botha and Smuts in Africa* (London: Cassell, 1917), p. 184.
15. Paice, *Tip and Run*, p. 37; Whittall, *With Botha and Smuts*, pp. 199–200; Francis Brett-Young, *Marching on Tanga* (London: W. Collins, 1917), p. 215; Deneys Reitz, 'Trekking On', in T.S. Emslie (ed.), *The Deneys Reitz Trilogy: Adrift on the Open Veld* (Cape Town, SA: Stormberg, 1999), p. 254; The National Archives (TNA), Cab 45/9, 'Actions of the Northern Rhodesian Police', p. 13; Cab 45/17 'Extracts from the letters of a South African Colonel, 1916–1917', p. 5.
16. Michael von Herff, ' "They walk through the fire like the blondest German": African Soldiers Serving the Kaiser in German East Africa (1888–1914)', MA Thesis (McGill University, 1991), p. 94.
17. Ibid., p. 570; for a specific account of a traditional offensive action see also Paice, *Tip and Run*, pp. 81–84; see also Lettow-Vorbeck, *My Reminiscences*, p. 42, pp. 57–58.
18. Anderson, *The Forgotten Front*, p. 28.
19. Charles Miller, *Battle for the Bundu*, pp. 15–19; Strachan, *The First World War Volume One*, p. 578.
20. Paice, *Tip and Run*, p. 37.
21. Malcolm Page, *KAR: A History of the King's African Rifles* (London: Leo Cooper, 1998), pp. 26–27; TNA, Cab 45/27 'Preliminary Studies of the Operations in East Africa indicating certain general lessons', p. 2; see also W. Lloyd-Jones, *K.A.R.: Being an Unofficial Account of the Origins and Activities of The King's African Rifles* (London: Arrowsmith, 1926).
22. Lettow-Vorbeck, *My Reminiscences*, pp. 18–19.
23. Ibid., p. 21.
24. The best single-volume account of the battle is Anderson, *The Battle of Tanga 1914*.
25. TNA, Cab 45/6, 'Battle of Tanga 1914'; Cab 45/7, 'Battle of Tanga 1914'.
26. Heinrich Schnee, *Deutsch-Ostafrika im Weltkriege* (Leipzig, Quelle und Meyer, 1919), p. 60; Paice, *Tip and Run*, p. 17.
27. Schnee, *Deutsch-Ostafrika*, p. 58.
28. Anderson, *The Forgotten Front*, pp. 37–38.

29. Some communications were possible but irregular and contingent upon the weather and receiver position; see Eckard Michels, *Paul von Lettow Vorbeck: Der Held von Deutsch-Ostafrika* (Paderborn, DE: Ferdinand Schöningh, 2008), p. 177; Lettow-Vorbeck, *My Reminiscences,* p. 34.
30. C.P. Fendall, *The East African Force 1915–1919* (London: Witherby, 1921), p. 129; also quoted in Strachan, *The First World War Volume One* (2001), p. 574; an interesting comparison of the importance of Lettow's and Schnee's logistical preparations can be found in R.H. Beadon, *The Royal Army Service Corps: A History of Transport and Supply in the British Army Volume II* (Cambridge: Cambridge University Press, 1931), pp. 295–299.
31. Lettow-Vorbeck, *My Reminiscences,* p. 70.
32. Ibid., p. 70; Schnee, *Deutsch-Ostafrika,* p. 166.
33. Schnee, *Deutsch-Ostafrika,* pp. 280–291; Strachan, *The First World War Volume One,* pp. 592–593.
34. TNA, Cab 45/18 'Administration in Occupied Territory: German Currency, Martial Law, Instructions to Politicals etc.'
35. Strachan, *The First World War Volume One,* p. 593.
36. Lettow-Vorbeck, *My Reminiscences,* p. 53.
37. Strachan, *The First World War Volume One,* p. 570; Douglas Porch, *Counterinsurgency: Exposing the Myths of the New Way of War* (Cambridge: Cambridge University Press, 2013), pp. 85–86.
38. Leonard Mosley, *Duel for Kilimanjaro* (London: Weidenfeld and Nicolson, 1963), p. 109, pp. 146–147; Samson, *World War One in Africa,* pp. 120–121.
39. Anderson, *The Forgotten Front,* p. 297.
40. Fendall, *The East African Force,* p. 85.
41. For the political level see D. French, *Britain's Strategy and War Aims 1914–1916* (London: Allen and Unwin, 1986). Volumes on the military development during 1916 are numerous: Dan Todman and Gary Sheffield (eds), *Command and Control on the Western Front The British Army's Experience 1914–1918* (Staplehurst: Spellmount, 2004); Andy Simpson, *Directing Operations: British Corps Command on the Western Front 1914–1918* (Stroud: Spellmount, 2006) and Paddy Griffiths, *Battle Tactics of the Western Front* (London: Yale University Press, 1994) perhaps cover the most important facets. For the social setting see Adrian Gregory, *The Last Great War* (Cambridge: Cambridge University Press, 2008).
42. W.K. Hancock and Jean van der Poel, *Selections from the Smuts Papers Volume One* (Cambridge: Cambridge University Press, 1966), p. 3.
43. Ibid., pp. 407–444; Thomas Packenham, *The Boer War* (London: Weidenfeld and Nicolson, 1979), pp. 532–533.
44. Strachan, *The First World War Volume One,* pp. 550–553; internal political divisions within the Union are well covered in Bill Nasson, 'South Africa', in Peter Liddle, John Bourne and Ian Whitehead (eds), *The Great World War 1914–1945 Volume Two: The People's Experience* (London: Harper Collins, 2001), pp. 243–256.
45. Dan Todman, 'The Grand Lamasery Revisited: General Headquarters on the Western Front, 1914–1918', in Todman and Sheffield (eds), *Command and Control on the Western Front,* pp. 39–70.
46. W.K. Hancock and Jean van der Poel, *Selections from the Smuts Papers Volume Three,* (Cambridge: Cambridge University Press, 1966), p. 374.

47. Ibid., pp. 401–402.
48. Ibid., p. 404.
49. Ibid., pp. 390–391.
50. Ibid., p. 310.
51. Anderson, *The Forgotten Front*, p. 127.
52. War Office, *Statistics of the Military Effort of the British Empire During the Great War* (London: HMSO, 1922), p. 302.
53. Fendall, *The East African Force*, p. 77.
54. A.G. Doherty, 'The Veterinary Services in East Africa', in L.J. Blenkinsop and J.W. Rainey (eds), *The Official History of the Great War: Veterinary Services* (London: HMSO, 1925), pp. 412, 417; Strachan, *The First World War Volume One*, p. 609.
55. Farwell, *The Great War in Africa 1914–1918*, p. 309.
56. J.H.V. Crowe, *General Smuts' Campaign in East Africa* (London: John Murray, 1918), pp. 3–5; Doherty, 'The Veterinary Services in East Africa', p. 412.
57. Ian Malcolm Brown, *British Logistics on the Western Front 1914–1918* (Westport, CT: Praeger, 1998), pp. 103–104, p. 120, p. 133, p. 139.
58. Whittall, *With Botha and Smuts*, pp. 256–257.
59. Beadon, *The Royal Army Service Corps*, pp. 303–306; Fendall, *The East African Force*, p. 66.
60. TNA, Cab 45/16 'Problems of Supply 1916' 'Ewart to Dobbs, 20 October 1916'.
61. Ibid.; the DST was Percy Hazelton, although he was not a signatory on the note.
62. Ibid., 'DDOS to AA & QMG, 23 September 1916'.
63. Ibid., 'Ewart to Dobbs, handwritten note, 29 September 1916'.
64. Reitz, 'Trekking On', p. 258; Doherty, 'The Veterinary Services in East Africa', p. 412.
65. Beadon, *The Royal Army Service Corps Volume II*, pp. 297–298; Fendall, *The East African Force* (1919), p. 42; he considered this a positive feature and a reasonable allocation of individual specialisms.
66. TNA, Cab 45/16 'Problems of Supply 1916' 'Ewart to Dobbs, 9 September 1916'.
67. Ibid., 'Ewart to Dobbs 2 October 1916'.
68. Ibid., 'Ewart to Dobbs' 9 September 1916.
69. Ibid., 'Ewart to Dobbs, handwritten letter 22 June'.
70. Hancock and van der Poel, *Smuts Paper Volume Three*, pp. 406–407.
71. J.C. Smuts, 'Introduction', in J.H.V. Crowe (ed.), *General Smuts' Campaign in East Africa*, p. xi.
72. Samson, *World War One in Africa*, pp. 118–119; Doherty, 'The Veterinary Services in East Africa', p. 417.
73. Beadon, *The Royal Army Service Corps Volume II*, pp. 293–294; Doherty, 'The Veterinary Services in East Africa', p. 418.
74. Beadon, *The Royal Army Service Corps Volume II*, p. 301.
75. TNA, Cab 45/27 'Preliminary Studies of the Operations in East Africa' (1933), p. 6.
76. War Office (1909), *Field Service Regulations* (London: HMSO, 1909), pp. 131–140.
77. Strachan, *The First World War Volume One*, p. 626.

78. Hancock and van der Poel, *Smuts Papers Volume One*, pp. 430–437, pp. 470–471; Packenham, *The Boer War*, p. 524; Reitz, 'Commando', in Emslie (ed.), *The Deneys Reitz Trilogy*, pp. 138–139, p. 142, p. 158.

79. Hancock and van der Poel, *Smuts Papers Volume Three*, pp. 269–271; J.J. Collyer, *The Campaign in German South West Africa, 1914–1915* (Pretoria, SA: Government of the Union of South Africa, 1937), pp. 167–169.

80. Ibid., p. 337.

81. Strachan, *The First World War Volume One*, p. 614.

82. Fendall, *The East African Force*, p. 63.

83. Ibid., pp. 85–86.

84. Hancock and van der Poel, *Smuts Papers Volume Three*, p. 346; Smuts's despatches were greeted with praise in Britain and published widely in the press. See Lt.-Gen. The Hon. J.C. Smuts, *The London Gazette*, Tuesday 20 June 1916; Wednesday 17 January 1917; 18 April 1917; and for press reception and praise see *The Spectator*, 24 June 1916, p. 2.

85. Lettow-Vorbeck, *My Reminiscences*, pp. 108–111 gives a good account of both his fears of being cut off from his lines of communication and his desire to set up a decisive encounter.

86. Ibid., p. 141.

87. Ibid., pp. 154–155.

88. Anderson, *The Forgotten Front*, pp. 146–147.

89. Hancock and van der Poel, *Smuts Papers Volume Three*, p. 409.

7

The Egyptian Expeditionary Force and the Battles for Jerusalem: Command and Tactics in the Judaean Hills, November– December 1917

Christopher Newton

The photograph of the Commander-in-Chief of the Egyptian Expeditionary Force (EEF) General Sir Edmund Allenby entering Jerusalem on 11 December 1917 is one of the most iconic of the First World War and the British effort in the war. The capture of Jerusalem offered the British government and public some relief at a time of setbacks and disappointments on the Western Front. The capture of Jerusalem was a tangible, significant and symbolic gain, and it was a clear sign that the Turkish army was being defeated. This historic moment of British forces entering the Holy City has, however, not been matched by historical interest, and the Palestine Front in general in the First World War has often been described as a 'forgotten front'.[1] Although interest is picking up, albeit gradually over the past 20 years, and with new works being produced during 2014, the immediate military operations that led to the capture and consolidation of Jerusalem have not received a great deal of scholarly attention.[2]

The capture of Jerusalem was a hard-fought campaign. The city was gained at some cost to the EEF, and adjusting to the environment of the Judaean Hills was also a considerable challenge. This chapter seeks to explore how effectively the EEF adjusted to the changing conditions of the campaign, and will argue that the EEF's doctrine and training did allow it to cope with the new environment well, but the campaign did also reveal some tactical weaknesses that EEF commanders were identifying. The chapter will first outline the current areas of neglect in histories of the Palestine campaign, as well as the key features of the battles for Jerusalem. It will then evaluate EEF performance, examining the constraints it faced, and how effectively the organisation and individual commanders coped with these challenges.

Debates on the Palestine campaign

Traditional operational histories of the Palestine campaign have largely been criticised on two key grounds. First, as noted, they have largely centred on generalship of the main commanders, and in particular Allenby.[3] Early historians of the campaign, such as Archibald Wavell and Raymond Savage, have portrayed Allenby as the central figure in turning around the fortunes of the EEF and its success from late 1917 onwards.[4] Allenby is traditionally credited for modernising the EEF, especially for boosting its morale, and for ensuring that the attack at Third Gaza was well supported by artillery.[5] This view has undergone some revision. Jonathan Newell has argued that our perception of Allenby in the Palestine campaign has been shaped by those with particular interests in portraying him in a positive light. Wavell, for example, was Chief of the Imperial General Staff General Sir William Robertson's liaison officer with Allenby.[6] The questioning of Allenby's generalship by Clive Garsia, and later by Newell, has derived in a large part from his decision to concentrate his efforts at Beersheba rather than Gaza for the late 1917 offensive.[7] Jonathan Newell also argued that the achievements and preparations made by Allenby's predecessor, General Sir Archibald Murray, have been underplayed.[8] However, Newell's focus on Murray meant that historical focus still centred on the high command, and this continues to be a dominant theme. Moreover, despite attempts to challenge the early works, Allenby's reputation has remained intact, although modern scholars take a more nuanced, balanced approach. For example, James Kitchen has questioned the very notion of a decline in EEF after the Second Battle of Gaza.[9]

The second key criticism is the overemphasis by historians on the role of the cavalry at the expense of the achievements of the infantry and artillery. As well as reflecting the different characters of warfare between the Western and Palestine Fronts, it also reflected the preoccupations of and debate among inter-war theorists about the role of manoeuvre and the roles of cavalry and mechanised forces in British doctrine.[10] This focus on the cavalry has not gone unnoticed by infantry veterans of the theatre, and within the correspondence of the official historian of the Palestine campaign, Cyril Falls, are complaints, not least from XXI Corps commander Lieutenant-General Sir Edward Bulfin, that his narrative at that stage put a disproportionate amount of weight on the exploits of the cavalry.[11]

Despite the continuation of operational narratives, such as those by Anthony Bruce and John Grainger, there has been a shift of sorts away from the traditional themes of the Palestine campaign.[12] Many works started to take a thematic approach and examine aspects of the EEF's organisation. For example, Yigal Sheffy has examined the role and development of deception and intelligence.[13] Eran Dolev has examined the medical service and Allenby's role in ensuring there were adequate medical provisions.[14]

Most recently, the shift has moved even further to the soldiers' and officers' experience of the campaign. Given the plethora of studies examining the experience and combat motivation of soldiers on the Western Front, much-needed attention has now been finally turned to the British Imperial soldiers in the Egypt–Palestine theatre. These new works include Michael Mortlock's narrative of the experience of soldiers from the 54th Division.[15] David Woodward and Edward Woodfin have recently carried out insightful studies into British experiences of the theatre.[16] In 2014, James Kitchen published his study into the experience and motivations of the different contingents that made up the EEF. This emphasis on the different contingents in the EEF is reflected in a growing interest in the significant and vital Indian contribution to the campaign, especially given that British soldiers were transferred back to the Western Front during early 1918. Dennis Showalter, for example, illustrated how the Indian cavalry developed into an effective, modern force.[17]

Despite this, there are still three aspects of the Palestine campaign that modern academic study could focus on more. The first area concerns the roles of commanders below the level of commander-in-chief, their units, and their tactics, especially below divisional level. To be clear, some of these commanders have been studied. As noted, the role of Lieutenant-General Sir Phillip Chetwode in campaign planning, particularly for the Battle of Beersheba, has been analysed.[18] There have been other studies, such as that into Desert Mounted Corps commander Lieutenant-General Sir Henry Chauvel.[19] There has also been more detailed study into certain units; for example, Kitchen examined some of the aspects of the 54th and 10th Divisions. However, far more work needs to be done, and this is hopefully just the start.

The second area that requires more investigation stems from an observation made by Woodfin. Woodfin has emphasised how the experience of soldiers changed rapidly, and that the war in this theatre underwent five distinct phases. The phases relevant to this chapter include the third phase, the trench deadlock in Gaza during 1917; the fourth, the break-out from Gaza and operations in the Judaean Hills; and, last phase, the operations in the Jaffra–Jordan valley and the final breakout and defeat of the Turkish forces.[20] What has often been neglected are these transitional periods from one phase to the next, and how commanders adapted to the military and tactical challenges posed by the immediate onset of these different phases.

This leads to the third aspect that requires more attention, that is, some of the key operational aspects and, in particular, the operations in the mountainous terrain, especially in the Judaean Hills. It must be acknowledged that Kitchen's examination of the Indianisation of the EEF in early 1918 does include some examination of mountain warfare, although much of the attention in his analysis was on 10th Division. Kitchen showed how commanders inculcated aggression within the Indian units in that division, how British units trained and worked alongside newly transferred Indian ones, and how the British inculcated this aggressive ethos into Indian units.[21] Kitchen is very illuminating on how these small operations contributed to the eventual success of the Indian forces at Megiddo. But scholarly analysis on operational aspects needs to be continued, and this especially includes an analysis of command and tactics during the more neglected battles, such as the Battles for Jerusalem.

The Battles for Jerusalem

Despite attention in some works on the Palestine theatre,[22] how the EEF captured and consolidated Jerusalem is worthy of detailed considera-tion, as the campaign illustrated how the EEF reacted to the immediate onset of new environmental and tactical conditions and how it learned lessons during an important phase of the Palestine campaign. The Battles for Jerusalem have especially been considered as an impressive feat of arms; Wavell described the campaign as 'the climax of the most brilliant campaign'.[23] However, in recent years historians have acknowl-edged some of the deficiencies of the EEF effort. John Grainger has pointed out that the official history does not focus on the first phase of the Jerusalem campaign known as the Battle for Neby Samwil, and very much treats it as a victory, as the imposing height of Neby Samwil itself was captured and retained. But Grainger describes it as a 'very expensive defeat', as the attacks on El Jib had all failed, and the British suffered a cumulative loss of over 2,000 men. The battle was, according to Grainger, 'a convincing Turkish victory' despite the British outnumbering the Turks at least three to one.[24] Moreover, writing about the late 1917 campaign overall, Edward Erickson also stated that in late 1917 'Allenby's Egyptian Expeditionary Force had not yet evolved the tactical and operational techniques necessary to defeat decisively the Turks in Palestine.'[25]

In early November, the EEF broke through the Gaza–Beersheba line. With the Turkish army mounting a fighting retreat, Allenby faced a dilemma. David Lloyd George wanted the EEF to take Jerusalem quickly, and by Christmas.[26] Allenby also believed that the hills surrounding Jerusalem needed to be quickly occupied in order to prevent the Turks developing on and consolidating their defences there. However, Allenby's supply lines were increasingly being stretched, and his troops needed a rest. Nevertheless, the political, grand strategic and strategic situation demanded that the EEF should press on, and this was what was decided.

The Turkish forces were split into two armies: Eighth Army was positioned on the plains, while the Seventh Army was positioned in the Judaean Hills surrounding Jerusalem. Allenby's plan was to keep the two armies separated, and he aimed to force the Seventh Army to withdraw from the city through the difficult eastern route by cutting off the northern road access to it. This was, however, no easy task for the EEF, as the hilly terrain surrounding Jerusalem favoured the defenders. The EEF force leading the initial main drive to capture Jerusalem was XXI Corps, commanded by Lieutenant-General Sir Edward Bulfin. This force consisted of 75th Division, 52nd (Lowland) Division on the left, as well as the Yeomanry Mounted Division. Components of the Australian Mounted Division also made contributions. The main push into the hills began on 19 November, and by 21 November the EEF took the commanding height of Neby Samwil. There followed some strong Ottoman counter-attacks in which Neby Samwil was seriously threatened, but the EEF managed to consolidate its hold on it. XX Corps then tried to take El Jib, north of Neby Samwil, however these attacks were ultimately unsuccessful. Further attempts by the EEF to make progress were now resisted by the Ottomans, and XXI Corps troops were by now completely exhausted. Allenby therefore called a temporary halt of operations. Given the state of XXI Corps at this time, this was the right thing to do, although political reasons necessitated a renewal of the attack by an equally weary XX Corps.[27]

Marshal Erich von Falkenhayn, formerly commander-in-chief of the German army, now commanding the Turkish force, launched a counter-offensive on 27 November. The Turks aimed to exploit a five-mile gap in the EEF line. Reserves consisting of the 7th Mounted Brigade, the Australian Mounted Division and a brigade of 52nd Division managed to close the gap.[28] The Turks continued to attack into the first days of December, and the EEF managed to repulse these attacks. On 3 December, 74th Division tried to recapture Beit Ur el Foqa but was unable to hold on to it.[29] The EEF soon turned its attention to its next attack, and by 7 December XX Corps (commanded by Lieutenant-General Sir Philip Chetwode) had taken over operations in the Judaean Hills. The relieving divisions included 60th (London) and the 74th (Yeomanry) Divisions and the 10th (Irish) Division, and they would be joined by 53rd Division (or a force known as Mott's Detachment, as it included other units including cavalry), which had been advancing up the Hebron road. Given the costly nature of the attacks around Neby Samwil, Chetwode decided to attack Jerusalem from the south and west: 60th and 74th Divisions would attack from the west, while 53rd Division on the right would attack from the south. The objectives of the plan were also changed, as the EEF was no longer seeking to force Seventh Army eastwards, but now force it to retreat northwards.[30] An early morning attack was launched on 8 December; 60th Division captured Deir Yesin, but 74th Division had encountered some resistance (enfilade fire from Neby Samwil), and the weather had slowed the progress of 53rd Division.[31] Despite the difficulties encountered by the EEF, by the early morning of 9 November, the Ottoman Seventh Army evacuated Jerusalem, and the EEF entered it that same day. 60th Division also captured the Mount of Olives on 10 December. Allenby's entrance took place on 11 December.

The campaign did not end there. Turkish artillery could still reach Jerusalem and Allenby needed to consolidate his positions. While the EEF was planning its next move, the Ottomans launched a counter-attack on 26-7 December. Despite its initial progress, the counter-offensive was defeated. On 27 December, 74th and 10th Divisions launched their attacks, and had managed to advance 4,000 yards on a six-mile front.[32] On 28 December XX Corps launched a general attack, taking key positions such as El Jib and Beituna. By 30 December, Jerusalem was secure.

The performance of the EEF

In order to assess the performance of the EEF force, and the various assessments of Falls, Wavell, Grainger, and Erickson, three sets of questions need to be addressed. First, what were the challenges and constraints that the EEF was facing? Second, what were the EEF's key organisational assets and qualities, and how well were they utilised during the campaign? Lastly, how effectively did commanders use their initiative, and how speedily did the EEF adapt to new situations and circumstances, despite the limitations commanders were facing?

Challenges and constraints

The first set of issues concerns the constraints and challenges that the EEF was operating under and confronting. There were three main types of challenges. The first arose from political and strategic constraints under which the EEF was placed. First, the capture of Jerusalem was a key political objective, and preoccupied Allenby's attention when there was the possibility of destroying the Turkish Eighth Army on the plains.[33] The political and religious significance of Jerusalem, and the significance that the British, Turks and Germans, and David Lloyd George, placed on its capture meant that it was too much of a significant objective to miss out.[34] The entire basis and the subsequent operations were the consequence of that political imperative. Second, as noted, there was considerable political and strategic pressure to capture Jerusalem quickly, and therefore the initial operations were mounted with a tired force that could not wait for adequate artillery support or provisions to catch up with them. There were other political constraints, such as the initial order for the British not to fight within six miles of Jerusalem, which also affected the first phase of the campaign.

The second key set of challenges comprised those resulting from the environment and terrain. Climbing the rocky hills was a considerable physical challenge in itself, slowing progress. It was noted by 75th Division that 'progress was slow owing to the steepness of the ground, and the physical exhaustion involved, and owing to the difficulty of giving any artillery support'.[35] The weather was also a major factor that soldiers had to contend with. During periods of the fighting in November, the troops endured torrential downpours.[36] Soldiers fought while they were soaked through,[37] and the downpours could be so hard that they could cause the collapse of trenches.[38] Cold temperatures were also an element that troops had to contend with, especially since they were wearing their summer uniforms.[39] These natural difficulties added to the logistical problems, particularly in the transportation of food and artillery, as well as battlefield communication difficulties.[40] Prior to the Battle of Neby Samwil, 52nd Division found that the rain and mist made visual signalling impossible and the terrain also made communication by wire impractical. Units, therefore, especially in the early phases, had to rely on runners.[41] There were also tactical difficulties that were largely the result of the physical difficulties of the terrain. The initial difficulties with artillery have already been mentioned, but this was also not ideal ground for cavalry and camels.[42] For example, the Yeomanry Mounted Division, who were tasked with an initial strike to cut off the Nablus–Jerusalem road, found the terrain tough to traverse and it was difficult to keep the horses and men supplied.[43]

These tactical difficulties were exacerbated by the Turks themselves and this was the third key challenge. While the Turkish army had been weakened, it nevertheless still challenged the EEF, especially when it came to hill fighting. They were trained in the tactics that the Germans had been developing on the Western Front, including storm troop tactics, and German units and commanders also contributed to the force in Palestine. Edward Erickson argues that the Turks had demonstrated during the Battle of Beersheba–Third Gaza that they could hold their own against the British. [44]

Often it was a combination of these that affected EEF progress. First, as noted, the pressure to capture the city as soon as possible meant that the EEF attacked without adequate supplies. The decision not to fight within six miles of Jerusalem led to the initial concentration by XXI Corps to fight around the Neby Samwil defences. However, the strength of these defences meant that the rule had to be broken and XXI Corps did eventually fight south of Neby Samwil.[45] There were also a number of challenges to which the command system still had to adapt. For example, a combination of time pressure and misjudgement on the part of senior commanders meant that objectives were sometimes over-ambitious, and the time it would take for troops to trek over the difficult terrain was underestimated. An example of this was that the high command wanted the divisions to reach Bireh on 20 November, yet his nearest infantry was six miles away from this objective.[46]

Second, the combination of the terrain and the determination of the Turkish defenders also hampered the use of certain weapons. Logistical and terrain challenges meant that the XXI Corps operations were especially conducted with inadequate artillery support, while the Turks were well equipped with heavier weapons.[47] The terrain also posed difficulties for lighter supporting weapons, and this made arms and infantry co-operation problematic. For example, Shea noted that 'in the action in front of JERUSALEM, Machine Guns were much hampered by the precipitous nature of the country. Machine guns could be man-handled for very short distances.'[48] The report of 10th Division reflected this point, stating that machine gunners 'move slowly and while on the move are out of action, present a big target and may come across obstacles that mules cannot easily negotiate', although machine guns were still invaluable as 'from well selected positions they are often able to continue firing on the enemy's works almost till the moment they are rushed by our infantry'.[49]

In terms of the use of Lewis guns, 180th Brigade noted that 'over this hilly country it has been most difficult for the Lewis Gun and ammunition to keep up the attack'. However, 'the extraordinary good work...done by the Lewis Gunners in getting two guns and S.A.A. up the precipitous slopes of SHAB SALAH with the leading infantry shows what can be done by determined teams'.[50] The most effective means of getting round these problems was to coordinate Lewis gun and machine gun fire when possible: 74th Division noted that

> it was found advisable to have a Lewis Gun placed close to a Machine Gun in order that it could take on close range targets and fill gaps if by any chance the Machine Gun had a stoppage. This was found especially necessary on the steep slopes of the hills encountered, consisting of numerous stops, where enemy snipers and bombers could creep up quite close to the Machine Guns.[51]

This point was reinforced in 10th Division's tactical notes document, which noted that 'Lewis Guns cannot keep up a rapid rate of fire for long and they should be used to supplement M.G.'s, but not replace them'.[52] Nevertheless, coordinating machine guns and Lewis guns was not an easy task: 60th Division found that 'in the attack on the defences of JERUSALEM, the ground was so steep that the machine guns were unable to scale the heights in time to co-operate with Lewis Guns, and distances were too great for machine guns to support from the rear to the flank'.[53]

Lastly, trench mortars encountered similar problems. According to Shea, mortars were 'particularly useful in searching dead ground, which is bound to exist in the country',[54] and 180th Brigade found that at Neby Samwil 'they materially helped the break-up of two attacks and also proved of use against enemy snipers hidden behind thick stone walls'.[55] However, 'they are sometimes useful in the initial stages of an attack, but their camel transport prevents their use during the latter stages'.[56]

Doctrine and organisation

Against those challenges, the EEF possessed a number of inherent qualities and flaws that affected its reactions to the new conditions. Adapting its organisational qualities to the Judaean Hills was also a challenge in itself. The EEF was wrestling with applying the principles it was developing for 'modern' warfare as well as those it had developed for colonial hill fighting.[57] First, the EEF was applying the principles that it had been developing concerning mountain warfare, gained through its extensive experience of colonial warfare.[58] These principles included the importance of occupying flanking high ground ('crowning the heights'), piqueting, and the construction of *sangars* (rock defences).[59] In recent years increasing emphasis was placed in British doctrine on scouting, skirmishing tactics and the use of initiative.[60]

Veterans of these campaigns noticed the similarities between the North-West Frontier and the Judaean Hills. Mounted Yeomanry Division commander Major-General George Barrow noted that the hills resembled the Himalayas on a small scale.[61] The commander of 60th Division, Major-General Sir John Shea, also observed that the front they were engaged in was 'in many ways the terrain of the North-West Frontier of India',[62] and that 'the Turk is much akin to the Pathan both in characteristics and in tactics'.[63] Moreover, units such as the 58th Rifles and 2/3rd Gurkhas in 75th Division had considerable experience fighting in the North-West Frontier.[64] Meanwhile, 53rd and 54th Divisions had served in Gallipoli, while 60th Division had served in Salonika and 10th Division had served in Salonika and Gallipoli.[65] This doctrine and experience enabled commanders to understand the importance of deploying in artillery and small column formations in the hills.[66] Moreover, numerous commanders and historians have observed that this experience served the EEF extremely well during this campaign, and there were effective examples of the use of turning movements and covering fire to methodically capture each height.[67] However, there would be a limit to the utility of this experience, at least in terms of the Indian experience. In his 1918 tactical notes, Shea, while comparing the Turks to the Pathans, nevertheless stressed that the Turk 'has the advantage over the Pathan of possessing Artillery and Machine Guns', and that the Turkish defence system was one that prevented them from 'dissolving into thin air'.[68] This was where British doctrine for 'modern' warfare came into the equation.

Second, the EEF was also incorporating modern tactics and weaponry in this different setting. Prior to the Third Battle of Gaza, the EEF had been undergoing considerable organisational reforms. It was operating under the new command system, which was now organised along the lines of corps – XX Corps, XXI Corps and the Desert Mounted Corps. New commanders were also appointed; some, such as 60th

Division commander Major-General Shea, had served under Allenby in France.[69] The key tactical challenge the EEF faced was the practical implementation of the tactical principles that had been developed on the Western Front. The doctrine placed increased emphasis on all-arms co-operation, especially between the infantry and artillery, and co-operation between specialists within the infantry, including riflemen, bombers, rifle grenadiers and Lewis gunners.[70]

There were crossovers between trench warfare and mountain warfare, and this was something that was understood. For example, Major-General Mott (although it should be noted that he was also drawing from his experience of the earlier Khuweilfe operation) noted that 'in the rocky and precipitous country "mopping up" has proved just as necessary as in Trench Warfare', and that 'special parties must be detailed to search the captured ground for snipers overlooked by the first rush. If this is not done considerable inconvenience is caused to ammunition carriers and stretcher bearers.'[71] However, as noted earlier, despite this experience, the ground often provided difficulties for the effective coordination of artillery, machine guns and Lewis guns. Nevertheless, the coordinated use of modern weapons was still extremely effective in this theatre, often enabling modifications to existing tactics. For example, a 74th Division report stated that 'in this form of fighting it was also found that the employment of Lewis Guns allowed the number of infantry necessary for picketting the hills to be greatly reduced [sic]'.[72]

In terms of the artillery, when it could be used in greater numbers during the later stages of the campaign, there were many examples of its effective use in conjunction with the infantry. On 31 December, the left group of 10th Division 'encountered resistance from a hill about P.14.c. The Divisional Artillery bombarded this hill and it was taken and the advance continued.' The advance took place 'over extremely difficult country intersected with deep ravines. The enemy had numerous machine guns cunningly hidden among the rocks.' However, 'the pace of the Infantry advance nevertheless exceeded all expectation, and they received the support from the Artillery, who by their quick and accurate shooting saved many casualties'. Moreover, 'several enemy concentrations were also effectively shelled by the Artillery'.[73] The artillery also performed an effective close support role during 60th Division's capture of the 'extremely precipitous' Shab Saleh position.[74] Divisions also learned to adapt in using their artillery effectively; for example, Shea noted that 'in the Turkish attack on Jerusalem on Dec. 27th the guns were mostly placed in the front line. This is unusual, but the local circumstances pointed to this being the correct policy and results entirely justified it.'[75]

In terms of organisation, while there had been significant improvements in the EEF command and staff system, there were still some deficiencies. While there were examples of effective intelligence, for example the discovery that the Turks were intending to attack on 27 December, through decoding wireless messages and examining agents' and prisoner reports, there were some significant limitations.[76] Partly, this was due to administrative problems; for example, the forces lacked accurate maps, and there were also difficulties in aerial reconnaissance due to the weather.[77] On occasions this lack of information about the local geography led to confusions in the issuing of orders. During 231st Brigade's relief of the 8th and 6th Brigades near Beit Duqqu on 29–30 November, 25th Royal Welsh was ordered to take up positions in advance of any post held by 6th Brigade to Point 1750. Yet in reality there was no hill at Point 1750, and the order meant Point 2297 or Signal Hill.[78] There were also examples of a lack of proper reconnaissance. A 10th Division report commented: 'the necessity of careful reconnaissance has been emphasised, and some of the failures are directly traceable to lack of reconnaissance'. The 10th Division report also stressed that the area to be attacked must be reconnoitred from different points as, for example, 'a series of hills one behind the other may appear to be a continuous ridge, whereas in reality the hills are separated by deep wadis'.[79]

Lastly, co-operation between units was mixed during this campaign. During combat, there were numerous positive examples at brigade and battalion levels. For example, during the Turkish attack on Neby Samwil on 22 November, 2/4th Hampshires assisted 3/3rd Gurkhas, who had been pushed back, and the Gurkhas managed to regain their position.[80] On 20 November, 233rd Brigade had sent two battalions to support the attack of 3/3rd Gurkhas towards Qaryat el-Inab.[81] Nevertheless, in the hilly terrain, co-operation remained a challenge. The commander of 10th The Buffs stated:

> very great difficulty was experienced during the last operations in keeping touch with units on the flanks, especially during a night advance, when it was well nigh impossible to locate one's position on a map, and exceedingly difficult to keep direction when advancing in hilly country such as this. It was felt that Battalion Liaison Officers would have been of value in spite of the difficulties of the country.[82]

Also, 180th Brigade reported that the 'lack of liaison between flank Bns of different Brigades has led to delays e.g. on 8/12/17, the whereabouts of the 179th Brigade on our right was not known until the morning'.[83]

Initiative

The last element is whether the EEF used its initiative effectively and adapted to circumstances. The mobile nature of the operations meant that the initiative of commanders lower down the chain of command could be more important than those on the Western Front.[84] As Major-General Shea would note in June 1918, 'the training and initiative of Platoon Commanders and Section leaders is all important' in this country, and the commanders at these levels must take full advantage of opportunities.[85] Some good displays of initiative were exhibited at the lower levels of command. For example, during the 75th Division operations on 20 November, commander of 233rd Brigade Brigadier-General Colston took advantage of the mist to mount a surprise attack on the Turks. The brigade was also effectively covered by a mortar battery on a nearby crest (Hill 2486).[86] Furthermore, the commander of 180th Brigade was also instrumental in organising the brigade reserve to assist the attack around Deir Yesin on 8 December.[87]

It also has to be mentioned that the EEF was aided by the decisions and lack of initiative of Turkish commanders. For example, while Yeomanry Mounted Division commander Major-General Barrow was right to abandon the attack on Zeitun Ridge on 22 November, covering units were very slow to arrive and Falls makes an admission that it was 'very fortunate the enemy did not attempt a pursuit.'[88] Moreover, there were some aspects of lower commander initiative that needed improving, especially using the ground more effectively for defence. Brigadier-General Watson of 180th Brigade felt that 'the Turks made more use of natural cover than our men. Our tendency is to make long lines of walls and sangars. These provide good targets.'[89] This indicates that EEF troops were still making the transition from trench warfare to hill warfare, although it must be also considered that this was Turkish territory, and therefore a degree of adjustment from the EEF side would be inevitable. Furthermore, historians have questioned the basis of some attacks. For example, on the 74th Division attack on 3 December, Falls concedes that 'local attacks of this nature were not worth their cost.'[90]

Nevertheless, despite these flaws, the EEF had an effective post-battle learning process in place. The records of these lessons gained from recent experiences have been preserved better in some units than in others. This chapter has already noted ideas from commanders concerning the

co-operation of machine and Lewis guns. On the issue of unit communication, Brigadier-General Watson echoed the suggestion of 10th The
Buffs, ultimately recommending that 'the system of liaison should be
extended down to companies.'[91] Other suggestions included means to
improve the rapidity and speed of advances. For example, 10th Division's tactical notes stated: 'it is surprising how rapidly infantry can
move over these mountains provided they travel as lightly laden as
possible.'[92] Of course, this particular lesson was not new, and was one
that was understood by colonial troops in India, and this illustrated that
some commanders and units still had much to learn about fighting in
the Judaean Hills.[93]

The keys to Jerusalem

This chapter has provided just a few observations on how the EEF performed, adapted and learned from its experiences of hill fighting during
the Jerusalem campaign. The EEF did face a number of constraints and
challenges. XXI Corps was initially constrained by political and strategic demands. The strategic demands of following up the success at Gaza
and capturing Jerusalem forced the EEF to take some costly risks and
to attack in extremely unfavourable circumstances, such as the initial
attacks on El Jib. The hilly terrain also constrained tactics, flexibility,
and unit coordination. To counteract these constraints, commanders did
display flexibility and initiative. Initial costly assaults forced the higher
command to rethink its approach, and adopt a theoretically less costly,
but less decisive, plan devised by Chetwode. Furthermore, the EEF was
able to draw upon its developing doctrine for 'modern warfare' as well as
its colonial hill-fighting experience. This doctrinal base provided more
than adequate foundation. However, inevitably, such doctrine needed
further development and adaptation, and the campaign therefore did
expose some weaknesses. These included organisational weaknesses,
unit cooperation (although this was a problem that was not unique to
this front, and the hilly terrain did present particular difficulties), and
the use of terrain for defensive means.

The research in this chapter does justify some balance such as that
provided by Grainger and Erickson when evaluating EEF performance
in this campaign; but it should be stressed this is only to some degree.
There were some tactical weaknesses. Yet many of these were the result
of strategic and operational constraints, and commanders identified
lessons and improvements, illustrating that there was an effective learning process in place. This learning and adaptation process was complex,

and despite the different environments this also reflects recent findings on the British army on the Western Front.[94] However, the process in Palestine would take on additional complexities, and it would be disrupted by the reorganisation of the EEF in 1918, which would bring with it a series of new challenges.

Overall, the EEF used its qualities of experience and flexibility to help adjust to the Judaean Hills. The commanders were engaged in what could be described as a multi-dimensional learning process in which learning to fight 'modern war' was just one component of what it needed to do in order to fight in these unique conditions.[95] James Kitchen makes an interesting point when he states that, while Montgomery led Eighth Army to victory in North Africa in the Second World War, Allenby *commanded* the EEF to victory.[96] This is not to say that the role of Allenby was not important; he was. But we can only obtain a full picture of how the EEF changed and how Allenby ultimately achieved victory if our attention continues to shift to the individual units and their commanders that made possible its successes, and important symbolic events such as Allenby's entrance into Jerusalem.

Notes

1. The blurb of Edward Woodfin's recent book described it as an 'oft-forgotten, but important campaign'. Edward Woodfin, *Camp and Combat on the Sinai and Palestine Front: The Experience of the British Empire Soldier, 1916–18* (Houndmills: Palgrave Macmillan, 2012).
2. James E. Kitchen, *The British Imperial Army in the Middle East: Morale and Military Identity in the Sinai and Palestine Campaigns, 1916–18* (London: Bloomsbury, 2014); Eran Dolev, Yigal Sheffy and Haim Goren eds., *Palestine and World War I: Grand Strategy, Military Tactics, and Culture in War* (I.B. Tauris, 2014). The latter was not published at the time of writing.
3. Kitchen, *The British Imperial Army*, p. 21; pp. 105–111. Kitchen provides a good overview of the debate.
4. Cyril Falls, *Military Operations: Egypt and Palestine: From 1917 to the End of the War* (London: HMSO, 1930); Sir Archibald Wavell, *Allenby: A Study in Greatness* (London: George C. Harrap & Co., 1940); Raymond Savage, *Allenby of Armageddon* (London: Hodder & Stoughton, 1925).
5. Matthew Hughes, *Allenby and British Strategy in the Middle East, 1917–1919* (London: Frank Cass, 1999), p. 48.
6. Jonathan Q. Newell, 'Learning the Hard Way: Allenby in Egypt and Palestine, 1917–19', *Journal of Strategic Studies*, Vol. 14, No. 3 (1991), p. 363.
7. Clive Garsia, *A Key to Victory: A Study in War Planning* (London: Eyre and Spottiswoode, 1940), p. 25.
8. Jonathan Newell, 'Allenby and the Palestine Campaign', in Brian Bond ed., *The First World War and British Military History* (Oxford: Clarendon Press, 1991), p. 216–219.

9. Kitchen, *The Imperial British Army*, p. 121.
10. Ibid., p. 108.
11. Ibid., p. 26.
12. Anthony Bruce, *The Last Crusade: British Campaigns in Palestine* (London: John Murray, 2002); John D. Grainger, *The Battle for Palestine 1917* (Woodbridge: The Boydell Press, 2006), pp. 227–278.
13. Yigal Sheffy, *British Military Intelligence in the Palestine Campaign* (London: Frank Cass, 1997).
14. Eran Dolev, *Allenby's Military Medicine: Life and Death in World War I Palestine* (London: I.B. Tauris, 2007).
15. Michael J. Mortlock, *The Egyptian Expeditionary Force in World War I: A History of the British-Led Campaigns in Egypt, Palestine and Syria* (Jefferson, NC: MacFarland & Company, Inc., 2011).
16. David R. Woodward, *Hell in the Holy Land: World War I in the Holy Land* (Lexington: University of Kentucky Press, 2006).
17. Dennis Showalter, 'The Indianization of the Egyptian Expeditionary Force, 1917–18: An Imperial Turning Point', in Kaushik Roy (ed.), *The Indian Army in the Two World Wars* (Leiden: Brill, 2011), pp. 145–164.
18. For example, Hughes, *Allenby and British Strategy*, p. 58.
19. A.J. Hill, *Chauvel of the Light Horse: A Biography of General Sir Henry Chauvel* (Melbourne: University Press, 1978).
20. Woodfin, *Camp and Combat*, p. 2.
21. Kitchen, *The British Imperial Army*, p. 206.
22. See, for example, Grainger, *The Battle for Palestine*.
23. Wavell, *The Palestine Campaigns*, p. 167.
24. Grainger, *The Battle for Palestine*, p. 193.
25. Edward J. Erickson, *Ottoman Army Effectiveness in World War I: A Comparative Study* (London: Routledge, 2007), p. 125.
26. Woodward, *Hell in the Holy Land*, p. 85.
27. Ibid., p. 145.
28. Wavell, *The Palestine Campaigns*, p. 163.
29. Ibid., p. 164.
30. Grainger, *The Battle for Palestine*, pp. 204–205.
31. Wavell, *The Palestine Campaigns*, p. 166.
32. Ibid., pp. 171–172; Grainger, *The Battle for Palestine*, p. 223.
33. Grainger, *The Battle for Palestine*, pp. 179–180.
34. Matthew Hughes, *Allenby in Palestine* (Stroud: Sutton Publishing/Army Records Society, 2004), p. 10.
35. 'Narrative of Operations', War Diary of 75th Division, TNA WO 95/4490.
36. Falls, *Military Operations*, p. 204; Lieutenant-Colonel R.R. Thompson, *The Fifty-Second (Lowland) Division* (Glasgow: MacLehose, Jackson & Co., 1923), p. 433.
37. Major-General John Shea, 'Narrative of Operations', December 1917, TNA WO 95/4660.
38. Kitchen, *The British Imperial Army*, p. 32.
39. Woodward, *Hell in the Holy Land,* p. 142.
40. Falls, *Military Operations*, pp. 185–186.
41. Thompson, *The Fifty-Second (Lowland) Division*, p. 436.
42. Henry Gullett, *Official History of Australia in the War, Vol. VII: Sinai and Palestine* (Sydney: Angus & Robertson Ltd, 1941), p. 490.

43. Woodward, *Hell in the Holy Land*, pp. 141–142.
44. Erickson, *Ottoman Army Effectiveness*, p. 124.
45. Grainger, *The Battle for Palestine*, p. 204.
46. Falls, *Military Operations*, p. 194; see also Allenby to Robertson, 26 November 1917, in Matthew Hughes (ed.), *Allenby in Palestine*, p. 98.
47. Grainger, *The Battle for Palestine*, pp. 185–195.
48. 'Experiences Gained in the Recent Fighting', War Diary of 60th Division, TNA WO 95/4660.
49. '10th Divisional: Tactical Notes on the Operations in Palestine', 13 February 2018, TNA WO 95/4567.
50. Brigadier-General F. Watson, 'Recent Observations', 13 February 2018, War Diary of 60th Division TNA WO 95/4660.
51. 'Notes on the Deployment of Lewis Guns in Recent Operations', War Diary of 74th (Yeomanry) Division, TNA WO 95/4673.
52. '10th Divisional: Tactical Notes on the Operations in Palestine', TNA WO 95/4567.
53. 'Experiences Gained in the Recent Fighting', TNA WO 95/4660.
54. Ibid.
55. Brigadier-General F. Watson, 'Recent Observations', TNA WO 95/4660.
56. Ibid.
57. James E. Kitchen also explores the notion of the EEF grappling with the demands of the environment in the Middle East and those of 'modern warfare'. Kitchen, *The British Imperial Army*, pp. 25–60.
58. For a good account of this, see T.R. Moreman, *The Army in India and the Development of Frontier Warfare, 1849–1947* (Houndmills: Macmillan Press Ltd., 1998).
59. Moreman, *The British Army in India*, pp. 16–18, p. 78.
60. Ibid., pp. 78–81.
61. Woodward, *Hell in the Holy Land*, p. 141.
62. Major-General Sir John Shea, 'Tactical Notes', June 1918, Shea Papers, LHCMA.
63. Ibid.
64. Kitchen, *The British Imperial Army*, p. 192.
65. Edward J. Erickson, *Ottoman Army Effectiveness in World War I: A Comparative Study* (London: Routledge, 2007), pp. 112–113.
66. 'Experiences Gained in the Recent Fighting', War Diary of 60th Division, TNA WO 95/4660.
67. Major-General John Shea, 'Lecture: Some Aspects of Lord Allenby's Campaign', Shea Papers, LHCMA.
68. Major-General Sir John Shea, 'Tactical Notes', LHCMA.
69. Erickson, *Ottoman Army Effectiveness*, p. 113.
70. For more information see Paddy Griffith, *Battle Tactics of the Western Front: The British Army's Art of Attack, 1916–1918* (New Haven: Yale University Press, 1994).
71. Major-General S.F. Mott, 'Tactical Notes', TNA WO 95/4615.
72. 'Notes on the Deployment of Lewis Guns in Recent Operations', TNA WO 95/4673.
73. 'XXth Corps Operations Subsequent to the Capture of Jerusalem up to December 31st 1917', War Diary of 20 Corps, 16 February 2018, TNA WO 95/4480.

74. Ibid.
75. 'Summary of Operations of LEFT Attack, December 26th to 31st', War Diary of 10th Division, TNA WO 95/4567.
76. Falls, *Military Operations*, p. 278; Sheffy, *British Military Intelligence*, pp. 282–3.
77. Wavell, *The Palestine Campaigns*, p. 157.
78. Falls, *Military Operations*, p. 232.
79. '10th Divisional: Tactical Notes on the Operations in Palestine', TNA WO 95/4567. The tactical development of 10th Division is explored in depth in Stephen Sandford, *Neither Unionist nor Nationalist: The 10th (Irish) Division 1914–18* (Sallins: Irish Academic Press, 2014). This was not published at the time of writing.
80. Falls, *Military Operations.*, pp. 202–203.
81. Ibid., p. 194.
82. 10th The Buffs, Letter, 23/1/18, TNA WO 95/4675.
83. Brigadier-General F. Watson, 'Recent Observations', TNA WO 95/4660.
84. Falls, *Military Operations*, p. 643.
85. Shea, 'Tactical Notes', LHCMA.
86. Falls, *Military Operations*, p. 194.
87. Grainger, *The Battle for Palestine*, p. 208.
88. Falls, *Military Operations*, p. 200.
89. Brigadier-General F. Watson, 'Recent Observations', TNA WO 95/4660.
90. Falls, *Military Operations*, pp. 235–236.
91. Brigadier-General F. Watson, 'Recent Observations', TNA WO 95/4660.
92. '10th Divisional: Tactical Notes on the Operations in Palestine', TNA WO 95/4567; For detailed analysis of 10th Division tactics, see Sandford, *Neither Unionist nor Nationalist*.
93. Moreman, p. 79.
94. For example, Jonathan Boff, *Winning and Losing on the Western Front: The British Third Army and the Defeat of Germany in 1918* (Cambridge: Cambridge University Press, 2012), p. 247. He and other recent historians have stressed that the concept of a 'learning curve' has often been misunderstood.
95. Kitchen, *The British Imperial Army*, pp. 27–46.
96. Ibid., p. 121.

8
A Picture of German Unity? Federal Contingents in the German Army, 1916–1917

Tony Cowan

> Most of the Bavarian army – especially the officer corps – entered the war as Prussia-friendly or at least imbued with strong confidence in the ability of the North German contingent and the feeling of its military superiority. During the campaign this feeling has completely changed. Above all, continuous association with each other has made us for the first time fully conscious of the complete difference between north and south and has had a repellent effect. The outstanding performance by Bavarian troops in all theatres has evidently very greatly increased their confidence; and it has also had the perhaps unmerited but natural effect of lowering their estimation of Prussia. In addition there have been infringements, arrogance and tactlessness by Prussian commanders. In short, inflammable material is piling up...[1]

This letter from the Bavarian Minister of War illustrates two important points. First, constitutionally the German army was a federal organisation comprising separate contingents. The largest was the Prussian army, but three others – from Bavaria, Saxony and Württemberg – were significant and retained autonomous rights. Second, relations between the contingents could be difficult. The key question here is not 'Did the Prussians and Bavarians (Saxons, Württembergers) like each other?', but 'Did the contingents' nature and interrelationships affect battlefield performance?' A possible comparison would be the relations between Australian and British formations: clearly there were tensions, but these did not prevent the Australians being among the most effective troops in the British Expeditionary Force.[2]

Martin Kitchen believes that the division of the German army into contingents did not prevent effective military unity, and that despite nominal concessions the predominance of the Prussian army was unchallenged.[3] It has also been suggested that co-operation between the Prussian, Bavarian, Saxon and Württemberg contingents was 'free of friction and tensions'. Similarly, explaining his selection of 11th Bavarian Infantry Division (BID) as a case study of a typical German formation, Christian Stachelbeck argues that its Bavarian provenance is not relevant because of the widespread standardisation and unification of the German army.[4]

This chapter will show that the German army was less homogeneous than such views allow; that although the contingents could co-operate effectively together, their continued existence increased administrative and operational friction; and that their quality and battlefield performance varied. After outlining the status of the contingents in peacetime, the chapter looks mainly at the period from late 1916 to mid-1917. This was the height of the trench warfare phase on the Western Front and included the crucial failure of the 1917 Entente spring offensive (the Battle of Arras and Nivelle Offensive).[5]

The 1871 German constitution recognised the military forces – the contingents – of the 25 federal states as the basis of the German army. In reality, however, 21 of these states ceded most of their military sovereignty to the Kaiser as King of Prussia through a series of military conventions and other agreements. Only formations from Hessen and Baden retained any form of separate identity within the Prussian army: these were the Grand Duchies which had signed the constitution as sovereign entities and they raised complete divisions for the army. In practical terms, by 1914 there were only four separate contingents: the Prussian, Bavarian and Saxon armies and the Württemberg army corps.[6] Table 8.1 shows the proportion of manpower each contributed

Table 8.1 Contingents' relative contributions to the German army (peacetime)

Contingent	%
Prussian army	77
Bavarian army	11
Saxon army	8
Württemberg army corps	4
Total	100

to the German army.[7] The overwhelming numerical predominance of the Prussian army is clear.

The three remaining non-Prussian contingents all retained significant rights, which varied according to their constitutional and treaty undertakings. Württemberg had the least autonomy, having signed an additional military agreement with Prussia in 1893; this in effect merged the two officer corps and facilitated cross-posting between the two contingents. The Bavarian army, as the largest contingent after Prussia, was the most determined and able to maintain its autonomy. This included independent appointment of its senior commanders, higher educational requirements for its officer corps, separate training of its general staff officers in its own staff college and a separate numbering system for all units. Saxony was more independent than Württemberg but less than Bavaria. Table 8.2 illustrates these different degrees of autonomy in terms of institutions.[8]

But the constitution and treaties also limited the contingents' autonomy. They were obliged to adopt conscription, with uniform terms of service, and to contribute their proportion of the agreed peacetime strength of the army and its costs. The Kaiser was the federal commander-in-chief (*Bundesfeldherr*) in peace and war, with the exception that the Bavarian army only came under his command on mobilisation. A key function was his authority to appoint or at least agree the appointment of senior commanders, again except for Bavaria. All contingents had to adopt Prussian standards in organisation, equipment, regulations and training. The *Reich* authorities had the right to carry out inspections to ensure implementation of these standards. Other measures also promoted integration. All three contingents seconded general staff officers to the Prussian Great General Staff. Bavarians were also seconded to the Prussian Military Technical Academy as well as to the artillery and small-arms testing commissions. Saxon officers had a broader choice of postings outside their own army, and Württembergers

Table 8.2 Independent institutions of contingents' armies

Contingent	Ministry of War	General staff	Officer corps	Staff college	Separate unit numbers
Bavarian	Yes	Yes	Yes	Yes	Yes
Saxon	Yes	Yes	Yes	No	No
Württemberg	Yes	No	No	No	No

had access to a range of positions at various levels in the Prussian army.[9]

Generally the aim of ensuring uniformity of standards and performance in peacetime was achieved, despite the contingents' autonomy. But it was not possible to eliminate all problems. Even Württemberg, which believed in co-operating fully on operational issues, was determined to maintain its rights. There were regular arguments over the command of the Württemberg army corps, and over delimiting the spheres of authority of its commander (usually a Prussian) and the Württemberg Minister of War. In Bavaria, keenness to develop the local aircraft industry impeded rationalisation of design and supply at a national (German) level.[10]

Once war came in 1914, the Kaiser's formal position as commander-in-chief meant in practice that the Prussian-dominated Supreme Army Command (*Oberste Heeresleitung*, OHL) controlled the contingents' field forces. By 1916 the Bavarian Minister of War was forced to concede that '*during the war* there is a certain internal contradiction between the unity and independence of the supreme command – which must be recognised as a military necessity – and the constitutionally reserved rights of Bavarian military sovereignty'.[11] Nevertheless the contingents retained important rights, including control of the forces in their homelands and administration. To defend these rights and in a continuation of peacetime practice, each contingent posted a senior officer as military plenipotentiary to the Kaiser's General Headquarters (of which OHL was part).

By early 1917, in terms of divisions in the field Prussia's relative contribution had increased slightly, whereas Bavaria's and Saxony's had fallen slightly (Table 8.3).[12]

Table 8.3 Contingents' relative contributions (number of divisions)

Contingent	Peacetime	% of German army	9 April 1917	% of German army
Prussian	38	76	177	78
Bavarian	6	12	24	11
Saxon	4	8	17	7
Württemberg	2	4	10	4
Total	50	100	228	100

The existence of the contingents and their rights undoubtedly affected the conduct of the war. At the political level the individual states had their own war aims, and these could impinge directly on military matters. For instance, Saxony hoped to gain territory in the east. Deploying troops there during the war would help bolster this claim in the post-war settlement. Saxony believed that it would be able to colonise the new territory with its 'excess' population. This would enable the kingdom to raise a third and maybe even a fourth army corps. Extra military strength would in turn allow Saxony to maintain the military convention with Prussia or even improve it along Bavarian lines, thus winning greater military sovereignty. Württemberg went through the same thought process over acquiring territory in Alsace-Lorraine.[13]

Political and dynastic considerations affected military organisation and probably operations. A characteristic of the Western Front in spring 1917, and a product of Germany's political structure, was that the three German army group commanders were heirs to the thrones of Prussia, Bavaria and Württemberg.[14] OHL reportedly wanted to make *Generalfeldmarschall* Crown Prince Rupprecht of Bavaria theatre commander for the whole Western Front. This did not happen because Crown Prince Wilhelm, heir to the imperial and Prussian thrones, could not be placed under Rupprecht, heir to the Bavarian throne.[15] A similar problem arose in early 1917. Fourth Army, on the coast, could not be brought into Army Group Rupprecht where it naturally belonged because its commander, *Generalfeldmarschall* Herzog Albrecht, heir to the Württemberg throne, could not serve under Rupprecht. This problem was only solved when the third Western Front army group was created and Albrecht given command. Fourth Army then moved into Army Group Rupprecht.[16]

Dynastic issues also affected operations, or at least were perceived to. As Sixth Army commander in August 1914, Rupprecht commanded almost the entire mobilised Bavarian army, which therefore remained largely under the Wittelsbach dynasty's control. The positioning of Sixth Army along the frontier in Alsace-Lorraine met the Bavarian desire to secure its Pfalz (Rhineland Palatinate) territory against invasion.[17] More than one senior Prussian officer commented that the need for the Wittelsbachs to gain military glory had influenced Rupprecht's conduct of operations in August 1914. Whether justified or not, these were serious allegations given the widespread view that the operations were a major factor in the defeat of the initial German offensive and therefore in the loss of the war.[18] The Prussians were clearly worried about Rupprecht. Erich Falkenhayn, head of OHL, described him as a 'particularist' or supporter of Bavarian autonomy. Falkenhayn arranged for *Generalleutnant* Hermann von Kuhl to be appointed Rupprecht's chief of staff (*Chef des Generalstabes*, CGS) as a Prussian chaperone.[19]

Nor were the Prussian Hohenzollerns immune from accusations of taking military action to promote their dynastic interests. Crown Prince Wilhelm was said to have asked permission to take the offensive in August 1914 to emulate Rupprecht's initial success in Lorraine.[20] Wilhelm's role commanding Fifth Army at Verdun in 1916 was especially controversial. It had been hoped that a great victory there by the heir to the Prussian throne would strengthen the monarchy. But by April 1917 damaging rumours were circulating that he was responsible for the overall failure at Verdun as well as the two serious local defeats in October and December 1916. Falkenhayn's successor as head of OHL, *Generalfeldmarschall* Paul von Hindenburg, ordered steps to be taken actively to counter the rumours. Recording this order, Rupprecht commented that it would be said nothing had been achieved on the Western Front since the beginning of trench warfare because the army and later the army group commanders there were chosen only for dynastic reasons.[21] Prussian dynastic considerations may also have had an important – and negative – influence on decisions relating to the German March 1918 offensive. Both at the time and later it has been alleged that *General der Infanterie* Erich Ludendorff, Hindenburg's chief assistant, selected the final attack plan and distorted the chain of command with a view to giving Crown Prince Wilhelm a spectacular victory.[22]

The existence of the contingents affected military effectiveness in other areas too, including personnel work and administration of the army. Many senior Prussian and Württemberg officers served in each others' contingents. But with very rare exceptions, only Bavarian and Saxon officers held command and general staff positions in their respective corps and divisions: control of these appointments is one of the clearest signs of the two kingdoms' continued military autonomy. Only a few Bavarian and Saxon officers held senior Prussian positions. The outstanding example is *Generalleutnant* Max Ritter von Höhn, who for six months commanded the Prussian 2nd Guard Infantry Division – a unique distinction for a Bavarian officer.[23] It was possible, however, to see a sinister Prussian plot in this, or at least Rupprecht did: he suspected that by offering commands to Bavarians the Prussians were skilfully manoeuvring to demand the right to appoint Bavarian generals.[24]

Both Bavarians and Saxons laid claim to one Army command or similar position. In 1914 the Bavarians saw Sixth Army as their preserve, the Saxons Third Army. After the Saxon *Generaloberst* Max Freiherr von

Hausen left command of Third Army in September 1914, the Saxons constantly pressed for one of their senior officers to hold an equivalent job.[25] Lower-level posts were also of concern. In April 1917, Bavarian Ministry of War approval had to be sought to appoint a Prussian as chief engineer officer in Sixth Army, a lieutenant-colonel's job; in return, a Bavarian would be nominated to the equivalent post in Second Army.[26] Such issues were often handled by the military plenipotentiaries at GHQ. In April 1917 the Bavarian military plenipotentiary assured Rupprecht that when a particular Bavarian major was appointed to a general staff job in First Army headquarters – basically a Prussian formation – Bavarian rights had been respected and authorisation requested.[27] These interventions with Ludendorff and other senior OHL staff on matters dear to the contingents' hearts took up time better spent on more important matters.

In terms of personal relations, naturally some officers got on well with their colleagues in other contingents, some did not. Similarly, officers had differing views on how much unification between the contingents was desirable. Whereas the Bavarian *Generalleutnant* Paul Ritter von Kneußl held increasingly strong anti-Prussian feelings, Höhn – who had had two postings to the general staff in Berlin as well as the Prussian divisional command – was a firm believer in greater Germany and loved Prussia's military tradition.[28] There was always the possibility of friction. While commanding Prussian and Bavarian divisions in October 1916, the Prussian *General der Infanterie* Max von Boehn said to the Kaiser that the enemy would not get through as long as there was still one Prussian soldier alive. Boehn was probably being tactless rather than malicious, but the Bavarians complained and he had to apologise.[29]

The Prussian Ministry of War controlled the army's general administration, but it had to consult with the Bavarian, Saxon and Württemberg Ministries and could only communicate its decisions to the contingents through them. Inevitably the Bavarians wanted more independence than the others. An example is the reorganisation of the corps system from late 1916. Corps was the highest-level military organisation controlled by contingents, originally comprising a fixed formation of two infantry divisions and supporting units. From late 1916 this organic link was broken: corps then became group (*Gruppe*) headquarters, controlling a fluctuating number of divisions from any contingent which moved in and out of its sector as required. The Württembergers and Saxons quickly agreed with the Prussians how this should be handled, but the Bavarians insisted on being consulted beforehand on a case-by-case basis.[30]

This corps reorganisation loosened the contingent system, but generally during the war the system was maintained or even strengthened. Pre-war, one Saxon and one Württemberg regiment were brigaded with Prussian troops as part of the garrison of Alsace-Lorraine. The rush to increase the number of combat formations in 1914–1916 led to the creation of many more mixed-contingent divisions as well as the sending of replacements outside their contingents. Falkenhayn ignored a complaint by Baden about this. However Württemberg commanders believed that the fragmentation of their contingent adversely affected communications and reduced the combat effectiveness of their troops. Their complaints led to a change of policy by Falkenhayn's successors at OHL in October 1916. Most mixed divisions were then reorganised so that each came entirely from one contingent. In moments of crisis after that, OHL might try to send men from one contingent as replacements to another, but this led to complaints from the contingents citing OHL's October 1916 policy and the original military conventions.[31]

Bavarian military leaders including Rupprecht, the Minister of War and the military plenipotentiary at GHQ all worked towards maintaining Bavaria's 'special position' as it came under increasing threat in 1916–1917. Their efforts included resisting sending any more Bavarian divisions to the Somme; pressing for divisions to be reunited in Bavarian corps and for more to be allocated to Sixth Army, still seen as the Bavarian army in the field; and if Sixth Army could not be Bavarian, asking for another Army headquarters to be set up which would be. They also determined to oppose Prussian encroachment by retaining the monopoly on posting Bavarian officers, inculcating the feeling that the Bavarian army was a separate entity and taking practical steps to strengthen the connection between Bavarian troops and their homeland – meaning Bavaria, not Germany.[32]

Did the contingent system described here affect battlefield performance? Some background explanation will be helpful. A crucial factor in performance was fighting power, or combat value (*Kampfwert*) as the Germans usually called it. The German official history commented that 'nowhere near all divisions were suited for major combat'.[33] The importance of assessing divisions' combat value accurately was dramatically demonstrated by the case of 39th Bavarian Reserve Division at Verdun. This had been organised only for trench warfare on quiet fronts; it had no experience of major combat; and it had stated frankly that it was not fit for deployment to Verdun. It was deployed anyway and not surprisingly overrun during the successful French December 1916 attack.[34]

If anything, the question of combat value became even more pressing by spring 1917: the introduction of new tactics placed heavier demands on the troops, at a time when the quality of the army was perceived to have declined.[35] Analysis shows that when the Entente spring offensive opened on 9 April, over 40 per cent of divisions in the field were viewed as intrinsically not up to the demands of major battle on the Western Front. Included in this category were divisions deployed long-term to the Eastern Front, which had become a backwater. It was possible to use formations there whose combat value prevented their employment in the west except in emergency.[36] From winter 1916 at the latest, all units which were less effective in battle were being sent to the Eastern Front and conversely the best divisions were being sent west.[37]

Commenting on contingents' overall performance, Ludendorff wrote that though they bickered they all did their duty; all had their good and less good divisions, with the exception of those from Württemberg and Baden which were all high quality. 'In spite of the variety of peoples composing it, the [German] Army held together well.'[38] Evidence from early 1917 lends some support to Ludendorff's comments. In particular, the contingents were part of an integrated military system. Two examples will demonstrate this. The first is operational and organisational. In May 1917, Gruppe Liesse in the Aisne sector was controlled by Generalkommando 54. This was a Prussian corps headquarters with a Prussian commander and CGS, commanding one Bavarian and four Prussian divisions. Three of the Prussian divisions were in the front line, and units supporting them included Bavarian and Württemberg artillery. The Bavarian division, 11th BID, was completely integrated into the *Gruppe* organisation. Its first role was as a counter-attack division (*Eingreifdivision*) and at one point it had detached two of its regiments to support a Prussian division. Later, it replaced this division in the front line. Kneußl, 11th BID's commander, strongly disliked Prussia, but there is no evidence that the Bavarian provenance of his division caused organisational or tactical problems.[39]

The second example comes from the area of doctrine and training. In late 1916 the Bavarian Höhn was specially chosen to produce the first draft of the new defensive doctrine. OHL finalised and circulated this to the whole army. It then set up a school to train divisional staffs on the doctrine. The first two commandants of the school were the Württemberg *Generalleutnant* Otto von Moser and the Bavarian *Generalleutnant* Karl Ritter von Wenninger; the first demonstration units were Bavarian and Württemberg divisions. Moser later wrote that his staff, comprising officers from Prussia, Bavaria and Württemberg, was 'a picture of German unity'. Students came from all parts of the German army, and the school taught an integrated doctrine.[40]

There is also evidence supporting Ludendorff's statement about the excellent quality of Württemberg troops. Six divisional commanders were awarded the *Pour le Mérite*, the top Prussian decoration, for their performance against the 1917 Entente spring offensive. Two of them were Württembergers, a high proportion for so small a contingent. The award of *Pour le Mérites* to two further senior Württemberg officers for their role in defeating the offensive – Moser, then commanding Gruppe Arras, and *Oberstleutnant* Walter Reinhardt, Seventh Army's CGS – must have further strengthened the reputation of the contingent. Describing an action slightly later in the year, the Prussian *General der Infanterie* Otto von Below wrote that 'as ever' the Württemberg divisions had fought brilliantly, and he praised a Württemberg commander who had performed excellently on the Somme. Even Württemberg formations could struggle occasionally though, as shown by disciplinary problems in 26th ID that autumn.[41]

Bavarian formations had a mixed record against the Entente spring offensive. On the one hand, 3rd BID's part in the Battle of Arras was viewed as a model implementation of the new defensive tactics; its commander, Wenninger, lectured to the assembled officers of two Armies; and his talk was circulated more broadly on the Western Front. Other Bavarian divisions had performed less well, especially 14th BID which was regarded as having failed in the severe defeat at Arras on 9 April.[42] This led to a temporary Bavarian loss of confidence in their military reputation, particularly when the division was sent to the Eastern Front to recover. At this moment of crisis, Ludendorff had to spend time reassuring the military plenipotentiary that the move did not reflect badly on the Bavarians.[43]

The battlefield failure of 14th BID illustrates another characteristic of the contingents, that they were not homogeneous within themselves. Explaining the failure, a regimental commander from the division included the point that there were many men from the Pfalz in it.[44] No evidence supports this explanation of the defeat, but negative views of the Pfälzer were common in the rest of the Bavarian army. The next month, Kneußl of 11th BID commented in his diary on one of his regiments which was performing badly:

> I've never had a really high opinion of the 22nd Regiment. From the Pfalz of course! But they've now gone so far that they can barely be used in the defence, that's to say that in an enemy attack they *may* stay where they are, but…only because retreating would be

even more dangerous. The Pfälzer really don't have much guts, except when it comes to talking...[45]

Prussian commanders too had definite views on the combat value of troops from different areas of the Prussian army. Ludendorff clearly thought highly of troops from Baden. In contrast there had been widespread doubts before the war, including at a senior level, about the reliability of Rhineland troops.[46] Incidents involving a number of divisions from the region in late 1916 and 1917 would have fed such concerns, whether justified or not. There were serious disciplinary and morale problems in 15th ID from its second deployment on the Somme to at least autumn 1917, leading to a series of court martial cases and the sacking of two successive divisional commanders. 16th ID was also viewed as having failed in action on the Somme; there was an investigation and the divisional commander was removed.[47] A regiment of 15th Reserve Division (RD) was seen as having failed at Arras in May 1917, 'and not for the first time'.[48] OHL raised concerns, unfairly, about the performance of a fourth Rhineland division, 16th RD; a fifth, 185th ID, suffered from morale and disciplinary problems in late 1916 and summer 1917.[49]

Some of the sources describing these incidents refer to Rhinelanders gratuitously or with ironic exclamation marks, perhaps reflecting the pre-war doubts.[50] There is a temptation to see such remarks as mere gossip or prejudice: in an echo of British martial race theory, officers often commented on the characteristics of troops from different regions.[51] However there clearly was high-level concern about the Rhineland cases. The CGS of the corps in which 15th ID was serving contrasted the tough northern troops in the corps with the Rhinelanders. He backed up his comments with references to whole companies of Rhinelanders refusing to advance and to men shooting at their officers.[52] Similarly, the courts martial and sackings demonstrate official recognition of the problems. Tellingly, four of the five Rhineland divisions mentioned were sent to the Eastern Front for a few months to sort themselves out in quieter circumstances.

Statistical analysis of German divisions engaged against the Entente spring offensive illuminates German commanders' assessment of the combat value of different contingents (Table 8.4). Just under half of all divisions were committed to the battle. The percentage of Prussian divisions reflects this closely. Bavarian divisions figure more prominently, not least because the battle of Arras was fought by Sixth Army

Table 8.4   Deployment of divisions facing the Entente spring offensive, April–May 1917

Contingent	No. of divisions engaged	Total divisions available	% participation
Prussian	88	177	50
Bavarian	14	24	58
Saxon	3	17	18
Württemberg	6	10	60
Total	111	228	49

in which many Bavarian formations were still concentrated. No such reason applies to the Württemberg divisions, and their 60 per cent participation rate is well above average. But what stands out is the low participation rate of Saxon divisions. Even combining participation in the battle of Messines in June with the spring offensive, the rate only rises from 18 per cent to 29 per cent, and it fell slightly at Third Ypres that autumn.

This is all the more striking because Saxon divisions had been heavily engaged in the 1916 battles: 85 per cent had fought at Verdun or the Somme or both, roughly the same as the Bavarians and Württembergers. Their casualties were also about average; and as with other contingents their performance varied – some divisions were reported as fighting excellently, others as having completely failed. Comment from outside the Saxon contingent apparently focused on the negative aspects. Senior Württemberg officers were especially critical, *Generalleutnant* Wilhelm Herzog von Urach commenting that the Saxons did not exactly enjoy the best reputation.[53] The influential head of the Prussian Military Cabinet wrote that a Saxon division in particular was responsible for a serious defeat on the Somme. Other officers contented themselves with ironic remarks when describing Saxon successes or failures.[54] There are suggestions in British reminiscences too that the Saxons were a softer touch than the Prussians and Bavarians.[55]

In early 1917 specific problems with Saxon formations emerged. Sixth Army's operations officer described the Saxon XII Reserve Corps as 'bad'. Two weeks before the battle of Arras began, it was removed from the line and replaced by Prussians; its CGS was sacked.[56] The incoming Prussians had no hesitation in blaming the Saxons for the poor development of the defences they had inherited, which they saw as a large part of the reason for their defeat on 9 April: 'It's a real pity that our wonderful corps had to eat this soup which our Saxon predecessors deserved as they had prepared nothing. Frankly if we had not replaced them the British would now be in Valenciennes.'[57] Reporting an OHL briefing on the first day's fighting in the Champagne, the only detail the head of the Military Cabinet mentioned was that a Saxon division had given way.[58] This was 58th ID, which had an indifferent reputation in 1916 and was shortly after sent to the 'sin bin' on the Eastern Front. Kuhl recorded that regrettably all Saxon divisions had to be taken out of the front line just before the British attack at Messines in June.[59] The corps commander there was the Saxon *General der Kavallerie* Maximilian von Laffert, who was believed to have mishandled the defence; he was not sacked, but his corps headquarters was removed and sent to a quiet sector.[60]

The corollary of the low Saxon participation in the Western Front battles of 1917 was a noticeable build-up of divisions on the Eastern Front (Table 8.5). For comparison, in October 1917 only one-fifth of Bavarian and one-tenth of Württemberg divisions were on the Eastern Front. The concentration of formations there suited Saxon war aims, but there may have been other reasons for it. The British assessment was that among the units sent to the east were those the Germans wanted to save from heavy casualties for political reasons, including the Saxons.[61]

More likely, they were part of the transfer of less capable formations to the Eastern Front. Only one of the five Saxon divisions raised in late 1916–1917 served on the Western Front, in a quiet sector, before moving east. In contrast, many of the other contingents' divisions formed at this time took part in the heavy western fighting of late 1917. This suggests that these new Saxon divisions were of low quality. The reason for this is not clear, but one factor may be that between 1871 and 1913 Saxony was the state which saw the largest increase in its army. Infantry battalions almost doubled in number and artillery batteries more than

Table 8.5 Saxon divisions by front at different periods

Date	Total Saxon divisions	Western	Eastern	% of Saxon divisions on Eastern Front
July 1916	12	12	0	0
April 1917	17	11	6	35
October 1917	18	7	11	61

trebled; the corresponding figures for Bavaria were much lower. There was a perennial shortage of officers, many of whom had to assume posts for which their experience did not qualify them.[62] It is possible that Saxony had simply outstripped the manpower resources needed to properly maintain the units it had raised by 1917. It is also possible that Saxon formations had suffered lasting damage from their heavy engagement in the 1916 battles. Finally, restricting senior command and general staff posts to officers from the relatively small Saxon contingent seriously limited the available pool of talent. This may have contributed to the performance problems.

The influential Inspector of Aviation Troops, *Oberstleutnant* Wilhelm Siegert, wrote that the particularism of the individual federal states had disastrous effects on Germany's conduct of the war and in fact was one of the nails in its coffin.[63] The traditional view is diametrically opposite, claiming that there was effective military unity despite the existence of the federal contingents, and that co-operation between them was free of friction and tensions. The analysis here has shown that both these views are exaggerated and that the truth lies somewhere in between. There was effective military unity, but the existence of the three non-Prussian contingents increased administrative and operational friction. Their combat value and reputation in late 1916 and 1917 varied: contemporaries perceived the Württemberg formations as best, the Bavarians as average and the Saxons as worst.

The contingent system remained significant in military terms because it was part of a bigger political picture, the *Kaiserreich*'s dynamic between centralising and particularist tendencies. Specific military points should be viewed in this context. As an example, underlying criticism of units from the Pfalz was the difficult relationship between the region and the rest of Bavaria. Similarly, Bavarian and Saxon restriction of command and general staff posts to officers of their own contingents was part of their overall effort to retain military sovereignty; in turn, this was an important aspect of their struggle for political autonomy in a united Germany.[64]

Against this background, it is not surprising that there were both centripetal and centrifugal forces acting on the military during the war. Centripetal forces included the army working together as a whole in a way it did not during peacetime. Mobilisation gave the Kaiser – and therefore OHL – greater authority over the contingents. Especially after the fixed corps structure was abolished, divisions were moved round as operations required. In addition, the new defensive tactics often necessitated the ad hoc deployment of regiments and other sub-units regardless of their contingent affiliation. The contingents co-operated at least well enough to run this system effectively.

On the other side of the coin, various factors increased the significance of the contingents during the war. Chief of these was OHL's decision in October 1916 to reunite units with their parent contingents. As the quote opening this chapter suggests, the strain of a long war and military necessity aggravated the tensions between non-Prussian contingents and the centre which had existed in peacetime. The contingents, especially the Bavarians but including smaller ones like the Badenese, strove to maintain their rights under the original military conventions and other agreements. This could always lead to disputes and cause effort which would have been better deployed elsewhere. The contingents' views of their own interests might lead them to oppose measures which were militarily sensible: Rupprecht's (eventually unsuccessful) attempts to avoid sending Bavarian formations to the Somme are an example.

The analysis here has focused on late 1916 and early 1917. Some evidence suggests that relations between the contingents deteriorated later in the war. Ludendorff wrote that from summer 1918 the separatist spirit in Bavarian troops increased and only a few divisions fought as well as before. Postal censorship also showed that as the war continued, troops from different regions increasingly distrusted Prussian dominance.[65] Summing up, then, despite the German army's unification and generally successful measures for standardisation, it was ultimately unable to overcome particularism. We should therefore not exaggerate the role it played in creating national unity. In fact, during the war problems arising from the army's regional composition had a major effect on its character and performance and so contributed to its eventual defeat.[66]

Notes

1. Bavarian Minister of War to *Generalfeldmarschall* Rupprecht, Crown Prince of Bavaria, 5 April 1917, Bayerisches Hauptstaatsarchiv, Abteilung III Geheimes Hausarchiv, München (hereafter HAM), Nachlass Rupprecht Nr. 614.
2. Not least in their own estimation.
3. Martin Kitchen, *The German Officer Corps 1890–1914* (Oxford: Clarendon Press, 1968), p. 15.
4. Wiegand Schmidt-Richberg, 'Die Regierungszeit Wilhelms II', in Militärgeschichtliches Forschungsamt (ed.), *Handbuch zur deutschen Militärgeschichte 1648–1939*, Vol. V: *Von der Entlassung Bismarcks bis zum Ende des Ersten*

Weltkrieges (1890–1918) (Frankfurt am Main: Bernard & Graefe, 1968), p. 53 (hereafter MGFA, *Handbuch*); Christian Stachelbeck, *Militärische Effektivität im Ersten Weltkrieg: die 11. Bayerische Infanteriedivision 1915 bis 1918* (Paderborn: Ferdinand Schöningh, 2010), p. 4.

5. For other aspects of the German army's composition, such as the reliability of troops from Alsace-Lorraine and ethnic Polish areas, see Alan Kramer, '*Wackes* at war: Alsace-Lorraine and the failure of German national mobilization, 1914–1918', in John Horne (ed.), *State, Society and Mobilization in Europe during the First World War* (Cambridge: Cambridge University Press, 1997), pp. 105–121; and Alexander Watson, 'Fighting for Another Fatherland: the Polish Minority in the German Army, 1914–1918', *English Historical Review*, Vol. CXXVI, No. 522 (October 2011), pp. 1137–1166.

6. Paul Laband, *Das Staatsrecht der Deutschen Reiches*, 4 vols, Fifth Edition, Vol. IV (Tübingen: Verlag von J.C.B. Mohr, 1914), pp. 4–76. For the historical background, see Manfred Messerschmidt, 'Die politische Geschichte der preußisch-deutschen Armee', in MGFA (ed.), *Handbuch*, Vol. IV, *Militärgeschichte im 19. Jahrhundert 1814–1890* (München: Bernard & Graefe, 1975), pp. 36–44, 205–215.

7. Based on Ottomar Freiherr von Osten-Sacken und von Rhein, *Preußens Heer: Von seinen Anfängen bis zur Gegenwart*, Vol. III (Berlin: E.S. Mittler, 1914), p. 403.

8. Württemberg's general staff existed only as a body of general staff officers, not as a functioning organisation.

9. On these points see especially F.F. Campbell, 'The Bavarian Army, 1870–1918: the Constitutional and Structural Relations with the Prussian Military Establishment', unpublished PhD thesis (Ohio State University, 1972), p. 53–55. For the Saxon army, see J. Hoffmann, 'Die sächsische Armee im Deutschen Reich 1871 bis 1918', unpublished PhD thesis (University of Dresden, 2007); and for Württemberg, R.T. Walker Jr, 'Prusso-Württembergian Military Relations in the German Empire, 1870–1918', unpublished PhD thesis (Ohio State University, 1974).

10. Walker, 'Prusso-Württembergian Military Relations', pp. 105–107, 113–116; John H. Morrow, Jr, *German Air Power in World War I* (Lincoln, Nebraska: University of Nebraska Press, 1982), pp. 9–10, 66–68.

11. Bavarian Minister of War to Rupprecht, No. 90849, 22 August 1916, HAM, Nachlass Rupprecht Nr. 614.

12. These and subsequent figures exclude ten cavalry divisions. For simplicity, they aggregate nine mixed-contingent divisions to the contingent which supplied most of the manpower; and two naval divisions to the Prussian contingent, which also contained the Hessian and Badenese divisions. The date chosen for the total of divisions available, 9 April 1917, was the first day of the Entente spring offensive. Details of officers' careers and divisional deployment are from the author's databases.

13. Hoffmann, 'Sächsische Armee', pp. 327–334; Württemberg military plenipotentiary to Herzog Albrecht [no reference], 14 May 1917 and 12388, 18 June 1918, both Archiv des Hauses Württemberg, G331/548. For federal states' war aims, see Karl-Heinz Janßen, *Macht und Verblendung: Kriegszielpolitik der deutschen Bundesstaaten 1914–1918* (Göttingen: Musterschmidt Verlag, 1963).

14. The Crown Prince of Saxony was too junior for such a job; he was serving as a staff officer in Fifth Army.
15. Hermann von Kuhl, unpublished manuscript, 'Persönliches Kriegstagebuch des Generals der Inf. a.D. von Kuhl (Nov 15–Nov 18)', BA/MA, RH61/970, p. 24 (diary entry for 8 September 1916) (hereafter, Kuhl, 'Kriegstagebuch').
16. Robert T. Foley, 'The Other Side of the Wire: the German Army in 1917', in Peter Dennis and Jeffrey Grey (eds), *1917 – Tactics, Training and Technology* (Australia: Australian History Military Publications, 2007), p. 157.
17. Campbell, 'Bavarian Army', p. 227. The Pfalz was a Bavarian territory geographically separate from the main part of the kingdom.
18. Markus Pöhlmann, *Kriegsgeschichte und Geschichtspolitik: Der Erste Weltkrieg: Die amtliche deutsche Militärgeschichtsschreibung 1914–1956* (Paderborn: Ferdinand Schöningh, 2002), pp. 301–303.
19. Kuhl, 'Kriegstagebuch', p. 4; Pöhlmann, *Kriegsgeschichte*, p. 251.
20. Sewell Tyng, *The Campaign of the Marne* (Yardley: Westholme Publishing, 2007), p. 81.
21. OHL to all commanders down to division level, Nr. 2125, 2 April 1917, Bayerisches Hauptstaatsarchiv, Abteilung IV Kriegsarchiv, München (hereafter KAM), HGr. Rupprecht neue Nr. 378, f. 62. Kronprinz Rupprecht von Bayern, *Mein Kriegstagebuch* (ed. Eugen von Frauenholz) (3 vols.) (München: Deutscher National Verlag, 1929), II, p. 130 (diary entry for 5 April 1917).
22. David T. Zabecki, *The German 1918 Offensives: A Case Study in the Operational Level of War* (London and New York: Routledge, 2006), pp. 164–165; Kuhl, 'Kriegstagebuch', p. 106 (diary entry for 22 January 1918).
23. Fritz von Loßberg, *Meine Tätigkeit im Weltkriege 1914–1918* (Berlin: E.S. Mittler, 1939), p. 167.
24. Rupprecht, *Kriegstagebuch*, I, p. 514 (diary entry for 4 August 1916).
25. Hoffmann, 'Sächsische Armee', pp. 329, 336; Campbell, 'Bavarian Army', pp. 147–149.
26. OHL to Army Group Rupprecht, 1c No. 2937, 24 April 1917, KAM, HGr. Rupprecht neue Nr. 378.
27. Bavarian military plenipotentiary to Rupprecht, 15 April 1917, HAM, Nachlass Rupprecht Nr. 614.
28. Stachelbeck, *Militärische Effektivität*, p. 47; Generaloberst von Einem, *Erinnerungen eines Soldaten 1853–1933* (Leipzig: K.F. Koehler, 1933), p. 182.
29. Kuhl, 'Kriegstagebuch', p. 33 (diary entries for 21, 22 and 25 October 1916).
30. OHL circular, Ic Nr. 44492 op., January 1917, BA/MA, PH1/10, p. 124.
31. Walker, 'Prusso-Württembergian Military Relations', pp. 132–136; Hoffmann, 'Sächsische Armee', pp. 334–335.
32. Rudolf Ritter von Xylander, unpublished diary, KAM, R. Xylander Nachlass, Bd. 12, p. 663 (diary entry 19 August 1916; hereafter, 'Xylander diary'). Xylander was Sixth Army's operations officer). Bavarian Minister of War to Rupprecht, 5 April 1917 and Nr. 205014A, 4 December 1917; Rupprecht to Bavarian Minister of War, 13 June 1917, all on HAM, Nachlass Rupprecht Nr. 614. Rupprecht unpublished diary, HAM, Nachlass Rupprecht Nr. 705, p. 2414 (diary entry for 12 April 1917) (hereafter 'Rupprecht, unpublished diary'); Rupprecht, *Kriegstagebuch*, I, p. 518 and II, p. 196 (diary entries for 15 August 1916 and 12 June 1917).

33. Reichsarchiv, *Der Weltkrieg 1914 bis 1918: Die militärischen Operationen zu Lande*, Vol. XI: *Die Kriegführung im Herbst 1916 und im Winter 1916/17* (Berlin: E.S. Mittler, 1938), p. 481. Detailed analysis of combat value in T. Cowan, 'Genius for War? German Operational Command on the Western Front in Early 1917', unpublished PhD thesis (University of London, forthcoming).

34. Reichsarchiv, *Weltkrieg*, XI, pp. 151–152 and 160–161. The division's commander and general staff officer were among those sacked after the debacle. In other words, they were held responsible for the division's part in the overall defeat, whether fairly or not.

35. Marshal Paul von Hindenburg, *Out of My Life*, trans. F.A. Holt (London: Cassell & Co, 1920), pp. 262–263.

36. Ibid., p. 133.

37. Rupprecht, unpublished diary, p. 2065 (diary entry for 3 November 1916); Reichsarchiv, *Der Weltkrieg 1914 bis 1918: Die militärischen Operationen zu Lande*, Vol. XII: *Die Kriegführung im Frühjahr 1917* (Berlin: E.S. Mittler, 1939), p. 546.

38. General Ludendorff, *My War Memories 1914–1918* (London: Hutchinson & Co., 1919), pp. 260–261.

39. Paul von Kneußl, unpublished diary, KAM, Nachlass Kneußl, Bd. 13 (diary entries for 5–9 May 1917).

40. Otto von Moser, *Feldzugsaufzeichnungen 1914–1918*, Third Edition (Stuttgart: Chr. Belser Verlagsbuchhandlung, 1928), p. 269; Tony Cowan, 'The Introduction of New German Defensive Tactics in 1917', in William Philpott and Jonathan Boff (eds), *Mastering the Industrial Battlefield: Military Transformation on the Western Front, 1914–18* (Farnham: Ashgate, forthcoming).

41. Otto von Below, 'Lebenserinnerungen', unpublished manuscript in BA/MA, N87/61, f. 134 (diary entry for 27 August 1917). Loßberg, CGS of the Württemberg army corps from 1913 to 1915, offers a reasonably convincing explanation for the high quality of Württemberg troops: Loßberg, *Meine Tätigkeit*, p. 1. 26th ID: Alexander Watson, *Enduring the Great War: Combat, Morale and Collapse in the German and British Armies, 1914–1918* (Cambridge: Cambridge University Press, 2008), pp. 169–171.

42. Army Group Rupprecht to OHL, Ia 2857, 21 April 1917, BA/MA, RH61/1890.

43. Bavarian military plenipotentiary to Rupprecht, 19 April 1917, HAM, Nachlass Rupprecht Nr. 614.

44. Ibid.

45. Kneußl, unpublished diary, Bd. 13 (diary entry for 12 May 1917). Benjamin Ziemann, *War Experiences in Rural Germany, 1914–1923* (Oxford: Berg, 2007), p. 142 describes widespread problems between 'real' Bavarians and men from the Pfalz.

46. Hans von Felgenhauer and Wilhelm Müller-Loebnitz (eds), *Das Ehrenbuch der Rheinländer. Die Rheinländer im Weltkrieg* (Stuttgart: Vaterländische Verlagsanstalt Oskar Hinderer, n.d.), p. 6.

47. The investigations into 15th and 16th ID's performance are in Generallandesarchiv Karlsruhe (hereafter GLAK) files 456 F1/430, 431, 432 and 547. Gerhard Tappen, 'Meine Kriegserinnerungen', unpublished manuscript in BA/MA, RH61/986, f. 191–192 records serious problems in 15th ID in autumn 1917.

48. 15th RD: Below, 'Lebenserinnerungen', f. 13 (diary entry for 3 May 1917).

49. 16th RD: OHL to Army Group German Crown Prince, Ic Nr. 2985, 27 April 1918, GLAK 456 F1/249. 185th ID: HQ Sixth Army record of general staff discussion, 17 September 1917, KAM, AOK 6 Bd. 369.
50. Xylander diary, p. 635 (diary entry for 16 July 1916); Below, 'Lebenserinner-ungen', f. 13 (diary entry for 3 May 1917).
51. For martial race theory, see Tan Tai Yong, *The Garrison State: the Military, Government and Society in Colonial Punjab, 1849–1947* (New Delhi: Sage Publications, 2005), especially Ch. 2.
52. Albrecht von Thaer, *Generalstabsdienst an der Front und in der O.H.L. Aus Briefen und Tagebuchaufzeichnungen 1915–1919* (Siegfried A. Kaehler, ed.) (Göttingen: Vandenhoeck & Ruprecht, 1958), pp. 91–92 (letter, 13 October 1916).
53. Wilhelm Herzog von Urach, letter to his family, 11 August 1916, HSAS, GU117 Bü 1072; for other Württemberg criticism see Walker, 'Prusso-Württembergian Military Relations', pp. 131, 143.
54. *General der Infanterie* Moriz Freiherr von Lyncker to his wife, 13 September 1916, in Holger Afflerbach, *Kaiser Wilhelm II. als Oberster Kriegsherr im Ersten Weltkrieg: Quellen aus der militärischen Umgebung des Kaisers 1914–1918* (München: R. Oldenbourg Verlag, 2005), p. 428; Xylander diary, pp. 643–644 (diary entry for 25 July 1916).
55. Tony Ashworth, *Trench Warfare 1914–1918: The Live and Let Live System* (London: Pan Books, 2000), pp. 34, 150.
56. Xylander diary, p. 803 (diary entry for 19 March 1917); HQ Fourth Army telegram to Army Group Rupprecht, 2a 210/17 pers., 27 April 1917, KAM, HGr Rupprecht neue Nr. 378, f. 92–93.
57. Thaer, *Generalstabsdienst*, p. 113 (letter, 19 April 1917).
58. Lyncker to his wife, 17 April 1917, in Afflerbach, *Kaiser Wilhelm II*, p. 482.
59. Kuhl, 'Kriegstagebuch', p. 69 (diary entry for 5 June 1917). Two Saxon divisions did in fact fight in the battle.
60. Brigadier-General Sir James E. Edmonds, *Military Operations: France and Belgium 1917*, Vol. 2, 7th June-10th November. *Messines and Third Ypres (Passchendaele)* (London: Macmillan and Co., 1948), p. 94 (hereafter, BOH 1917, II).
61. GHQ France 'Note on the Strategic Situation With Special Reference to the Present Condition of German Resources and Probable German Operations', 11 June 1917, BOH 1917, II, p. 427.
62. P. Camena d'Almeida, *L'armée allemande avant et pendant la guerre de 1914–1918* (Nancy: Berger-Levrault, Éditeurs, 1919), pp. 42–44; Thomas Freiherr von Fritsch-Seerhausen, 'Das sächsische Offizierkorps 1867–1918', in Hans H. Hoffmann (ed.), *Das deutsche Offizierkorps, 1860–1960* (Boppard am Rhein: Harald Boldt, 1979), p. 68.
63. Georg Paul Neumann, *Die deutschen Luftstreitkräfte im Weltkriege* (Berlin: E.S. Mittler, 1920), p. 312.
64. On the Pfalz, see Celia Applegate, *A Nation of Provincials: The German Idea of Heimat* (Berkeley, CA: University of California Press, 1990). Roger Chickering, *Imperial Germany and the Great War, 1914–1918*, Second Edition (Cambridge: Cambridge University Press, 2004), pp. 4–6 gives a succinct account of Germany as a federal state and the ensuing constitutional, cultural and ethnic issues. Stig Förster, *The Battlefield: Towards a Modern History*

of War (London: German Historical Institute, 2008) makes important points about synergies between military and other branches of history.

65. Ludendorff, *War Memories*, p. 643; Stachelbeck, *Militärische Effektivität*, pp. 290–291.
66. Walker, 'Prusso-Württembergian Military Relations', p. 170.

9
Out of the Trenches: Hitler, Wagner and German National Regeneration After the Great War 1914–1918

David Ian Hall

The sudden end to the war in November 1918 was both a shock and, at least for a brief moment, a relief to the civilian population of Germany. Severe food shortages and general war weariness were the two most dominant concerns on the home front, and most Germans longed to return to a life that in some degree resembled their pre-August 1914 normality. The armistice and the peace, however, brought more, not fewer, hardships. Severe economic and social problems were exacerbated by domestic political turmoil, revolution and violence. International disapprobation added to the growing sense of fear, isolation and humiliation that left even the most apolitical Germans wondering what was to become of them and their shattered country. Extreme politics filled a void created by both the war's end and the terms of the peace settlement, but did not offer real and immediate solutions to the deep divisions and multitude of problems that beset post-war republican Germany. Many Germans wondered how all of this had happened. The left and the right used the *Dolchstoßlegende* (stab in the back legend) to explain both the military defeat and the dissolution of the Empire in November 1918 and the harsh peace imposed at Versailles at the end of June 1919. Germany's failings were also seen by some, particularly the radical *völkisch* right, as resulting from an inveterate metaphysical illness. One obscure extreme nationalist politician in post-war Munich, Adolf Hitler, believed that 'the political collapse...was culturally indicated'. He was confident in his belief that national decline and defeat in the Great War were the direct result of a spiritual degeneration that could be seen in nearly every field of art and culture in Germany since 1900. Hitler was equally certain that the only way out of this downward spiral was to reclaim German art – characterised by the unique heredi-tary traits of the German people – 'since there was always a common cultural foundation' on which to rebuild a truly united Germany: a Germany that had never really existed, either during the 1914–1918 war or even immediately after unification in 1871.[1]

Hitler's vision of a new reborn and united Germany further required that class, confession, party and regional divisions be swept away and replaced with a German national consciousness that had inner spir-itual strength. For Hitler, this was attainable only through a revered and widely shared German culture, beginning with core German artis-tic values such as those portrayed in the music-dramas and writings of Richard Wagner. The connection between a people's art and the strong national community that Hitler sought is expressed most clearly in Wagner's opera *Die Meistersinger von Nürnberg* (one of Hitler's favourite operas). On one level, a basic and benign interpretation, the opera is a glorious affirmation of humanity and the value of art. But it can also be seen as a musical–political crusade to revive the 'German spirit' by purging it of alien elements, chief among them the Jews.[2] Philosopher and Wagner expert Michael Tanner has written that *Die Meistersinger* is 'about the connections between life and art, between individuals' lives and the art they produce, and between the life of a community and its attitude to art'.[3] Hitler accentuated the importance of art in the national community and politics in the Nazi party's manifesto as early as 1920 and he reconfirmed that art was not 'auxiliary to politics' but must 'become a functioning part of the National Socialist political pro-gramme' in a defining cultural speech at the party's annual meeting in Nürnberg in September 1934.[4] *Kunst* (art) – German art in all of its var-ious forms – was Hitler's solution to Germany's historical weakness as well as the basis for a solid foundation on which to rebuild the coun-try after the disasters of 1918 and 1919. Drawing on the writings of Richard Wagner and the early cultural–political ideas of Adolf Hitler, as well as Thomas Mann, Houston Stewart Chamberlain, Dietrich Eckart, Rudolf von Sebottendorff and other members of the *Thule-Gesellschaft* (Thule Society), this chapter examines how and why Hitler and the early National Socialists saw art (*Kunst*) as the essential factor in their struggle to restore German greatness after the debacle of the Great War 1914–1918.

During the period immediately before and during the First World War, many Germans saw themselves as part of a national community that was loosely defined by its art and culture.[5] Art, in all of its various forms, was an affirmation of what was beautiful and noble, the supreme form of human activity by gifted men (geniuses) conditioned by the unique hereditary traits of the people from which they came. It was this prevailing view of art in Germany that led Max Weber, the founder of modern sociology, to write in 1915: 'all culture today is and remains bound to a nation'.[6] Germans had *Kultur* (culture) whereas France and Great Britain had *Zivilisation* (civilisation). *Kultur* in this sense referred positively to the shared traditions and values of the *Volk* (people) in a national community. *Zivilisation* was mildly pejorative and signified the overly formalistic and calculating habits and attitudes characteristic of a courtly society (France) or an obsessively commercial and materialistic society (Britain).[7] The contrast between *Kultur und Zivilisation* was a leading topic in German journalism and cultural–political writing, and it was portrayed as the main underlying cause of conflict between Germany and the Entente powers, Britain and France. On 4 October 1914, a group of 93 prominent German artists and intellectuals published a manifesto in which they claimed that the war against Germany was not a war against German militarism, as foreign propaganda asserted, but a war against German culture. They believed that France and Britain, in pursuit of their commercial and imperial interests, had set out to destroy the unique German spirit – the essence that inspired and united the *Volk* and was the link between the German people and German *Kunst und Kultur*.[8] Thomas Mann, the renowned German cultural, political and social critic, novelist and essayist, made an even clearer and simple distinction between the two terms *Kultur und Zivilisation*: 'Culture binds together; civilization dissolves'.[9] Later on, towards the end of the war, Mann warned that the war between Germany and the Entente powers was, in fact, civilisation waging a war of annihilation against German culture.[10]

The struggles that the Germans had with national identity and national unity in the late 19th and early 20th centuries were a salient feature in the troubled history of their newly unified state in the centre of Europe and a key contributing factor to the causes of both the First and the Second World Wars. Throughout July 1914 – after the assassination of the Austrian heir to the throne, Archduke Franz Ferdinand, and his wife Sophie, in Sarajevo, and the ensuing diplomatic crisis between the European powers over Austria's response and the possibility of a general European war – large crowds of Berliners gathered on the Unter den Linden and in front of Kaiser Wilhelm II's palace eager to learn what was going to happen. Was Germany going to go to war? The vast majority of the assembled crowds sang national anthems and patriotic songs: *Die Wacht am Rhein* (The Watch on the Rhine),

Deutschland, Deutschland über Alles (Germany, Germany, Over All), and the Austrian national anthem, *Gott erhalte Franz den Kaiser* (God Save Franz the Kaiser). Their patriotic fervour symbolised the nationalism of the masses, and yet, despite similar public demonstrations of patriotism in Paris, Moscow and, later, London, the events in Berlin have subsequently been portrayed as proof of monolithic German militarism. The so-called 'unparalleled' German militarism as well as the 'total and unconditional' German national unity that provided support for the war, accusations first spread by enemy propagandists both before and during the war, are long-perpetuated Germanophobia that has deflected attention away from the real fears many Germans had in 1914 for their culture and way of life as well as the negative consequences of war.[11]

Not all Berliners, and not all Germans, supported war in the summer of 1914, and these people also took to the streets to voice their concerns. On 28 July, the Social Democrats organised a number of 'peace meetings' in the proletarian neighbourhoods of Berlin. Over 100,000 working-class men and women participated and many of them made their way into the city centre to join the crowds on the Unter den Linden. They too sang songs, mainly the *Marseillaise*, to counter the patriotic anthems of those who supported war. Similar counter-demonstrations occurred in other German cities, but once war began a wider national consensus on fighting and winning the war emerged. War fever also produced a mass industry of public participation. Daily newspaper coverage, postcards, pamphlets, cheap novels and memoirs, photographs, ashtrays, flags, neckties and scarfs, china mugs, and war-themed Christmas ornaments brought the war experience into virtually all German homes. Public events supporting the war and scrapbooking at home created, in the words of historian Peter Fritzsche, a 'peoples' archive' that transformed their intimate involvement in the war into a German identity.[12]

Thomas Mann had no illusions about a patriotic war that would end in a triumphant German victory. He compared 1914 to 1756 (the long seven years' war fought by Frederick the Great that ended in 1763 with little tangible gain for Prussia), not 1870 with its emphatic victory over the French and German unification. He blamed all of the belligerent powers equally for the outbreak of war in 1914, stating: 'this war is just as much a common European action as it is a European catastrophe'. The Great War was a catastrophe for Mann mainly because it was a war of ideas as much as a war for the conventional prizes of power, commerce or territory. The battle between culture and civilisation, as he viewed it, would change Europe irrevocably, and, regardless of the outcome, 'after the war everything would be different' and 'no one would be able to continue his life in the old style'.[13]

The unexpected totality of defeat in November 1918 came as a severe shock to most Germans, but it was soon surpassed by hardship and deprivation, unprecedented financial crises, national humiliation and international condemnation. Few would have believed Admiral Alfred von Tirpitz, one of the founders of the *Deutsche Vaterlandspartei* (German Fatherland Party), when he warned: '[t]here is a danger that this war that has been forced upon us may end in a peace that will do the utmost harm to our people'.[14] The physical and psychological traumas of the war affected all Germans, but they were felt even more acutely by the cultural and intellectual elites. Richard Wagner's descendants in Bayreuth, Winifred and Siegfried Wagner, his English-born daughter-in-law and the only son of the composer and his wife Cosima, were better off than most, but they too struggled to obtain nourishing food for their young family.[15] They also watched nervously, as did most Germans, the birth of the new republic, with the leader of the Social Democrat Party, Friedrich Ebert, its first chancellor. Earlier in the war Winifred had renounced her English heritage and British nationality in favour of her new German homeland. By November 1918, she spoke for many of her disillusioned German countrymen and women when she described the political triumph of the left-wing republicans in a letter to her friend Lenchen Boy: 'My God, who would have thought that such a turn of events was possible! How proud we were of our German Fatherland, and how ashamed we are that a worm at the core could produce such degradation.'[16] The 'worm at the core' was Ebert and the Social Democrats. Support for Ebert's government and the republic was further weakened by the armistice and the harsh terms of the Versailles Treaty, along with the Bolshevik revolutions and counter-revolutions led by the *Freikorps* and the right.[17]

Out of this turmoil and violence emerged the *Dolchstoßlegende* (stab in the back legend). It asserted that the undefeated army in the field had been betrayed by Communists and Jews; that revolution, the unfair peace settlement and the destruction of German traditions and values had been brought about by enemies of the Fatherland, who for cowardly and selfish reasons had destroyed the German *Reich* in order to gain power themselves. Bolshevism quickly became a catch-all condemnation for left-wing politicians, pacifists, the liberal press, Jews and anyone else who could be blamed for Germany's defeat and the multitude of problems that beset post-war Germany. The term was also used to stigmatise new trends in art, architecture, literature and music. Both nationalists and traditionalists feared the end of the German *Reich* and German art. Fighting against the Bolsheviks and the socialists became increasingly intertwined with fighting for the nation.[18]

For German nationalists, particularly those who were either members of or supportive of the racial nationalist views of the various pan-German organisations,[19] it also reinvigorated their anti-Semitic beliefs. Cosima Wagner, Richard Wagner's influential widow, expressed such views when she wrote to a royal friend, Crown Prince Ernst zu Hohenlohe-Langenburg, 'as always and everywhere it is the Semitic element that is responsible for agitation and subversion'.[20] The Wagners stood firmly in the nationalists' camp and provided substantial support for those who campaigned for the old German values and order in both art and the state. They, along with most German nationalists, believed that a strong authoritarian government was needed to halt the degenerative forces that were tearing Germany apart. After reading General Erich von Ludendorff's memoirs, Cosima felt that he was the man to save Germany. She said as much in another letter to Hohenlohe-Langenburg: 'Ah, if only Ludendorff could be our dictator.'[21]

While not necessarily wanting Ludendorff to run the country, the remnants of the Great General Staff shared Cosima's yearning for a strong national leader as they set about rebuilding the army and planning to restore Germany to its position as a Great Power. General Walther Reinhardt, newly appointed Chief of the Army Command following the disbandment of the General Staff,[22] believed that national renewal was dependent on the regeneration of the army. Moreover, he was fully aware of the historical precedent that supported his view. Reinhardt drew his inspiration from the triumvirate of Prussian generals and military reformers – Clausewitz, Gneisenau, and Scharnhorst[23] – who rebuilt the army and the nation following the strategic shock of defeat in the Napoleonic Wars. Reinhardt's reading of Clausewitz told him that the recovery would come from the state drawing on the power of the *Volk* (the people) united in a common purpose. The purpose was the 'life-threatening struggle for [Germany's] existence' and this required large military forces that were capable of waging and winning a *Völkskrieg* (peoples' war). Reinhardt also appreciated the administrative and financial benefits of centralised political power and he supported the new civilian bureaucratic system of the Weimar Republic. What was required to make it all work, according to Reinhardt and many of his fellow generals in the clandestine General Staff, was a strong and charismatic leader who promoted military values and who could be trusted to provide decisive leadership in war.[24]

Kunst und Kultur (art and culture) were not matters that occupied either Reinhardt's or the other generals' attention in their efforts to rebuild Germany. Reinhardt, however, did believe that national unity was essential if Germany was to recover and regain her former glory and status in the world. Germans, he urged, had to count on Germans and not look to alliances or foreign elements within the *Reich* for their salvation. 'The danger of Bolshevism for Germany', warned Reinhardt, 'is not to be dismissed or underestimated.'[25] Reinhardt espoused a course of action that fostered internal unity based on military purpose and military service that culminated with the full militarisation of German society. His views were more extreme than those of General Hans von Seeckt, the unofficial Chief of the General Staff, but they were endorsed by other senior military officers, including General Wilhelm Groener and General Kurt von Schleicher.[26] Many nationalists and members of right-wing organisations loosely grouped together in the *Völkischer Bund* (German Nationalist League) supported a strong leader and a strong military, but they regarded the army more as a product of national unity than as the source of its creation. National renewal required cultural regeneration. One of the leading advocates of this thinking was Houston Stewart Chamberlain.

Chamberlain was the son of a British admiral and was married to Eva, Richard and Cosima Wagner's daughter. He was also the intellectual leader of *Wahnfried* (Wagner's family home in Bayreuth) and the Bayreuth Circle (an active and influential group of pan-German intellectuals, editors and writers, who promoted Wagner's ideas and work).[27] Wagner's music converted Chamberlain to a love of German art and culture, and he repaid this debt by writing a substantial and widely-read biography of his father-in-law as well as a number of other works that explained the unique German spirit that had been captured and released by Wagner through his *Gesamtkunstwerk* (total art work).[28] Wagner was an idealist and a Romantic. He was also a cultural and political revolutionary, and his music and his writings were controversial both at the time they were produced and subsequently to the present day. His mature music-dramas are demanding and emotional, both for the audience and the performers, but most of all they are a glorious affirmation of humanity and of the intrinsic value of art. Wagner expressed his passions for what was noble, heroic and German in his writings as well as his music. His essay, *Was ist deutsch?*, first published in 1865, saluted the German spirit as the quest for what is beautiful and noble. It also raised a warning, controversially stating that Germans needed to protect their culture from alien elements, particularly Jews, otherwise the German spirit would be extinguished. Wagner's *Deutschtum* was an aesthetic born of genius and will: his genius and the indomitable German spirit. It had political purpose, too, in reaching out to the *Volk* and providing an enduring foundation on which the small and squabbling German principalities and states could finally attain national unification. These views were expressed in another major essay, published in 1867, entitled *Deutsche Kunst und deutsche Politik*.[29] Chamberlain drew on his extensive knowledge of Wagner's work and his own deeply felt mission to save his beloved adopted homeland. In 1917, along with Heinrich Claβ and Georg von Below, he started a journal, *Deutschlands Erneuerung* (*Germany's Renewal*), to provide a forum for German nationalists and anti-Semitic writers. Chamberlain was already famous in these circles for his *Die Grundlagen des neunzehnten Jahrhunderts* (*The Foundations of the Nineteenth Century*), published in 1899, which was an important text for the pan-German movement and *völkisch* anti-Semitism. Chamberlain's main intellectual contribution to the post-war debate on national unity and regeneration was to link Wagner's doctrine of regeneration, based on the unique characteristics of Germanness, with an elimination of all things Jewish. Chamberlain also looked longingly, as did Cosima and the generals, for a saviour, a strong man who would lead a reborn Germany back to its rightful position of prominence in the world. The man he eventually found – or, more correctly, the man who found Chamberlain – was Adolf Hitler.[30]

Hitler was a Wagnerian from an early age. He was only 12 when he attended a full performance of *Lohengrin*, his first Wagner music-drama, at the Linz Landestheater. 'I was captivated at once,' he wrote in the opening pages of *Mein Kampf*. 'My youthful enthusiasm for the master of Bayreuth knew no bounds. Again and again I was drawn to his works....'[31] In addition to his love of Wagner's music, just like Chamberlain before him, Hitler was completely besotted with German art, culture, music, architecture, and virtually anything else if it could be regarded as quintessentially German. *Mein Kampf* cannot be taken as a factually accurate autobiography of Hitler's life, but it does offer a telling glimpse into the Romantic and idealistic imagery that he employed to give colour to his political development and passionate expression to his *Weltanschauung* (world view). Hitler's description of his first visit to Munich is a perfect example of his highly emotional and Romanticised style: 'there was the heartfelt love which seized me for this city [Munich] more than for any other place that I knew, almost from the first hour of my sojourn there. A *German* city!' Hitler went further with his praise for the city where his political career and National Socialism began, and later was venerated by the Nazis as the *Hauptstadt der Bewegung* (Capital of the Movement). Munich, he claimed, was a 'metropolis of German art' and you could not know Germany if you did not know Munich. Moreover, 'one does not know German art if one has not seen Munich' – its architecture, its art galleries, museums and theatres, its parks and gardens, its festivals, and its beer halls and beer gardens.[32] Hitler was content in Munich. It was where he felt most German. He felt that the city had a German soul, and that it was the true manifestation of German culture.[33] Defeat in the war and the unacceptable peace agreed to by Ebert's Social Democrat government were, for Hitler, obvious symptoms of decay brought about by a cultural decline that had to be arrested and reversed if Germany was to recover her greatness. To 'master this disease', Bolshevism in all its forms – politics, cubism, Dadaism – and all its proponents – leftist, socialists and Jews – had to be resisted and destroyed.[34] Reclaiming German art, freed from foreign contamination, would heal the German soul and restore the German spirit. Only a true *Völksgemeinschaft* (national community) based on racial purity and imbued with an authentic German culture, led by a heroic leader, could see Germany successfully through this historic struggle.[35] Hitler saw himself as this leader, the combination of Siegfried and Parsifal, armed with Siegfried's sword Nothung and the holy Spear of Longinus.[36]

It is unlikely that any *Müncheners* recognised Hitler, the inconspicuous soldier guarding the *Hauptbahnhof* in the summer of 1919, as one of Richard Wagner's Germanic heroes predestined to save Germany and the German people. Nonetheless, Hitler had acquitted himself well as 'an able and courageous soldier in the Great War', a fact recognised by his entitlement, wholly on merit, to wear the Iron Cross, both first and second class.[37] The war also increased his fanatical devotion to Germany and his belief in a strong national community that only required reawakening to overturn defeat and rejoice in 'the final victory over our enemies'.[38] His journey to becoming their *Führer* and fulfilling his self-declared destiny began formally on 12 September 1919 at the *Sterneckerbräu* on the Tal in central Munich, when he attended a meeting of Anton Drexler's *Deutsche Arbeiterpartei* (German Workers Party, DAP).[39] The account of this meeting is well known: Hitler's initial indifference, his explosive reaction to a speaker (Professor Baumann) advocating Bavarian separatism, and Drexler's alleged remarks '*Mensch, der hat a Gosch'n, den kunnt ma braucha*' ('Goodness, he's got a gob. We could use him').[40] Hitler went to the meeting expecting to hear Dietrich Eckart, a well-known journalist, *völkisch* poet and playwright, but Eckart was ill and he was replaced by Gottfried Feder, a pan-German economic expert, who gave a lecture on the 'breaking of interest slavery'. Hitler was familiar with both the lecturer and the content of his lecture, having recently taken courses at the Ludwig-Maximilians-Universität where Feder was a professor. The meeting, however, was much more important to Hitler's political future than the surface events that have attracted so much historical attention. Hitler had come to the attention of the leading political agitators in the *Thule-Gesellschaft* (Thule Society).

The DAP was established as a new workers' debating society by Karl Harrer, a leading member of the *Thule-Gesellschaft*, to draw Munich's working classes away from Bolshevism and into the *völkisch* sphere of public politics. Drexler, 'a genuine worker', was a co-founder of the DAP and its first 'party leader'. The Thule Society was a revived offshoot of a larger national and older anti-Semitic *völkisch* secret society, the *Germanen-Orden*, which was established in the 1890s. The Munich-based Thule Society began life in January 1918, and it was the first influential organisation to give Hitler assistance.[41] Rudolf von Sebottendorf, its founder and leader, claimed that 'Thule people were to whom Hitler first came, and it was Thule people who joined him in the beginning.'[42] Sebottendorf was an occultist, and the Thule Society's insignia was Siegfried's sword Nothung imposed on a Swastika. The Lodge, as the society was openly called in public, had rooms in the luxury hotel *Vier Jahreszeiten* on the Maximilianstraße, one of the most exclusive streets in Munich. At its height membership exceeded 1,500, with influential and wealthy connections throughout the highest ranks of Bavarian society. Membership was strictly controlled and members had to prove that they were of pure 'Aryan blood'. Future leaders in the *Nationalsozialistische Deutsche Arbeiterpartei* (National Socialist German Workers Party, NSDAP), including Hans Frank, Alfred Rosenberg and Rudolf Heß, were members. The society's mandate was to combat the Jewish–Bolshevik terror and to promote the rebirth of a pure *völkisch* utopia. The Thule Society also had its own newspaper to disseminate its ideology and political programme, the *Münchener Beobachter*, which Hitler purchased for the NSDAP, with Eckart's financial assistance, in 1920, and renamed the *Völkischer Beobachter*.[43] The *VB*, as it was more commonly called, became the official newspaper of the party, announcing party meetings, rallies and speaking engagements, publishing the speeches given by Hitler and other party leaders, and generally reinforcing the National Socialist message with a running commentary on the day's political and social events.

Dietrich Eckart also introduced Hitler to wealthy right-wing sympathisers, including Count Ernst zu Reventlow, the publisher Hugo Bruckmann (Chamberlain's publisher) and his wife Else, and the famous piano manufacturer Edwin Bechstein (Winifred's guardian) and his wife Helena. Helena Bechstein was instantly captivated upon meeting the young Hitler. She threw herself into supporting him in every possible way – her wealth, her contacts and her reputation – and she did not hesitate to tell her many friends and acquaintances that there was hope for the future: at last 'Germany's young Messiah' had been found. The Bechsteins and Eckart also had summer homes on the Obersalzberg, above Berchtesgaden. Hitler was a frequent visitor. He mixed with the *völkisch* musicians, singers and writers high up the mountain on the Vorderbrand and absorbed the many mythical legends of the region. It was on the Obersalzberg that he completed *Mein Kampf* upon his release from prison in 1924, and later built the Berghof, his private and official country residence. Before these notorieties occurred, Hitler – publicly by quoting Wagner in his speeches and privately through his deep knowledge and passion for the master of Bayreuth's ideas and music – proved his Wagnerian credentials to Helena Bechstein, and she in turn opened for him the door to *Wahnfried*, Wagner's home and the spiritual headquarters of the Bayreuth Circle.[44]

Hitler's first visit to *Wahnfried* on Sunday 30 September 1923 was an auspicious one. He was the principal speaker at 'German Day' in Bayreuth, organised by nationalists and right-wing paramilitary groups to protest the French occupation of the Ruhr and the 'shameful Treaty of Versailles'. Bayreuth's nationalist mayor, Albert Preu, welcomed more than 5,000 guests to his 'old town with a world reputation as a centre of art and the home of Wagner'. He said it was an honour to host the 'German Day' but it also brought great responsibility. 'It is the spirit of Siegfried that we need', urged Preu, 'so that like our Master, Richard Wagner, who triumphed over all hostile forces, we can once more achieve respect in the world.'[45] Hitler's speech was measured and without any anti-Semitism. He told his large audience in the town's overfull *Reithalle* (riding school) that Germany needed an authoritative leader and that the nation would be better when the only German citizens were 'those who are and feel German, and everyone else should go to Moscow'.[46] As soon as he finished his speech, he hurried off to *Wahnfried* to see the Wagners.

Winifred, Siegfried and all the children stood outside the front door of the house when Hitler's large Mercedes rolled up the drive. Introductions were formal and a bit stiff, but all of this changed when they

were inside the house, in the great two-storey salon with Wagner's
pianos and other precious mementoes of the composer's life and career.
Ever since Hitler had heard *Lohengrin* he had looked upon Wagner as
'the greatest German who ever lived'.[47] This is how Wagner's grand-
daughter Friedelind remembered Hitler's famous visit. Afterwards, Hitler
viewed Wagner's grave, at the back of the spacious garden behind the
large house, and he spent a considerable amount of time alone in con-
templation before his evening meeting with Chamberlain. The two
men spoke until late in the evening. Chamberlain was delighted by
the visit and he asked Hitler to return the next morning to continue
their talk. When Hitler arrived Chamberlain was already outside, sit-
ting in his wheelchair and covered by a thick blanket to keep out
the early morning cold, waiting for him. There is no detailed record
of their discussions or the topics they addressed, but Chamberlain
was more than satisfied that Hitler was the man to take forward
Wagner's doctrine of regeneration.[48] Pure German art enriching and sustaining the indomitable German spirit would bring about Germany's
rebirth. Writing to Hitler a week later, Chamberlain told him that he
had expected to meet a fanatic but instead he found a saviour, the
key figure of the German counter-revolution.[49] Hitler had obtained
Chamberlain's blessing and with it the full support of *Wahnfried*
and the Bayreuth Circle. This encounter was memorialised by the
Nazis:

> Adolf Hitler and Houston Stewart Chamberlain clasped hands. The
> great thinker, whose writings went with the Führer on his journey
> and laid the intellectual foundations of the Nordic German world-
> view, the genius, seer and herald of the Third Reich, felt that through
> this simple man of the people Germany's destiny would achieve a
> glad fulfilment.[50]

The circle was now complete. Hitler's own views of a *Kulturstadt* had
been enhanced and endorsed by the guardians of Richard Wagner's life
work.[51] National unity required a strong national identity, which came
from being and feeling German, not simply from the total war ideology
advocated by the generals. Armies needed a reason to fight if they were
going to fight and win. German art and German culture was Hitler's
answer to establishing a strong national identity that would also give
the nation and the armed forces the necessary will to fight to change
the political landscape of Europe and restore Germany to its rightful
position as a Great Power.

Notes

1. Adolf Hitler, *Mein Kampf*, trans. Ralph Manheim (Boston: Houghton Mifflin Company, 1971), pp. 257–259.
2. Barry Millington (ed.), *The Wagner Compendium. A Guide to Wagner's Life and Music* (London: Thames & Hudson Ltd., 1992), pp. 304.
3. Michael Tanner, *Wagner* (London: Flamingo, an imprint of HarperCollins Publishers, 1997), pp. 160.
4. Peter Watson, *The German Genius* (London: Simon & Schuster, 2010), pp. 629–630.
5. Peter Adam, *The Arts of the Third Reich* (Thames and Hudson Ltd, 1992), pp. 28–32; Richard Weikart, *Hitler's Ethic* (Basingstoke: Palgrave Macmillan, 2009), pp. 77–81.
6. Max Weber, *Wirtschaft und Gesellschaft* (Tübingen, Verlag J.C.B. Mohr, 1972), pp. 242, 527ff.
7. Raymond Geuss, *Morality, Culture, and History. Essays on German Philosophy* (Cambridge: University of Cambridge Press, 1999), pp. 31–32.
8. Wolf Lepenies, *The Seduction of Culture in German History* (Princeton: Princeton University Press, 2006), pp. 16–17.
9. Thomas Mann, *Reflections of a Nonpolitical Man*, trans. Walter D. Morris (New York: Frederick Ungar Publishing Co., Inc., 1983), p. 123.
10. Ibid., pp. 331–334. Clear definitions for *Kunst und Kultur* as well as the German Spirit are difficult to provide. It is actually easier to state what they are not rather than what they are. All three concepts, however, were well understood in a fairly loose way by contemporary Germans; hence the wide use of these terms in cultural, political and social writing of the time (c. 1890–1939), including newspapers, novels, pamphlets and more academic essays and monographs. The terms can also overlap and address in the broadest manner art (in all of its various forms), identity and history. Cf. Mann, *Reflections of a Nonpolitical Man*, ch. 12, 'Irony and Radicalisation', pp. 419–435; Geuss, *Morality, Culture, and History*; Jost Hermand, *Old Dreams of a New Reich: Volkish Utopias and National Socialism*, trans. Paul Levesque (Bloomington: Indiana University Press, 1992); Joan L. Clinefelter, *Artists for the Reich. Culture and Race From Weimar to Nazi Germany* (Oxford: Berg, 2005); Jonathan Petropoulos, *Art as Politics in the Third Reich* (Chapel Hill: University of North Carolina Press, 1996); Frederic Spotts, *Hitler and the Power of Aesthetics* (Woodstock, NY: The Overlook Press, 2003).
11. Peter Fritzsche, *Germans Into Nazis* (Cambridge, MA: Harvard University Press, 1998), pp. 13–19. Cf. Princess Evelyn Blücher, *An English Wife in Berlin* (New York: E.P. Dutton & Company, 1920); Richard Scully, *British Images of Germany* (Basingstoke: Palgrave Macmillan, 2012); Max Hastings, *Catastrophe: Europe Goes to War 1914* (London: William Collins, 2013).
12. Fritzsche, *Germans Into Nazis*, pp. 19–24, 40.
13. Mann, *Reflections of a Nonpolitical Man*, pp. 150–155.
14. Admiral Alfred von Tirpitz as quoted in Brigitte Hamann, *Winifred Wagner. A Life at the Heart of Hitler's Bayreuth*, trans. Alan Bance (London: Granta Books, 2005), pp. 33–34. The *Deutsche Vaterlandspartei* (German Fatherland Party) was founded in Berlin on 2 September 1917 and dissolved on 10 December 1918. One of its founding members was Anton Drexler, later

a member of the *Thule-Gesellschaft* (Thule Society) and co-founder of the *Deutsche Arbeiterpartei* (German Worker's Party).

15. Siegfried and Winifred Wagner had four children between 1917 and 1920: Wieland (1917), Friedelind (1918), Wolfgang (1919) and Verena (1920).

16. Winifred Wagner to Helena (Lechen) Boy, 17 November 1918 in Hamann, *Winifred Wagner*, 35.

17. For a detailed history of the *Freikorps* and its role in the revolutions and counter-revolutions in Germany after the Great War see Nigel Jones, *The Birth of the Nazis. How the Freikorps Blazed a Trail for Hitler*, rev. ed. (London: Constable and Robinson Ltd, 2004).

18. Oliver Hilmes, *Cosima Wagner. The Lady of Bayreuth*, trans. Stewart Spencer (New Haven: Yale University Press, 2010), p. 298; Hamman, *Winifred Wagner*, pp. 36–41.

19. For a detailed study of the Pan-German League see Roger Chickering, *We Men Who Feel Most German. A Cultural Study of the Pan-German League, 1886–1914* (Boston: George Allen and Unwin, 1984).

20. Correspondence between Cosima Wagner and Crown Prince Ernst zu Hohenlohe-Langenburg, 14 February 1918, in *Briefwechsel zwischen Cosima Wagner und Fürst Ernst zu Hohenlohe-Langenburg* (Stuttgart: Cotta, 1937), p. 368.

21. Correspondence between Cosima Wagner and Crown Prince Ernst zu Hohenlohe-Langenburg, 11 September 1919, in Cosima Wagner, *Das zweite Leben: Briefe und Aufzeichnungen 1883–1930*, ed. Dietrich Mach (München: Piper, 1980), p. 747f.

22. This was one of the terms of the military restrictions imposed on Germany by the Versailles Treaty. For all the military restrictions placed on Germany, see *The Treaty of Versailles*, Part V (English version, HMSO, 1920).

23. Gerhard von Scharnhorst, Carl von Clausewitz and Count August von Gneisenau were three of the most influential senior Prussian general officers responsible for reforming the army after the Napoleonic Wars. Scharnhorst and Clausewitz were first to advocate the founding of a *Kriegsakademie* (war academy), where Clausewitz was the director from 1819 to 1830.

24. William Mulligan, *The Creation of the Modern German Army. General Walther Reinhardt and the Weimar Republic, 1914–1930* (Oxford: Berghahn Books, 2005), pp. 198–204.

25. Bundesarchiv-Militärarchiv Freiburg, Nachlaß Walter Reinhardt, N 86/16 Reinhardt decree 11 February 1920.

26. General Wilhelm Groener was the Chief of the Great General Staff after the Great War until the imposition of the Versailles Treaty in July 1919. General Kurt von Schleicher, in addition to a prominent military career in the clandestine General Staff, was the last chancellor of the Weimar Republic.

27. The Bayreuth Circle is described in detail in Hilmes, *Cosima Wagner*, pp. 195–201.

28. Cf. Houston Stewart Chamberlain, *Richard Wagner* (München: Verlagsanstalt F. Bruckmann, 1901); *The Wagnerian Drama* (London: John Lane The Bodley Head Ltd, 1923); *Political Ideals*, trans. Alexander Jacob (Lanham, MD: University Press of America, Inc., 2005).

29. Cf. Richard Wagner, *Was ist deutsch?* (1865) and *Deutsche Kunst und deutsche Politik* (1867). Barry Millington, *Wagner* (Oxford: Oxford University Press,

2000), p. 253; Hannu Salmi, *Imagined Germany. Richard Wagner's National Utopia* (New York: Peter Lang Publishing, Inc., 1999), p. 61.

30. Hamann, *Winifred Wagner*, pp. 26–29; Hilmes, *Cosima Wagner*, pp. 257–258.
31. Hitler, *Mein Kampf*, 17.
32. Ibid., pp. 126–127; Peter Miesbeck, 'Hitler und München 1913 bis 1918', in *München – Hauptstadt der Bewegung. Bayerns Metropole und der Nationalsozialismus*, Richard Bauer, Hans Günter Hockerts and Brigitte Schütz (eds), *Wolfgang Till und Walter Ziegler* (München: Minerva, 2002), pp. 20–24.
33. A dissenting view on the importance of Munich to Hitler's political career and *Weltanschauung* is presented in an extensively researched but disappointingly polemical book by Thomas Weber. Cf. Thomas Weber, *Hitler's First War. Adolf Hitler, The Men of the List Regiment, and the First World War* (Oxford: Oxford University Press, 2010).
34. Hitler, *Mein Kampf*, pp. 257–263, 300–327.
35. Ian Kershaw, *Hitler 1889–1936: Hubris* (London: Penguin, 1998), pp. 289–290; Joachim Köhler, *Wagner's Hitler. The Prophet and His Disciple*, trans. Ronald Taylor (Cambridge: Polity Press. 2000), pp. 225–227; and Joachim Fest, *Hitler* (London: Penguin, 1974), p. 354 (Hitler's speech at the NSDAP Christmas celebrations 18 December 1926). See also Point 23 in the 25-point Programme of the NSDAP presented by Hitler in a speech given in the Munich Festsaal of the Hofbräuhaus on 24 February 1920.
36. Nothung is Siegfried's sword, broken but reforged by the pure hero Siegfried and used to kill the dragon Fafner. Parsifal's holy spear is the Spear of Longinus, a Roman legionnaire, who used it to wound Christ when he was on the cross. Parsifal, a pure and noble hero but also a naïve fool, defeats the evil sorcerer Klingsor, wins back the spear and returns it to the Knights of the Grail. Having reunited the spear and grail, the knights crown Parsifal the new King of the Knights of the Grail.
37. John Williams, *Corporal Hitler and the Great War 1914–1918. The List Regiment* (London: Frank Cass, 2005), pp. 7–8.
38. Werner Beumelburg, *Von 1914 bis 1939: Sinn und Erfüllung des Weltkrieges* (Leipzig: Verlag P. Rellam, 1939), pp. 15, 41.
39. The *Deutsche Arbeiterpartei* (DAP) was formed on 5 January 1919 and dissolved on 24 February 1920, when it was succeeded by the *Nationalsozialistische Deutsche Arbeiterpartei* (NSDAP).
40. Kershaw, *Hitler*, pp. 126–128; Cf. Hitler, *Mein Kampf*, pp. 221–223; Fest, *Hitler*, pp. 117–118.
41. Cf. David Luhrssen, *Hammer of the Gods. The Thule Society and the Birth of Nazism* (Washington: Potomac Books, 2012); Köhler, *Wagner's Hitler*, pp. 147–151; Tyson, *Hitler's Mentor: Dietrich Eckart* (Bloomington, IN: iUniverse, 2008), pp. 107–125; Fest, *Hitler*, pp. 115–117.
42. Rudolf von Sebottendorf, *Bevor Hitler Kam* (München: Deukula-Verlag Graffinger and Co., 1933), p. 13.
43. The *Völkischer Beobachter* (*VB*) was the official national newspaper of the NSDAP from 1920 to 1933, after which it became the main daily newspaper of the Nazi regime until the collapse of the Third Reich in May 1945. Hitler acquired the *Münchener Beobachter* in December 1920, and its relaunch as the *VB* was the day before the refounding of the Nazi Party on 27 February 1925. Hitler and Joseph Goebbels believed that a mass audience could be reached

through a party newspaper and that such a paper was a potent means of communicating their *völkisch* propaganda (people's message).

44. Obersalzberg Institut Archiv, Berchtesgaden, Dietrich Eckart Private Papers and Publications. Cf. Ernst Hanfstaengl, *Hitler: The Memoirs of a Nazi Insider Who Turned Against the Führer* (New York: Arcade, 2011; first published 1957), pp. 38–54; John Toland, *Adolf Hitler* (London: Hutchinson, 1979), pp. 101; Köhler, *Wagner's Hitler*, pp. 159–161; and Hamann, *Winifred Wagner*, pp. 51–54.
45. *Oberfränkische Zeitung*, 1 October 1923.
46. Ibid.
47. Friedelind Wagner's recollection of Hitler's arrival at *Wahnfried*. She has the day being a Sunday morning in May 1923, but it was actually Sunday 30 September and Monday 1 October 1923 when Hitler visited the Wagners at their family home for the first time. Cf. Friedelind Wagner and Page Cooper, *Heritage of Fire* (New York: Harper and Brothers Publishers, 1945), pp. 3–8.
48. Nationalarchiv der Richard-Wagner-Stiftung, Bayreuth (NRWB). Nachl. Chamberlain (Houston Stewart Chamberlain, diary entries 30 September and 1 October 1923).
49. NRWB. Chamberlain, Briefe 3, ii.124–125 (letter from Houston Stewart Chamberlain to Adolf Hitler, 7 October 1923).
50. *Bayerische Ostmark*, 25/26 July 1936.
51. Hilmes, *Cosima Wagner*, pp. 302–304; Fest, *Hitler*, p. 181; Hamann, *Winifred Wagner*, pp. 58–59.

10
Training, Morale and Battlefield Performance in the Italian Army, 1914–1917

Vanda Wilcox

'The worst defect of the Italian army was the small amount of attention given by its commanders to the serious training of the troops and their failure to appreciate the necessity for it.'[1] This was the damning judgement of General Sir Herbert Plumer, sent to command the British forces which helped to stabilise the Italian positions in November 1917 after the disastrous Italian defeat at Caporetto. Plumer's view was echoed in a telegram sent on 10 November 1917 from the Earl of Cavan, who reported that

> The King of Italy told me ... that lack of training in open warfare is the great fault. The men would attack from trench to trench if led by an officer, but were completely lost if expected to act as a rear-guard or independently.[2]

On their arrival in Italy in late 1917, the British troops were inclined to criticise everything about the Italian army, and made a number of negative judgements they were later forced to revise. But these comments on training merit further investigation, not least in the light of ongoing debates over the battle of Caporetto. Recent scholarship rejects claims that the Italian defeat was primarily caused by a collapse in morale, rather seeking operational explanations for the battle's outcome; the existence of serious shortcomings in Italian training could be an important element in this argument.[3] A better knowledge of training policies and practices will further enhance our analysis of Italian battlefield performance more generally: between May 1915 and October 1917 Italy fought 11 largely unsuccessful battles on the Isonzo front (as well as achieving mixed results in the Alps) and her armed forces have often been harshly criticised.[4] Training methods are an important element in understanding and re-evaluating the performance of the Italian army in combat.

Morale and training

Training is vital not only for analysing battlefield performance but also for explaining troop morale, as Hew Strachan has convincingly argued.[5] The cohesion and loyalty of primary groups, long the dominant narrative for explaining troop morale, breaks down during combat on the modern dispersed battlefield and is undermined by casualties (and replacements). Political or ideological motivations, though significant in both mobilising and sustaining morale, cannot fully account for high morale in combat.[6] Rigid disciplinary systems may keep men in line, and certainly in the Italian forces in the First World War military discipline played an important role.[7] However, following S.L.A. Marshall, Strachan shows that training must be integrated with primary groups, ideology and discipline in any model of combat motivation. When effective, training reduces fear – or makes it easier to manage – provides familiarity with the experiences of battle and helps to prepare men to kill.[8] In particular, men who know themselves to have been well trained have greater confidence in themselves and their comrades. Good training instils the comforting belief that it increases men's chances of survival 'precisely because it implie[s] a high degree of control over their outcomes in combat'.[9] To achieve this, training must simulate combat as closely as possible: by 1914, the close-order drill which had prepared men for war before the late 19th century was no longer useful for more than the most basic purposes of inculcating obedience and generating unit cohesion. Developing more complex training which reflected modern tactical and technological requirements was challenging for all armies. This essay will examine the theory and practice of training in the Italian in the period up to Caporetto, under the leadership of Luigi Cadorna (1850–1928), chief of the general staff from 1914 to 1917. It will explore the challenges faced by the army, analyse its doctrines and theories about training, and evaluate the successes and failures of the system in action.[10] If inadequate training is correlated with low morale, then traditional arguments about the failure of the Italian army at Caporetto may need to be revisited.

Pre-war debates on training

Many of the five million Italians who served in the First World War received their basic training before the war, during their compulsory military service, so pre-war policies and practices are important. In this period, training and military education were major areas for debate within the Italian army: service journals dedicated numerous articles to the issue and there was a clear perception that major changes were needed. One of the main problems was a lack of time to train troops effectively, especially after the reduction of military service from three years to two in 1910.

The inadequacy of infantry training in this period had already been highlighted by the war against the Ottomans for Libya in 1911–1912. Italian conscripts trained in simplistic and rigid tactics found themselves facing small, mobile bands of skilled and committed Turkish and Arab forces, which repeatedly inflicted tactical defeats on the invaders. The Italians were pressured into using cautious, hesitant tactics which were ill-suited to their ambitious strategic goals, and their victory was due more to the weakness of the Ottoman Empire than to Italian military prowess.[11] Unfortunately, the victory served to obscure the army's many problems and was instead read by many in government and military circles as a confirmation of current policies, including those on training and preparation: even reform-minded critics saw the Libyan war as 'comforting proof of the success of our patiently developed educational work'.[12] The tactical implications of the conflict were unclear, and in any case the authorities were reluctant to apply lessons from a colonial war in a European conflict. Efforts to identify areas for improvement were still under way when the Great War began.

Preparing for war: 1914–1915

When war broke out in August 1914, it was apparent to Comando Supremo that, despite Italy's declaration of neutrality, the army needed to be prepared for the possibility of war, and that one of the main problems was a severe shortage of both officers and men. In their haste to get as large a force as possible into the field, training was often seen as an area which could legitimately be curtailed. Officer training in particular suffered: commissioning courses at the military academies of Turin, Modena and others[13] were 'accelerated', so that cadets completed only one year instead of two as required by the syllabus.[14] Many new officers were commissioned directly after their first year of study – meaning that they missed out the more advanced material. The original infantry officers' course had included such topics as geography, topography, chemistry, riding, horse care, hygiene, German, French and Italian literature, as well as fortification, tactics, 'military arts', mathematics, small arms use, introduction to artillery, military history, administration and staff work.[15] In 1915 the Military Academy of Modena, earning the nickname the 'officer factory',[16] introduced a new short '*corso pratico*'. This supposedly practical course placed little emphasis on tactical planning or staff work: organisation, administration and the formulation and communication of effective orders and reports were all neglected.[17]

Pre-war officer training and the courses provided through 1915 were clearly inadequate for the requirements of modern warfare: forced to prioritise quantity over quality, the army sent many newly commissioned officers into combat poorly prepared. But by the end of 1915 the deficiencies of this system were clear; the general staff demanded an increased emphasis on training and ability, as they saw the effect of untrained junior officers on the battlefield. While initially the curtailment of training had been necessary, given the urgent need for new officers during the period of neutrality, the accelerated academy courses actually grew longer and more thorough as the war progressed, as the army realised that sound military knowledge was crucial for military effectiveness.[18] More up-to-date training on the realities of trench warfare was included, to prepare officers for the physical obstacles and enemy firepower they would encounter, though man management and leadership skills were still neglected.[19]

How did officers educated in this system carry out the training of the troops under their command? Traditionally, an officer's role in training his men was focused primarily on 'education' rather than 'instruction': they were ordered to emphasise patriotism, discipline, faith, obedience and all the other elements of 'moral and psychological' preparation of the men.[20] Since contemporary doctrine emphasised *élan* and attacking fervour, building character was seen as the chief function of military service, and all training and military education designed for ordinary recruits worked to this end. Lectures on national history and a 'poetic conception' of persuasive discipline were most important, while literacy programmes, complex tactical instruction and anything which might encourage independent thought among peasant soldiers were discouraged.[21] Achieving high standards of morale and discipline was the key objective of training, resting on the assumption that this would determine the effectiveness of the infantry (an inversion of the argument that good tactical, physical and psychological preparation produces troops with high morale). Neither the development of tactical expertise and confidence based on ability, nor the reduction of fear through acquisition of familiarity with combat, were priorities for the army. It would be wrong to say that officers were uninterested in their men's training– but they may have been seeking solutions to the wrong questions.

Practical instruction in technical and tactical abilities was mainly provided by NCOs. They were responsible for drill, physical education and marksmanship – areas which officers perhaps perceived as beneath their notice.[22] However, it was widely acknowledged that the Italian army had major problems with its NCOs; even before the war this was an ongoing cause for concern. An article in April 1914 in the infantry journal *Nuova Rivista di Fanteria* argued that the Italian army was suffering a 'long-term incurable crisis' with regard to its NCOs, which it saw as the weakest part of the institution precisely because of their inadequate training.[23] The author suggested more dedicated training schemes and better efforts to develop and improve leadership qualities, as well as new recruitment policies to select better candidates. The debate continued in other military journals, with much discussion of how to select and train NCOs focusing on character and morality. Their ability to provide good-quality training and a positive example – disciplined, dutiful, enthusiastic – was seen as critical.[24] Army authorities were dissatisfied with both the quality and the quantity of NCOs at their disposal throughout the war, and it is hard to ignore the impact of this problem on the provision of effective training.

Learning lessons from other fronts

Naturally, Italian military attachés and observers reported back to the army authorities on the dramatic events taking place on the battlefields of Europe. But Comando Supremo was not convinced that the static entrenchment of the Western Front – rather than the still-mobile east – was the model likely to emerge on their own borders.[25] New recommendations on the use of the terrain and the construction of trenches were issued in February 1915,[26] but Cadorna's famous tactical manual *Attacco Frontale e Ammaestramento Tattico*, published a few days later, reasserted the importance of attacking *élan* in achieving breakthroughs. This was largely in keeping with the 1913 doctrinal manual *Norme per il combattimento*, which emphasised the necessity of an overwhelming assault, in line with Italian analyses of the Russo-Japanese war (and influenced to some extent by French thinking). Italian doctrine acknowledged the strength of modern firepower but considered that the importance of infantry attacks – including, where necessary, the bayonet – remained unrivalled.[27] An article on training methods by a senior officer at the Modena military academy was published in *Nuova Rivista di Fanteria* in January 1915, asserting confidently that 'the current war is demonstrating once again that manoeuvre is more important than fire, and that in order to manoeuvre well units and troops must acquire the necessary ability through practice'.[28] The same month, writing in the *Rivista Militare Italiana*, one Alderigo Redini (Captain) asserted that 'Faith: above all faith, that is the indestructible certainty in the victorious outcome of the war' was the single most important issue in effectively preparing the army for the conflict ahead.[29] Discipline and exemplary leadership were also critical, he wrote, though he was confident that Italian generals were among the best in Europe, and that the Libyan war had amply demonstrated the excellent standards of the officer corps in general. However, he acknowledged the need for specialised training for both officers and men to prepare for the likely war ahead: officers should focus on full tactical mastery, familiarity with maps of border regions and knowledge of their 'likely enemy' – in January 1915 it was still not politic to name this force in print. Meanwhile, infantry training should focus on long marches, building field fortifications, night exercises, marksmanship, manoeuvre, and lots of preparation for cold, snow, rain and mountain survival. He concluded with an important observation:

> It will be very useful to explicitly describe the long duration of today's battles, and the possibility of having to stay pinned down for many days in a trench. The Risorgimento and the Libyan war have inculcated the belief that fighting is resolved in a single day with a brilliant, bold bayonet charge. To avoid running into very bitter disappointments, it is extremely important to eliminate this belief.[30]

Other commentators at this time were noting the new importance of artillery and attempting to revise the norms for its use accordingly.[31] It was clear to Cadorna and others that closer co-operation between infantry and artillery, rather than a rigid division of the battle into distinct phases, would be necessary[32]; this would need careful preparation, and there was still a gulf between theory and practice. Some officers were perfectly capable of reading the signs in spring 1915 and of seeking to adapt doctrine and training accordingly – but time was short.

Standard infantry training up to 1917

As the war went on, army authorities gradually began to pay closer attention to the duration and method of infantry training. The system remained relatively decentralised: the design and implementation of most training exercises were handled at brigade level or below. In 1915, officers responsible for training were given manuals of doctrine but little advice on *how* the desired outcomes were to be achieved or what were the best methods for informing and preparing the troops. Not until early 1917 were more specific instructions on how to train regularly issued from Comando Supremo or Army commanders, and in practice there were considerable variations in practice throughout the armed forces up until 1918.[33]

Duration

Around 50 per cent of Italian infantrymen had received some military training during their regular two-year national service.[34] These men were usually somewhat better trained than those called up during the period of neutrality or once the war broke out, when standard infantry training was condensed into just two or three months. Basic training was already somewhat flawed before 1915, but wartime bought new pressures: time, money, experienced instructors and equipment were all in short supply.[35] Insufficient time was especially critical, since training, like rest and recreation, was rarely a priority for the army authorities in 1915–1916. The need to get fresh men into the lines quickly often overrode other considerations.

The impact of inadequate preparation was severe. To take one example, the Etna Brigade (223° and 224° Infantry Regiments) was formed on 2 December 1915 from Sicilians of the class of 1896, in other words who were newly eligible for military service and had no prior experience. Training began in Sicily in early January 1916 and the regiments received their official inauguration, complete with blessing of the regimental flag, in late March. In April they were sent north, via Messina, Bari and Ravenna, arriving in Padua on 11/12 April 1916. Assigned to XII Corps, they waited in Padua – apparently inactive – for three weeks, until on 1 May 1916 they were finally sent to the front. How did these new recruits perform after their three months' training? Just six weeks later, the brigade commander was sufficiently concerned about the performance of his regiments that he demanded reports from the two regimental colonels. Lt Col Francesco Rossi, of the 224° regiment, reported on 16 June that his men were undergoing a 'period of crisis' and were in urgent need of 'rest and reorganisation' before they would be fit to return to the front. Under the heading 'Level of Training' he observed:

> The unit is composed almost entirely of the class of 1896 whose hasty instruction (little more than three months) has not been sufficient to ensure an adequate preparation for the campaign, either with regard to technical training or with respect to physical endurance.[36]

He concluded that after a necessary period of rest, to help overcome minor health problems and fitness-related injuries, his men required a week of intensive tactical training before returning to any kind of active service. It is significant that the regiment's need for both 'technical and tactical' training had led it into a state of 'crisis'.

The complaint about lack of physical fitness was not unusual, since little emphasis was placed on this aspect of training beyond the use of gymnastics, on the Germanic system. This primarily entailed weight training and stretching exercises with little emphasis on building stamina or fitness; the idea of team-building through sports or games was not yet accepted, and the role of such events in building group cohesion during the training process was overlooked until 1918 or 1919.[37] Before the war, most infantry regiments lacked a proper gym and pursued physical education only in their 'free time' rather than in any structured fitness-building programme, often performing less than two hours' intensive activity each week. In the elite *bersaglieri* units, physical training was taken much more seriously – but, ironically, was perhaps less necessary, since candidates for these units were selected on the basis of physical health and robustness. Standard infantry recruits included those who were weaker, shorter and less developed (though there were considerable differences between urban and rural workers).[38] As the war went on, the inadequacy of this approach became ever clearer.

Rossi's request for an extra week of intensive tactical preparation may seem inadequate, but in reality it was hard to find any extra time for training for units already deployed. Once new units had been sent to the front they rarely received much additional training, since when they were rotated out of the front lines units were regularly sent off to perform other duties. Both before and during the war, police work and the suppression of strikes and protests cut into the time available for rest or training, as well as developing very different skills from those needed in battle.[39] Troops were consistently used for manual labour when outside the lines, and allocated to an assortment of tasks of doubtful necessity when they might have been receiving additional training. In January 1917, for example, the Minister for War approved the application of a number of city councils in northern Italy to use troops to clear snow and ice away from their streets.[40]

Tactical instruction

Training was not only brief; it was often ineffective in tactical terms, rarely corresponding to the realities of trench warfare. Conscripted into an infantry regiment in August 1914, Gino Frontali described his experiences of basic training:

> We received our first lesson in 'open order' and 'tactics.' Our lieutenant explained in minute detail the essential rules: be silent, obey signals, always look at the officer in charge, adapt movements to the ground, use shelter in order to offer the smallest possible target, never drop vigilance and observation in order to guard against any surprise.[41]

This description suggests that trainers acknowledged the need for greater tactical sophistication than close-order drill alone would permit (as any observer of the Libyan war could confirm), but emphasising the need to follow the officer closely in all things left infantrymen lost and unable to proceed without leadership – if officers fell during combat their men had no experience in taking the initiative themselves. This is an interesting echo of the comments attributed to the king by Cavan in November 1917. Even worse, the crucial word in this description is 'lesson'. Information was imparted through the lieutenant's detailed explanation – but was not demonstrated or practised. By contrast, the elite Alpini received a very different kind of training, with emphasis both on mountain skills and on tactics. Not until the Arditi stormtroop units were formed in the last 18 months of the war were other infantrymen systematically taught advanced or complex tactics; instead, they were mostly trained to attack in straightforward lines, even as late as 1917, unless they were fortunate enough to be under the command of a particularly energetic and innovative officer.[42] The acute shortage of experienced officers and NCOs who could conduct effective training was one major cause of these problems. Like many of his fellows, Alpini lieutenant Pinotto Garrone recorded that he was 'daunted' by the scale of his task in training his men, and complained that he had been given insufficient guidance and support.[43] Since officer training was itself weak on practical matters, tactical instruction and man management, junior officers' task was an unenviable one.

Familiarisation with equipment

Along with time and experienced instructors, the Italian army was critically short of equipment. Weapons handling and target practice, among the most fundamental elements of infantry training, were also deeply flawed – as many had acknowledged in the run-up to the war. In the decade before 1914 a raft of ministerial circulars, army directives, expert proposals and counter-proposals were produced, apparently without effect, while articles critically discussing the issue appeared most months in one or other of the service journals. In the view of one of the senior officers at the Modena Academy, the small arms training provided failed to take into account the circumstances of battle. The regulations, he wrote, 'could produce an excellent shot on the firing range but not a good soldier in combat.... Principles, lessons, commands and advice have only a relative usefulness for a soldier who may not have full control of himself [in battle].' He observed that

> technical preparation is indispensable, but it must be applied to the soldier who shall actually face battle, with fraught nerves, and not to an imaginary solder with a spirit of steel; it must be based on simple notions and easy movements because in combat, when memory becomes more or less paralysed, one can rely only on habit, deep rooted and simple habit.[44]

What was lacking was actual practice, especially under combat-simulation conditions – precisely the type of training now considered to be most useful and effective. In fact, any form of firing practice was difficult, given the acute shortages of equipment. In August 1914 the Italian army had at its disposal 750,000 rifles of the 1891 model, supposed to be the standard, and no hand grenades at all.[45] Training was therefore sometimes carried out with just one or two rifles per company, each man taking turns with the weapon. Gino Frontali described the situation in late 1914:

> Target practice suffered from a most serious defect. It was done in a great hurry...we fired two rounds (twelve shots each) every week. This exercise was sufficient to familiarise us with the use of the rifle, but not to establish any precision of aim. One saw progress only

rarely. Those who [already] shot well, who had a passion for hunting, improved a little after the first lessons. The others, the majority, hit the target only rarely, and no-one seemed concerned about it.[46]

As an anonymous writer complained in the *Nuova Rivista Fanteria*, in February 1915, training was extremely expensive in terms of cartridges – another area of acute shortages – and few men were able to fire a weapon often enough to gain real familiarity with it. In an effort to tackle this problem, Captain Bambara Domenico of the 23rd Infantry Regiment had developed a 'genius' invention allowing cartridge-less firing: a rifle fixed in a swivelling apparatus, mounted on a table-top. The article claimed that this would allow inexperienced recruits to practise aiming and firing 'in any part of a barracks, e.g. in the corridors', which would 'allow for dramatic improvements', the author concluded optimistically. The journal offered a picture of the apparatus, but there is no evidence that this idea was ever adopted.[47]

The shortage of weapons with which to train also affected machine-gun units and the artillery, some of whom were forced to practise manoeuvring their weapons with wooden models. Frontali reported an infantry major's comments in May 1915: 'We have no machine guns, they are running courses for machine gunners using wooden guns, and none of the gunners have ever fired a shot using a real weapon.'[48] As Italian industry responded to the challenge of producing the necessary quantities of weapons and munitions, this situation began to improve, but shortages of this kind continued to impede training throughout the war. A 1916 senatorial report on the artillery training camp at Bracciano, north of Rome, made similar criticisms: each company of around 70 men trained with only one piece and most never actually got to operate the gun. Training was mostly through lectures rather than exercises or practice, and a previous inspection to correct the problem had been cursory, leading to no improvement. Munitions were running short and no training at all was given on communication with artillery-spotting aircraft or observation balloons. The senators, moreover, found that facilities for officer training were poor: new officers trained alongside the men, who laughed at their superiors' mistakes, undermining hierarchical authority.[49] Material shortages were partly to blame for these failings, but the underlying problem was that, despite repeated criticisms, poorly devised courses bearing little relation to actual combat were still being delivered in 1916, showing minimal improvement on pre-war practice.

Training and the command culture

Devising and implementing programmes of training and tactical instruction was the responsibility of brigade commanders. It is perhaps unfair to say, as Hubert Plumer did in November 1917, that senior commanders 'failed to appreciate the importance' of training, since poor performances in combat were often blamed on inadequate training in internal army reports. To give one example among many, an official report on the March 1916 loss of an important position at S. Maria la Longo, on the Isonzo, blamed 'the tiredness and prolonged exertion of the troops, exacerbated by the brevity and infrequency of rest periods and lack of troops to provide relief, [as well as] the inadequacy of training and organisation, due in part to the frequent changes and removal of personnel'.[50] Despite such complaints, little had changed by the following summer. In June 1917, during the battle of the Ortigara, fresh troops of the 112th Infantry were sent to take part in the assault on Monte Mosciagh.

> They had been previously engaged mainly in manual labour and had never before fired rifles, used grenades or practised assault in waves. They were issued hand grenades ... of which they were frightened and which they abandoned in the communication trenches.[51]

This clearly shows how lack of familiarity with weaponry and equipment could affect men going into combat. Notably, General Luigi Capello, commander of Second Army – that most directly involved in the battle of Caporetto – spent the summer and early autumn of 1917 issuing repeated criticisms of his troops' standard of training and ordering urgent remedial instruction.[52] The problems were numerous. For example, 19th Division reported that specialised infantry troops and those assigned to use specific equipment such as grenade launchers were uncertain what to do and in urgent need of instruction, while training was being carried out by officers who were not experts. Divisional general Giovanni Villani had to insist that training should be entrusted only to officers who had received special instruction on the use of the relevant equipment. More generally, Villani considered that the troops were lacking in energy, and many had not been taught even basic hygiene norms.[53] General Alberto Cavaciocchi, commanding IV Corps (43rd, 36th, 50th Divisions), was similarly unimpressed with the quality and impact of the training he observed in August 1917, while he considered that 'moral and technical unpreparedness' was a major explanation for the failure to consolidate the initial gains made in that month's operations.[54]

In the light of these and other criticisms, Second Army headquarters decided to intervene, first ordering that men should not be left 'idle' during rest periods but must be appropriately employed at all times with training and fitness exercises.[55] On 30 August 1917, a new order for Second Army was issued to corps commanders setting out detailed criteria for instruction, which should:

(1) Imbue the troops with an aggressive spirit, embedding in them the concept of the overwhelming attack and the ability to manoeuvre in relation to the enemy's response. Familiarise them with the energetic use of hand grenades and ensure that the troops move in a succession of narrow waves.
(2) Dedicate attention to the use of grenades against machine-gun emplacements and developing coordinated flanking machines supported by machine-gun fire.
(3) Improve the connections between units alongside one another.
(4) Continue the 'conference' system of morale-boosting sessions.[56]

Leaving aside the question of whether, in August 1917, these were the most appropriate tactical instructions, it is interesting to observe how these very general orders were implemented, as revealed by unit diaries. The original order was simply forwarded on by corps commanders to their divisional generals exactly as received from the Army command – and, in many divisions, was then forwarded again without any comment to brigade commanders. No attempt was made to explain or expand on these instructions, or to suggest how they might be implemented in practice – or even to check that they would, in fact, be followed at all. Given what we have already seen about the paucity of officer instruction in how to provide training to men, this represents a serious deficiency. This culture of simply passing orders down without either making sure that they were effectively implemented or explaining to subordinates *how* to do so was infuriating both to the British, when they arrived in 1918,[57] and to many senior Italian officers. Capello himself complained about the problem:

> For example, in order to implement my orders on my homing pigeon service, it is not enough simply to send up to the front lines some unlucky nobody with a basket of birds and no instructions on how to use them. The order will have been followed only at the

moment in which a fully organised service has been established, with appropriately prepared and instructed personnel.[58]

Proof that his instructions were being ignored emerged rapidly. On 10 September Capello wrote:

This morning I saw a regiment being trained. It was pitiful. Training was carried out in closed order squads – the least appropriate method for current needs, and there was a complete failure to train men in flexible manoeuvres, the use of narrow waves, and in keeping position during attacks rather than bunching up, stopping or allowing gaps to open.

Instead, he witnessed 'squads and platoons immobile on the parade ground while officers stood gossiping'.[59] As a result of this infuriated letter, Capello's corps commanders finally bestirred themselves to inspect brigade-level training – even ordering night training – but there was still much more to be done, and the tendency to simply pass on generic orders without elaborating them into concrete activities continued. Orders handed down to divisional and brigade commanders were more likely to criticise the current system of instruction than to propose improvements.[60]

Successful training in this system, therefore, depended heavily on the initiative, competence and energy of battalion, regimental and brigade commanders, who were often ill prepared by their own training and education for this particular responsibility.[61] Worse still, the army hierarchy had worked to discourage individuals from taking initiative, and was much better at punishing those officers who erred than rewarding and encouraging those who succeeded. For both of these reasons, senior officers' repeated criticisms did not lead to significant improvements on the ground. This problematic command culture suggests that the Italian army suffered less an inability to correctly diagnose weaknesses and propose solutions than a systemic failure to effectively *implement* these solutions.

Conclusions

At the beginning of the war, Italian training methods were in line with pre-war tactical doctrine and would only slowly develop and change as new tactics for both offence and defence began to emerge. Military theorists were sometimes trying to answer the wrong questions: training priorities were not in line with the real demands of the conflict about to begin. Like other armies, the Italians did not respond rapidly to the new realities of industrialised trench warfare, and, unsurprisingly, the development of training mirrored the gradual tactical learning process. The need for new ideas and practices was clear quite early on, but it was much easier to identify that a problem existed than to fully diagnose it or to propose functional solutions. Even when better ideas were developed, implementing them effectively was the real difficulty. Both before and during the conflict, the army suffered from a number of serious shortages – of time for training; of experienced officers, and especially NCOs, to provide instruction; and, finally, of equipment with which to train, most notably weapons and munitions. These weaknesses were apparent to many, and efforts were made to improve training both for new recruits and for long-serving conscripts; however, the grave morale problems which existed in many units and which came to a head in October–November 1917 at Caporetto may in part be down to some of these serious deficiencies. Poorly trained troops lacked self-confidence and were ill prepared to take the initiative on the battlefield, a weakness which repeatedly caused problems during the battle. However, in the period before Caporetto there was no centralised effort to systematically improve the situation. Perhaps the most serious problem that the army faced in the effective development and implementation of new training methods was its command culture: the decentralised structure of training and the failures of close oversight (from above) and initiative (from below) meant that even when intelligent solutions were developed they had only limited impact. Ultimately, the Italian army struggled to manage training due to its logistical and organisational difficulties in coping with the unprecedented scale and nature of industrialised mass warfare.

Notes

1. J. E. Edmonds, *Military Operations in Italy 1915–1919*, British Official History of the War (London, 1949), p. 134.
2. National Archives, London (NA) WO 79/68, Further papers of the Earl of Cavan. Telegram 10 November 1917.
3. See G. Rochat, 'Caporetto. Le cause della sconfitta', in *Ufficiali e Soldati: l'esercito italiano dalla prima alla sceconda guerra mondiale* (Udine: Gaspari, 2000); R. Bencivenga, *La sorpresa strategica di Caporetto*, G. Rochat (ed.) (Udine: Gaspari, 1997).
4. For a concise analysis of the Italian army's performance see G. Rochat, 'L'efficienza dell'esercito italiano nella Grande Guerra', *Italia Contemporanea*, Vol. 206 (1997), pp. 87–105.
5. H. Strachan, 'Training, Morale and Modern War', *Journal of Contemporary History*, Vol. 41, No. 2 (April 2006), pp. 211–27, 211–214. See also C.H. Hammer,

Enduring Battle. American Soldiers in Three Wars, 1776–1945 (University of Kansas Press, 2011), especially Chapter 3, and J. Fennell, *Combat and Morale in the North African Campaign. The Eighth Army and the Path to El Alamein* (Cambridge University Press, 2011), Chapter 7.

6. John Lynn's distinction between initial motivation, sustaining motivation and combat motivation is central here: ideologies can at best feed the first two, while the third – critical – form of motivation is better explained by other forces such as comradeship or training. John Lynn, *The Bayonets of the Republic: Motivation and Tactics in the Army of Revolutionary France, 1791–94* (University of Illinois Press, 1984).

7. V. Wilcox, 'Discipline in the Italian army, 1915–1918', in Pierre Purseigle (ed.), *Warfare and Belligerence: Perspectives in First World War Studies* (Leiden: Brill, 2005), pp. 73–100.

8. Strachan, 'Training, Morale and Modern War', pp. 216–217; S.L.A. Marshall, *Men Against Fire: The Problem of Battle Command* (University of Oklahoma Press, 2000).

9. Hammer, *Enduring Battle*, p. 15.

10. In the final 12 months of the war, there were significant changes: under the leadership of Cadorna's replacement, Armando Diaz (1861–1928), new tactical and organisational doctrines were implemented, and army policies on everything from pay and pensions through to leave and troop rotation were reformed. On the Italian army's structural changes and tactical 'learning curve' after Caporetto, see F. Cappellano and B. Di Martino, *Un esercito forgiato nelle trincee: L'evoluzione tattica dell'esercito italiano nella Grande Guerra* (Udine: Gaspari, 2008), pp. 154–243. For the development of new propaganda techniques and attitudes to morale management, see G.L. Gatti, *Dopo Caporetto, Gli Ufficiali P nella Grande guerra: propaganda, assistenza, vigilanza* (Gorizia: Libreria Editrice Goriziana, 2000).

11. G. Rochat and G. Massobrio, *Breve storia dell'esercito italiano dall'1861 a 1943* (Turin: Einaudi, 1978). p. 86.

12. Capt. E. Bottini, 'La preparazione alla guerra e l'educazione militare della gioventù in Italia', *Rivista Militare Italiana* [hereafter RMI], LIX No. II (February 1914), pp. 278–304, 278.

13. In addition to the main academy at Modena – comparable to Sandhurst – specialist academies were located at Turin (artillery and engineers), Brescia (machine gunners and bombardiers), Naples (engineers) and Parma and Caserta (infantry).

14. Scuola Militare di Modena, *Annuario per il corso pratico degli allievi ufficiali e ufficiali di complemento*, 11 vols (Modena: Società tipografica Modenese, 1915–1926).

15. G. L. Balestra, *La formazione degli ufficiali nell'accademia militare di Modena, 1895–1939* (Rome: SME, 2000), pp. 99–100; Scuola Militare di Modena, *Annuario* (1915).

16. L. Gasparotto, *Diario di un fante* (Chiari: Nordpress, 2002), p. 39.

17. Scuola Militare di Modena, *Annuario*.

18. Scuola Militare di Modena, *Annuario*.

19. Inchiesta Caporetto, 'Relazione della Commissione d'Inchiesta, "Dall'Isonzo al Piave 24 ottobre–9 novembre 1917"', Rome: Commissione d'Inchiesta istituita dal R.D. 12 gennaio 1918, 2 vols, 1919 [hereafter RCI], Vol. II – Conclusion.

20. P. Daffinà, Lt, 'La ferma annuale', *RMI*, Anno LIX, issue IV (16 April 1914), pp. 721–742.
21. Bottini, 'La preparazione alla guerra e l'educazione militare', pp. 283–286.
22. Bottini, 'La preparazione alla guerra e l'educazione militare', p. 293.
23. Capt. Adami, 'Note sul problema dei sottufficiali', *La Nuova Rivista di Fanteria* [NRF], Vol. VII, No. 4 (1914), pp. 345–352. For an analysis of the performance of NCOs during the war, see L. Ceva, 'Riflessioni e Notizie sui sottufficiali', *Nuova Antologia*, Vol. 127 (1992), pp. 331–353.
24. G. Quirino, 'La crisi tra i graduati di truppa', *RMI*, Anno LX, No. I (16 January 1915), pp. 167–180.
25. On the extent to which developments from the Western Front were analysed in Italy before May 1915, see G. Rochat, 'La preparazione dell'esercito italiano nell'inverno 1914–15', *Il Risorgimento*, Vol. 13, No. 1 (1961), pp. 10–32.
26. Comando del Corpo di Stato Maggiore – Ufficio Difesa dello Stato, *Norme complementari all'istruzione sui lavori del campo di battaglia*, circular n. 250, 10 February 1915.
27. Cappellano and Di Martino, *Un esercito forgiato nelle trincee*, pp. 30–33.
28. Col. F. Coco, 'Influenza del meccanismo di scatto sull'efficienza del fuoco di fucileria in combattimento', *NRF*, Vol. VIII, No. 1 (January 1915), pp. 29–41. However, rapid and effective rifle fire was seen as being as much a technical issue as a training problem.
29. A. Redini, 'La Preparazione', *RMI*, Anno LX, No. I (16 January 1915), pp. 113–125.
30. Redini, 'La Preparazione', p. 123.
31. Cappellano and Di Martino, *Un esercito forgiato nelle trincee*, pp. 60–62.
32. Cappellano and Di Martino, *Un esercito forgiato nelle trincee*, pp. 66–67.
33. Cappellano and Di Martino, *Un esercito forgiato nelle trincee*, pp. 130–131.
34. Ufficio Statistico, *Sforzo militare*, p. xiv.
35. G. Rochat, *L'esercito italiano da Vittorio Veneto a Mussolini 1919–1925* (Bari: Laterza, 2006), p. 63.
36. Archivio dell'Ufficio Storico dello Stato Maggiore dell'Esercito Italiano [AUSSME] Fondo B1, 138D – 1517e Diario Storico [D. S.] (224° fant.) 'Relazione sulle condizioni del Reggimento al Comando della Brigata Etna', 224° Regg. N. 314, 16 June 1916, F. Rossi.
37. S. Giuntini, *Lo sport e la Grande Guerra. Forze armate e Movimento sportivo in Italia di fronte al primo conflitto mondiale* (Rome: Stato Maggiore dell'Esercito, 2000), pp. 91–93.
38. Bottini, 'La preparazione alla guerra e l'educazione militare', p. 300.
39. J. Gooch, *Army, State and Society in Italy, 1870–1915* (London: Macmillan, 1989), p. 136. On the role of the Brigata Sassari in suppressing the Turin bread riots in August 1917, see A. Gramsci, 'Alcuni temi della questione meridionale', in *Lo Stato operaio: Rassegna di politica proletaria*, Anno IV – n. 1, Bureau d'Editions, Paris, January 1930.
40. Archivio Centrale dello Stato, Rome [ACS], Presidenza del Consiglio dei Ministri, 1915–1918 [PCM] 102, fasc. 39.
41. G. Frontali, *La prima estate di guerra* (Bologna: Il Mulino, 1998), p. 7.
42. G. Rochat, *Gli arditi della Grande Guerra: Origini, battaglie e miti* (Gorizia: La Goriziana, 1990), p. 36.

43. G. and E. Garrone, *Lettere e diari di guerra 1915–1918* (Milan: Garzanti, 1974), pp. 163–164. Letters from Pinotto, September 1915.

44. Col. F. Coco, 'Influenza del meccanismo di scatto sull'efficienza del fuoco di fucileria in combattimento', *NRF*, Vol. VIII, No. 1, January 1915, pp. 29–41, 35.

45. L. Mondini, 'La Preparazione dell'esercito e lo sforzo militare nella prima guerra mondiale', in *L'esercito italiano dall'unita alla grande guerra*, Stato maggiore dell'Esercito, Ufficio storico (Rome: SME, 1980) p. 334.

46. Frontali, *La prima estate di guerra*. pp. 7–8. It is perhaps surprising to note that some British forces deployed to North Africa in 1942 were in a similar state: Fennell, *Combat and Morale in the North African Campaign*, pp. 231–232.

47. Anon., 'Armi e mezzi da combattimento della fanteria', *NRF*, Vol. VIII, No. 2, February 1915, pp. 230–233.

48. Frontali, *La prima estate di guerra*, p. 20.

49. ACS PCM 102/15.

50. AUSSME GM E2:5, Comando Supremo 28 March 1916 'Sunto dell'inchiesta su gli avvenimenti di S. Maria (18 e 19 marzo)'.

51. Report of Lt Col Avanzini, in A. Gatti, *Caporetto: Diario di Guerra* (Bologna: Il Mulino, 1964), pp. 125–126.

52. When brigades and regiments were temporarily separated and deployed in different places, as often happened, this meant that it was possible for some units to 'slip through the gaps'.

53. AUSSME Fondo B1 – 123S/486g, 487g – D.S., 19ˆ Division. 3 September 1917.

54. AUSSME Fondo B1 – 113/S.17d (vol. 6 & appendices), D.S., IV Corpo d'Armata. 7 August 1917 – Cavaciocchi went to watch training of Caltanisetta Brigade (147 & 148, created 1 May 1915) and was deeply unimpressed with their 'lack of energy'.

55. AUSSME Fondo B1 – 113/S.17d (vol. 6 & appendices), D.S., IV Corpo d'Armata. 19 August 1917 Comando della 2a Armata, Op. Prot. 4343, L. Capello.

56. AUSSME Fondo B1 – 113/S.17d (vol. 6 & appendices), D.S., IV Corpo d'Armata. 30 August 1917 Comando della 2a Armata, Op. Prot. 4437, L. Capello.

57. Edmonds, passim.

58. AUSSME Fondo B1 – 113/S.17d (vol. 6 & appendices), D.S., IV Corpo d'Armata. 05 September 1917 Comando della 2a Armata, All. 425, Op. di protocollo 4688, L. Capello.

59. AUSSME Fondo B1 – 113/S.17d (vol. 6 & appendices), D.S., IV Corpo d'Armata. 10 September 1917 Comando della 2a Armata, All. 478, Op. di Protocollo 4859, L. Capello.

60. AUSSME Fondo B1 – 113/S.17d (vol. 6 & appendices), D.S., IV Corpo d'Armata. See All. 453 Prot. Op. 5154 'Intensificazione delle istruzioni' and Prot. op. B. 5780 (Vol. 6C All.16)

61. With reference to the lack of uniformity or coherence in training methods, it is worth noting that other armies also tended to rely on a bottom-up model in this period: British army training was not centrally organised and stream-lined until the appointment of Sir Ivor Maxse in June 1918 as Inspector General of Training.

11
Seasoning the US 2nd Infantry Division

B. T. Smith

In the summer of 1918, the Allies were confronted with a series of German offensives, one of which appeared to threaten the capture of Paris. During this offensive, the inexperienced American Expeditionary Force (AEF) came to the aid of the French and British armies fighting to halt it. Although the United States' arrival in France was a blessing to the Allies, they still had concerns about whether the untested US soldiers and Marines possessed the ability to conduct modern warfare. The following is an account of how the French army and its leadership used one US division, the US 2nd Infantry Division, to help allay those concerns while at the same time giving the division the experience it needed to fight the war in France.

It was 4 July 1917, the United States' Independence Day in Paris. The United States had been at war with Imperial Germany for barely two months and, according to General John J. Pershing, the commanding officer of the AEF, '[t]he people of Paris had not yet seen any American troops'.[1] In a piece of stagecraft, Pershing and the 2nd battalion of the US 16th Infantry, a regiment of the US 1st Infantry Division (1st ID), marched down the famous *les Champs Elysées* in the centre of Paris, ending at Lafayette's tomb, where Pershing was mistakenly credited by the press as having said 'Lafayette, *nous sommes ici!*' or 'Lafayette, we are here!' The date, 4 July, was ostentatiously chosen to capitalise on the political theatre of the United States' Independence Day. The march of US troops through the streets of Paris on the anniversary was a purposeful attempt by both French and US politicians and generals to send a message to the French public that US soldiers were actually in France and to inspire the US public to support the Allied war effort. The march through Paris was the US military's dramatic 'entrance' to the war.

Three months after the spectacle in Paris, Pershing and General Philippe Pétain, commander-in-chief of the French army, held a meeting to discuss how US forces were to be used in the coming months. Pershing's French liaison officer Colonel Jacques De Chambrun, himself a descendant of Lafayette, later paraphrased the details of the discussion in a memorandum, which outlined Pétain's vision of a US sector in France and how French forces could help train US divisions to man that sector. During the discussion, Pétain stated to Pershing that he 'would not pass up any occasion to approve an auspicious entrance' for the AEF.[2] The phrase 'auspicious entrance' comes from the US translation of De Chambrun's memorandum. Pétain's statement could also be translated to read that he 'would not pass up an opportunity to celebrate the entry of [the AEF] onto the stage'. The 'stage' that Pétain referred to was the political stage of the Great War.

Regardless of the translation, Pétain was telling Pershing he wanted the entry of the AEF's soldiers onto the battlefields of France to be politically beneficial for both the United States and France. The US and French politicians and generals needed to demonstrate that the arrival of the United States meant the eventual defeat of Imperial Germany and its allies. As US Army Major General Hunter Liggett put it neatly, 'the realization of the German people that independent American divisions, corps or armies were in the field with determined purpose would be a severe blow to German morale and prestige'.[3] The Imperial German High Command did not miss this point. General Erich Ludendorff, the quartermaster general of the Imperial German army, realised that, if the AEF even temporarily gained the upper hand, it would have a most 'unfavourable effect' on the morale of Imperial Germany and its allies.[4]

The 'auspicious entrance' sought by Pétain for the AEF was designed to help shape a perception, a political perception for domestic consumption by both the US and French populations, as well as by Imperial Germany. Pétain and Pershing wanted the French and US armies to create a successful and triumphant entry of US soldiers onto the battlefields of France, in order to demonstrate to the US, French and German public that the AEF's prowess on the battlefield would eventually lead to victory for the Entente. The march down *les Champs Elysées* on 4 July was just the opening act.

The assurances created by this perception were especially important in the face of US domestic political opposition to the United States' entry into the war. While it was unlikely that those opposed to the United States' involvement possessed the influence to force the United States to withdraw from France, it was important for the AEF to assuage these doubters and encourage wider patriotic support for the war. In a January 1918 memorandum to the AEF's chief of staff, Lieutenant-Colonel Dennis Nolan, the chief for the AEF's Intelligence Section, expressed concern over the influence that 'anti-war agitators' and 'pacifists' had in the United States. Nolan felt that, if the views of the anti-war agitators and pacifists were to gain acceptance in the press, things such as the enactment of universal service, or the draft, would be directly threatened.[5] Nolan further expressed that there was a need by the AEF to present a positive view of itself on the battlefields of France, in order to help quiet these naysayers to its involvement in the war. Nolan's concerns were warranted; Imperial Germany made attempts to use US domestic politics as a means to undermine the French public's morale. British intelligence picked up a broadcast in French that stated:

> American Congressmen in Europe say people at home want war stopped. Strong pacifist sentiment sweeping US; but Representatives are muzzled by British and American militarists.[6]

But there were some genuine risks involved in ensuring that the AEF's entrance into the war was, indeed, truly 'auspicious'. The primary risk was that the AEF was very inexperienced in conducting modern warfare. In Pershing's own words, the United States had a vast number of soldiers, but they were 'ignorant of practically everything pertaining to the business of the soldier in war' and 'most of the officer personnel available had little or no military experience'.[7] Liggett said of the United States' allies after the war,

> If they feared the greenness of our men, they distrusted more the inexperience of our junior officers, and they had no faith whatever in our senior officers, whom they knew to be utterly without practical experience in high command…we had known no larger units than divisions since 1866, and had scant experience with divisions…I cannot blame them.[8]

If the AEF was going to create the positive perception it sought, the inexperience of its soldiers had to be properly managed.

Initially the United States' allies attempted to mitigate this by amalgamating US army units into their own, but Pershing repeatedly refused such attempts, based on his prerogative to form a US-only force in France. Pétain suggested to Pershing at the end of 1917 that the regiments of the US divisions in France be attached to French divisions, where they would be directed to the front to become 'seasoned'.[9] The 'seasoning' that Pétain spoke of was his way of mitigating the inexperience of the AEF while at the same time providing the unproven US soldiers with the necessary knowledge to successfully fight the Imperial German army.

Pershing disapproved of the idea. Although US regiments would train with French divisions, Pershing refused to have these same regiments fight within French divisions.[10] As a consequence of Pershing's decision, US divisions and their units would not see the type of serious combat that typified the Great War until July 1918. According to Colonel Harold B. Fiske, who would later become the chief of training for the AEF, the primary reason the AEF could not adopt Pétain's plan was because

> Our young officers and men are prone to take the tone and tactics of those with whom they are associated, and whatever they are now learning that is false or unsuited for us will be hard to eradicate later…The French do not like the rifle, do not know how to use it, and their infantry is consequently too entirely dependent upon powerful artillery support.[11]

Fiske's comments echoed Pershing's own views of the French and British armies. Pétain, faced with such stubbornness and ignorance towards French tactical doctrine, sought another way to 'season' the divisions of the AEF.

As the months of 1918 began to pass and with the anniversary of the United States' declaration of war approaching in 1918, the AEF in nearly a year of war had little to show for itself on the battlefields of France. In its first full year of war, the United States did not conduct a single attack with a unit larger than a battalion. The reaction to the AEF's inaction was not missed. The lack of US involvement on the battlefields of France created questions as to whether the United States was truly going to help end the war. One French soldier wrote: '[i]t is true that we have the Americans, but they have seen the war only in the movies'.[12] In February 1918, the AEF's Assistant Chief of Staff Colonel Fox Conner advocated that, 'for reasons of morale, both in our forces and at home', the AEF needed to conduct some form of offensive operation. The celebrated US Marine Corps Major General John A. Lejeune succinctly summed it up by writing: '[i]t was well known that America was assisting in the War, but the effect of her service was not yet in evidence…Some great moral effect was needed'.[13] Lejeune's 'moral effect' was just another way of conveying what Pétain expressed to Pershing:

a need for an 'auspicious entrance'. Along with Pétain, Lejeune and others realised that more was required of the AEF than simply coming to France; the AEF had to prove itself, and to do so ostentatiously.

In order to address this lack of action on the part of the AEF and to properly usher in the AEF to the battlefields of France, using the veteran US war correspondent and historian Emmet Crozier's own words, the French army and the US 1st ID put together '[a] set piece: a little exercise arranged for publicity purposes'.[14] Heavily supported by French soldiers, the US 28th Infantry, another regiment of the US 1st ID, attacked the German-held French village of Cantigny.[15] Supported by French tanks, artillery and aircraft, the attack was a success for the US regiment. According to Liggett, it was worth all 'previous preparations combined to the Allies' and 'it bucked up the morale' of the AEF.[16] Unfortunately for the AEF and its allies, the day prior, the German Seventh Army had launched the third German offensive of 1918 against *le Chemin des Dames*. As a consequence, the actions of the US regiment were drowned out by the roar of the massive battle and with it the opportunity for the Allies to develop the political perception they sought for the AEF.

Over five days, 27–31 May, the surprise attack unleashed by the German Seventh Army against the significantly outnumbered French and British divisions of the French Sixth Army created a massive bulge in the Allied lines that became known as the Marne Salient. Generalissimo Ferdinand Foch, the newly appointed Supreme Allied Commander, launched counter-attacks with French divisions specifically targeting the flanks of the German salient.[17] One of these counter-attacks was near the city of Reims. The defeat the German Seventh Army suffered on its left flank at Reims influenced its leadership to halt the offensive.[18] Foch's counter-attack prevented the German Seventh Army from securing further means to supply its advancing divisions.[19] Without further means to supply its advance, and with the flanks of the salient threatened, the German divisions at the tip of the Marne Salient were forced to stop. Foch had reinforced the flanks of the pocket with the greater portion of the Allies' reserves and of the remaining divisions available to him to contain the German Seventh Army; the US 2nd Infantry Division was one of them.[20]

The German offensive was devastating to the Allies, but it did present an opportunity for Allied leadership to once again create the political perception that they sought for the AEF. When the US 2nd Infantry Division (2nd ID) was ordered to the front to help bolster the defences of the French Sixth Army, its arrival at the Marne became a sensation in the press. The US 2nd ID was a unique division within the AEF. It was the only US division to contain one US Marine Corps brigade and one US army brigade, whereas all other AEF divisions in the Great War were solely made up of two US army brigades. The arrival of the US 2nd ID helped stiffen the defences around the salient, but, more importantly, it presented an opportunity for the Allied press. The German Seventh Army's offensive appeared to the Allies as if it were designed to take Paris. This was not the case, but, as Crozier put it, '[i]f Paris was to be saved, it was up to the Americans' and as such it 'might turn out to be quite a story after all'.[21]

The idea that Paris could be saved by the arrival of the US division at the front was a sensational one for the Allied press reporters. The United States had entered the war and, according to the overzealous Allied press, had done so spectacularly. One US press reporter wrote that 'the Second had came into position and stopped the Germans cold' and that there was '[n]o doubt about it, the Americans had saved Paris'.[22] Regardless of the fact that these accounts of the US division's arrival to the front by the press were not true, the US 2nd ID's arrival was enthusiastically publicised nonetheless. The third German offensive of 1918 genuinely brought the United States Army into the Great War and the US division's arrival gave the perception of victory, provided positive propaganda for both the French and US armies, and helped create the desired political perception that Pétain and Pershing had originally spoken of in 1917. Having a US division play a part in containing the salient gave the Allies the opportunity to further shape the positive political perception of a US division and that of the AEF.

The press helped create the 'auspicious entrance' for the US 2nd ID, but it had taken liberties with its description of the US division's entrance to the war. According to Crozier:

> A few of the correspondents, looking back, realized that in their enthusiasm they overplayed the situation along the Marne, giving the Americans too much credit for saving Paris... But at the time, they were caught up and swept along by events, and the events called for flag-waving and superlatives.[23]

Although this was the very perception that Pétain and Pershing sought, the inexperience of the US soldiers and Marines of the US 2nd ID threatened to undermine it.

Because of that inexperience, Pétain and his staff were particular in their placement of the US division. For the most part, Pétain placed the US division in a position that did not jeopardise the French army's efforts to contain the salient. The US division was not used to bolster the important flanks of the salient, nor was it used in the decisive counter-attacks against the German Seventh Army's flanks.[24] Instead, the US division was sent to augment the defences against overreaching German divisions at the tip of the salient. On the fourth day of the battle, the US 2nd ID was ordered from a quiet section of the French front to Château-Thierry, the tip of the Marne Salient, and attached to a French corps.[25] By positioning the US 2nd ID at the tip of the salient, Pétain's staff had placed the division at the most operationally manageable section of the active front for the French Sixth Army. Operationally, the tip of the salient benefited the French Sixth Army more than the German Seventh Army. The French Sixth Army had shorter supply lines and greater access to rail transportation. As a consequence, the French Sixth Army could reinforce this position more quickly than its overextended German counterpart.[26]

Additionally, the French Sixth Army's staff placed the US 2nd ID among French divisions that nearly all shared something in common: they had trained with US divisions in the last six months. Along with the *167e Division d'Infanterie* or the French 167th Infantry Division (167e DI), the US 2nd ID was transported to the rear of the *21e Corps d'Armée* or the French 21st Army Corps (21e CA). Three additional French infantry divisions, the 164e DI, the 43e DI and the 73e DI, were already present, bringing to a halt some of the advancing divisions of the German Seventh Army.[27] The French 164e DI had trained with the US 42nd ID in February and March of 1918.[28] The French 73^e DI had just finished training with the US 370th Infantry, a regiment of the US 93rd ID, on 19 May, and the French 167e DI had trained the US 3rd ID.[29] To the right of the US 2nd ID, there was the French 10th Colonial Infantry Division (10e DIC). This French division had helped train both the US 1st ID and 26th ID, in March and April, respectively.[30] Pétain and his staff were using divisions that had practical experience with their US counterparts. Along with French translators and French liaison officers, Pétain and his staff had created the necessary circumstances to help facilitate the co-operation that was needed between the French Sixth Army and the US 2nd ID.

The French 43e DI was the only division that had not trained with or worked alongside a US division by this point in the war. It was, however, unlike any other division in the French army. The French 43e DI was considered one of the French army's 'assault divisions', and was the only division to be nearly completely comprised of elite *chasseurs à pied* or light infantry battalions.[31] It was because of the division's make-up that Pétain was able to quickly despatch it in front of the advancing German Seventh Army. The French 43ᵉ DI helped maintain a cohesive front against the superior numbers of the German Seventh Army; executing a fighting withdrawal that eventually brought enough Allied divisions in to stop the German advance. By the time the US 2nd ID arrived, the French 43ᵉ DI, along with other French and British divisions, had finally stopped the German Seventh Army's advance. Once the front became stabilised, the French 43ᵉ DI ended its short-lived relationship with the US 2nd ID.

The US 2nd ID took command of a portion of that front, after it was stabilised by the aforementioned French divisions, by relieving the French 164ᵉ DI, which moved to the rear of the US division and joined the French 73ᵉ DI already in reserve. The French 167ᵉ DI took up positions to the left of the US 2nd ID, relieving the French 43ᵉ DI.[32] The US 2nd ID was now surrounded on three sides by French divisions that all possessed the knowledge of how best to coordinate their actions with the inexperienced US division. This particular arrangement meant that, if the Germans were able to break through the US defended positions, tactically and operationally the French divisions could coordinate their efforts with the US 2nd ID in order to quickly react and salvage the situation.

Once the 2nd ID was in position, Pétain ordered the US division, and other French divisions, to conduct local attacks all along the edges of the Marne Salient on 6 June. The US 2nd ID responded by launching an assault with its Marine brigade (4th Marine Brigade) against the German forces holding *le Bois de Belleau* or Belleau Wood.[33] During the 6 June attack, the Marines suffered over a thousand casualties in a single day without taking the wood. The date of 6 June saw the greatest loss of Marines in a single day for the US Marine Corps in its then 143-year history.[34] During the week that followed, the US division continued its attacks, suffering over 7,000 casualties, a quarter of its manpower – most of them Marines.[35] On 15 June, the exhausted Marines were relieved by a regiment of the US 3rd ID, the US 7th Infantry.[36]

As soon as the US 7th Infantry relieved the Marines, it too began to struggle.[37] The US regiment's 3rd battalion commander stated that the inexperience of his men was so great that, in one case, a company commander had actually set up his 'position facing in the wrong direction' to German defences.[38] In another instance, a junior officer stated that during an attack he became lost, lost control of his platoon and, in the process of regaining control of his unit, he inadvertently led them into a German ambush.[39] One US regimental commander commented that:

> platoon leaders as a rule are not equal to their task. They are willing enough, but ignorant. During excitement they take orders from anyone who ranks them, whether they belong to their units or not, regardless of what previous explicit orders had been given them.[40]

To further complicate matters for the US 2nd ID, the Marine Brigade failed to coordinate its artillery with the Army regiment.[41] The Army regiment's lack of artillery support contributed to, in the words of its commander, 'heavy casualties without any military result'.[42] Like the Marines before them, 25 per cent of the US 7th Infantry became casualties, this time in just four days.[43]

After a week away, the Marines returned to relieve the US 7th Infantry. On 23 June, and in front of Major General Liggett and his staff of the newly arrived US 1st Army Corps (1st AC), the Marines again attempted to take Belleau Wood.[44] Once again, forces of the German Seventh Army rebuffed them.[45] The principal reason for the failed attack was that the Marines did not coordinate their artillery with their infantry.[46]

Perception does not mirror reality, and the efforts of the US 2nd ID at Belleau Wood were certainly proving this to be the case. In the first three weeks of June, the 'saviours' of Paris had faltered in their multiple attempts to clear Belleau Wood, and what they did achieve was very little at great cost. The vacillating efforts of the US Marines and soldiers were creating a situation that could call into question their combat prowess, which in turn threatened to undermine the political perception of the AEF as an effective fighting force. Fiske and Pershing's refusal to understand the need for firepower and specifically train the AEF to utilise more artillery, as French officers had initially advocated to the AEF, was taking a toll on the US 2nd ID and preventing it from effectively removing the German forces that held Belleau Wood.

In the midst of this struggle to take Belleau Wood, Pétain was also trying to navigate the incorporation and seasoning of the newly arrived US 1st AC. This US corps was the first to be formed since the American Civil War, and as a consequence its staff had no practical experience whatsoever in the conduct of modern warfare at the corps level. To make matters worse, it had just observed the US Marine Brigade's actions at Belleau Wood, thus making it likely that the US 1st AC would adopt these ill-suited tactics. Needless to say, this was no model that Pétain wanted the US 1st AC to imitate, especially as the US corps was slated to eventually command French divisions. If the French army and the AEF were going to 'season' the corps, the US 1st AC needed to witness the use of tactics that were actually effective.

To preserve the political perception created by the US 2nd ID's 'auspicious entrance' at the Marne, French leadership chose to intervene in order to ensure that the 'seasoning' of the US division and corps was a success. Following the US 2nd ID's failed attack on 23 June, Pétain issued orders to all the French armies reiterating the importance of using artillery in attacking strongly held positions.[47] The French Sixth Army's commander, General Jean Degoutte, in turn directed the US 2nd ID's staff to follow this order, while explaining to them the need to minimise the use of infantry in an attack.[48] Degoutte wanted the US division to stop the suicidal infantry charges that were first used on 6 June by the US Marines. The US Marines did successfully use their artillery on at least one occasion during their first three weeks, but they were inconsistent with its application, as the episode with the US 7th Infantry proved. In essence, Pétain and Degoutte were asking the staff of the US 2nd ID to stop doing what both Fiske and Pershing had advocated and instead to 'take the tone and tactics of those with whom they are associated'.

So, after the intervention of the French army's leadership, the seasoning of the US 2nd ID continued on 25 June with the Marines once more attempting to sweep Belleau Wood of German forces. With the help of the French 167ᵉ DI's artillery, the US division finally succeeded in driving the last German defenders from Belleau Wood.[49] According to US reports, the 24-hour artillery barrage that preceded the attack allowed the Marines to clear the remainder of Belleau Wood of German forces 'with slight losses' to themselves.[50] The Marine Brigade finally slew its dragon with the French army's help and preserved the perception that the AEF was a capable fighting force.

In honour of the Marines' success, Degoutte renamed Belleau Wood *le Bois de la Brigade de Marine* or Marine Brigade Wood.[51] But the subsequent honour granted to the Marines did not sit well with the US army brigade (3rd Brigade) of the US 2nd ID, or with the regiment of the US 3rd ID, which had fought over that very same ground. Regular US army soldiers and officers felt that their efforts to help subdue Belleau Wood were being overlooked or even ignored. According to Crozier,

> The Marines got most of the credit and practically all the glory. The resulting discord, which was reflected in lowered Army morale, did

not become generally known, but the effects were serious enough to be analysed in official reports.[52]

The US Marine Brigade had, in fact, achieved its own 'auspicious entrance', so much so that the Marines' efforts were eclipsing those of the Regulars of the US army. The perception, so sought after by US and French generals, now possessed the potential of threatening the morale of the AEF itself.

The Regulars were not to be outdone by the Marines. Pershing kept the US 2nd ID at the front in spite of the division's requests to be relieved. The whole division, especially the US army Regulars, would see combat as Pétain had sought those many months prior. The Army brigade was ordered to capture the French village of Vaux as part of a wider US–French attack. The capture of Vaux was not the attack's sole goal. The attack, more importantly, was designed to 'season' the Army brigade and create the 'auspicious entrance' that the Regulars of the US army had sought a month earlier with the US 1st ID's attack on Cantigny.[53] Furthermore, the success of the attack would cement the perception of the division and the AEF that was created by the press when the US 2nd ID arrived at the front.

The basic concept of the US–French attack, led by the French 3ᵉ CA, was to have a regiment of the French 39ᵉ DI attack the tactically important woods on *la Côte 204* while the US army brigade of the US 2nd ID attacked and took the French village of Vaux.[54] The French 39ᵉ DI had just arrived at the front and took up positions to the right of the US 2nd ID, replacing the French 10ᵉ DIC. The French 39ᵉ DI was, just like the 43ᵉ DI, one of the French army's 'assault divisions'. This highly skilled division had served in every major engagement of the war, including the recent third German offensive, in which, again just like the French 43ᵉ DI, it helped execute the fighting withdrawal that stabilised the front. After two weeks of rest and training, the French 39ᵉ DI returned to the front only days prior to the US 2nd ID's attack on Vaux.

To prevent a situation similar to the one that had occurred during the three-week debacle the US Marines experienced, the French Sixth Army became more intimately involved in the planning and execution of the Army brigade's assault. Lapses in coordination had been the cause of the failed Marine attacks at Belleau Wood. The French Sixth Army wanted to ensure that the French 39ᵉ DI, along with the surrounding US and French artillery units, were properly coordinated for the US–French attack. On the afternoon of 24 June, after the renewed but failed

US Marine attack of 23 June, the French Sixth Army changed the conduct of the planning process of the attack to take Vaux.[55] The most striking difference was that the French 3[e] CA, which had earlier taken over the sector from the French 21[e] CA, ordered the US division to submit all its plans for the attack to the French corps for approval.[56] This had not occurred in the past with the US Marines.

To help the French 3[e] CA's efforts in managing and supervising the US 2nd ID, veteran French officers, rather benignly referred to as 'liaison officers', became actively involved in the planning and execution of the attack on Vaux.[57] The French army had placed 35 liaison officers within the US 2nd ID when it first arrived in France.[58] These liaison officers were actually instructors. In what could be considered an early form of political correctness, the French army called their instructors 'liaison officers', solely to avoid offending the self-esteems and egos of the US soldiers and the political temperaments of the US officers.[59] Although these French officers were extremely effective at facilitating liaison between the French and US armies, more so towards the end of the war, their primary function was to instruct US soldiers on how to conduct the type of warfare seen in France. The liaison officers translated and explained orders to their US counterparts and, as such, the French army essentially provided the US division with the needed experience it lacked.[60] For the attack on Vaux, these liaison officers were the crucial aspect for the success of the planning process.

The French 3[e] CA additionally established and standardised all communications to and from aircraft and between infantry units.[61] All aircraft squadrons and balloon companies were placed under the orders of the French corps.[62] French aircraft squadrons provided intelligence and, during the attack, they acted as artillery spotters and observers for both the US and French divisions.[63] And, in order to maintain liaison between the attacking regiment of the French 39[e] DI and the US army brigade as their forces advanced, a combat liaison group led by a French officer was created with platoons from both the US and French divisions.[64]

The most important contribution the French corps provided to the US division was artillery. A 12-hour artillery barrage for the US assault and a four-hour barrage for the French assault were planned for the attack.[65] All US plans regarding US artillery were submitted to the French corps for approval.[66] It was absolutely essential for the French Sixth Army to guarantee that the US division used its artillery properly and effectively. The French Sixth Army also provided nearly half the artillery for the US 2nd ID's assault on Vaux.[67] In fact, a French artillery regiment conducted the most difficult aspect of the US division's portion of the attack, the rolling barrage, which protected the US army brigade during its advance on Vaux.[68] The French commitment of artillery to the attack continued to grow as the plans took shape. By the time the attack was launched, almost 80 per cent of all the artillery used was French.[69]

The French army's intervention was a calculated and delicately executed move to address the spotty coordination and lack of tactical acumen demonstrated by the US 2nd ID. The French army wanted the division to be successfully 'seasoned', and in order for that to happen they left nothing to chance regarding the attack on Vaux, especially after witnessing the efforts of the Marines during the early weeks of June.[70] Nearly every aspect of the US division's assault on Vaux was based on plans that were previously screened by French officers and backed by French units.

Opposing the US–French forces was the *201. Infanterie-Division* or the German 201st Infantry Division (201.ID). Both French and US army intelligence determined that the German 201.ID was 'far from being up to strength' and its fighting ability was 'open to considerable doubt'.[71] German soldiers from the 201.ID later confirmed these assessments.[72] Of the three regiments that made up the German 201.ID, the regiment across from the US army brigade was the weakest, the *Infanterie-Regiment Nr. 402* or the 402nd Infantry Regiment (402.IR).[73] The 402.IR was described by German soldiers as 'very weak', 'not in fighting condition' and that its 'morale was decidedly low'.[74] With that said, though, whether it was through inexperience or an overriding cultural predisposition within the US army to see the enemy for more than it was, the US 2nd ID considered the 402.IR the best regiment in the German division.[75] Actually, the best regiment in the division was the 401.IR, which was opposite the French 39ᵉ DI on *la Côte 204*.[76]

The attack was set for 1 July and it began at 18.00 after the artillery barrages.[77] The US soldiers who followed the French artillery's rolling barrage later remarked on its 'excellent' and 'absolutely perfect' execution.[78] Fifteen minutes into the attack, elements of the US 2nd ID's Army brigade were already approaching Vaux, reporting that the German soldiers of the 402.IR were offering little resistance.[79] One US army report claimed that the troops of the German regiment 'were all hiding in their dugouts with no thought of an attack'.[80] The US 2nd ID's intelligence section characterised the German reaction as 'feeble' and stated that the Germans were making 'practically no defense of Vaux'.[81] Further reports claimed that many of the German soldiers 'appeared happy to be made prisoners of war' and that some 'induced' others to come out and give themselves up.[82] Before half an hour was up, the US brigade had passed through Vaux and began setting up its defensive positions north of the village.[83] Already waiting for them was the French-led liaison group, which had taken its objective ahead of the US brigade.[84] After an hour, Vaux and 200 soldiers of the German 402.IR were captured with minimal losses to the US 2nd ID.[85]

Unbeknownst to the French 39e DI and the other half of the US–French attack, the element of surprise had been lost days prior.[86] As soon as the pre-attack artillery barrage stopped, the single French regiment (*153e Régiment d'Infanterie*) was immediately met by German artillery and machine-gun fire.[87] Regardless, the regiment was able to flank the German 401.IR and nearly cut it off from the rest of its division.[88] As a result, the assault screened the efforts of the US 2nd ID's Army brigade by diverting the 201.ID's attention away from Vaux.[89] The near isolation of the German regiment on *la Côte 204* led the German division's operations staff to believe that the entire US–French attack's goal was to take the hill.[90] In the early hours of 2 July, units from all three German regiments (401.IR, 402.IR and 403.IR) of the 201.ID counter-attacked the outnumbered French regiment on the hill, leaving the US army brigade nearly unmolested to consolidate its positions in and around Vaux.[91] The French regiment stopped the German counter-attack but was unable to unseat the 401.IR from the wood atop *la Côte 204* as a consequence.[92] The French regiment became overextended and vulnerable to flanking fire from German positions as a result of the German counter-attack. Casualties increased for both sides as the night went on.[93] It was at this point that the French 39^e DI's staff made the decision to consolidate and discontinue attacking in order to prevent further casualties to its regiment.

Even though the French 39^e DI was unable to fully push the German 201.ID off the top of *la Côte 204*, the US–French attack had achieved its larger purpose: the US 2nd ID's Army brigade had conducted a successful attack and in the process became 'seasoned'.[94] The success of the US–French attack on Vaux was due in large part to the excellent coordination between French and US units in the planning and execution of the attack (as seen at Cantigny nearly a month earlier with the US 1st ID), the undeniable poor quality of the German regiment facing the US brigade, and the tactical expertise that the French army applied to the managing of its new ally. The artillery barrage used during the attack became near legendary for those in the US 2nd ID, as the US soldiers of the division testified afterwards in their accounts of the battle.

But the capture of Vaux was of little tactical significance. The staff of the German 201.ID decided that the recapture of Vaux was not 'absolutely necessary' and that no actual advantage could be gained from retaking it.[95] In the end, the tactical situation still favoured the German division, for it still contested the French and US divisions for the important crest of *la Côte 204*; hence the reason why it threw the weight of its reserves against the French portion of the attack.

The attack on Vaux was less about capturing a tactical position and more about creating a favourable political perception for the US 2nd ID and the AEF.[96] Although many battles in the Great War dwarfed Belleau Wood and Vaux in their size and strategic importance, the significance of these small attacks lay in that they demonstrated to the Allies and the United States that the AEF was ready for action.[97] The taking of Vaux helped ensure the perception of the US 2nd ID and the AEF as a capable fighting force. In the time-span of a week the US 2nd ID had obtained two concrete victories for itself by successfully launching attacks with both of its brigades that cleared German forces from Belleau Wood and the village of Vaux. Lejeune remarked that '[t]he psychological effect was tremendous... [a] handful of Americans had checked the Boche'.[98]

In addition to the positive political perception and the morale boost that these victories provided for the US 2nd ID and the AEF, the staff of the US division also gained valuable experience. The officers of the US 2nd ID learned from the mistakes they made at Belleau Wood and then began to understand how to fight a modern war when the division took Vaux. Both Liggett and Lejeune later succinctly summarised in their reports and memoirs this understanding gained. Liggett wrote:

> it was in the recklessness of our attack. The Marines took the machine-gun nests by hand and bayoneted the enemy out rather than wait for the slower method of sifting in behind (artillery). But if they paid heavily, it was one more proof of the drive of the American Army – that it could stand the gaff.[99]

Lejeune realised that the 25 June attack at Belleau Wood and the assault to take Vaux had both

> decisively shown the great importance of artillery to Infantry. Infantry alone without material makes little or no progress. If the enemy combines personnel and materiel, we must do the same or lose the game.[100]

It was the experience shared by the French army with the US 2nd ID at Belleau Wood and Vaux that helped the division achieve victory, as well as advancing the careers of both Liggett and Lejeune. Lejeune would go on to lead the US 2nd ID, and Liggett, who witnessed the attacks while commanding the newly created 1st AC, would eventually go on to take command of the US First Army by the end of the war.

Liggett's and Lejeune's comments reflected an understanding that Pétain had hoped to achieve with the AEF in 1917 but had been unable to because of Pershing. The US general's actions were influenced more by his mission to create a US-only force in France, and the political capital that it would bring to the negotiation table at Versailles, than by the advantages that could be gained from having a tactically proficient army as a result of fighting with French divisions. Pershing only needed to construct a political perception of the AEF as a rescuer that won the war for the Allies in order to achieve his goals. The efforts of the US 2nd ID at Belleau Wood and Vaux were ample to achieve what Pershing sought.

The German Seventh Army still had its doubts. In a German report concerning the US 2nd ID's efforts at Château-Thierry, German staff officers commented that the AEF's leadership was 'not yet up to mark' and that the AEF would 'not be able to dispense with French guidance for the time being'.[101] Although the Imperial German army was correct in its conclusion, it mattered little. The French army's adept placing of US forces in positions where they could be best used ensured that Pétain was able to season the US 2nd ID as well as achieve the political perception he and Pershing sought for the AEF. As General Hans von Boehn, commander of the German Seventh Army, put it:

> [it is] not a question of the possession of this or that village or woods, insignificant in itself; it is a question whether the Anglo-American claim that the American Army is equal or even the superior of the German Army is to be made good.[102]

With the French army's help, the US 2nd ID was able to make that claim.

Vaux became the US division's dénouement for its efforts around Château-Thierry; it was now 'seasoned'. The US 2nd ID was eventually relieved by a US National Guard division, the 26th ID. To help make the whole episode that much more 'auspicious', the 26th ID began its relief of the 2nd ID on the same day that the US 1st AC took command of both US and French forces for the first time. The date chosen by the French Sixth Army: 4 July 1918.

Notes

1. General J. J. Pershing, *Source Records of the Great War, Vol. V*, ed. Charles F. Horne, *National Alumni 1923* (New York: National Alumi, 1923), p. 91.
2. 'qu'il ne négligerait aucune occasion pour favoriser une heureuse entrée en scène de l'armée américaine'. *Les Armées Français, Tome V*, Vol. 2, Annexes, Vol. 2, Memorandum 'Agreement Relative Insertion of American Troops into Line', 18 October 1917. Historical Division-Department of the Army, *United States Army in the World War 1917–1919* [USAWW], Vol. 3 (Washington, DC: United States Government Printing Office, 1948), p. 250.
3. H. Liggett, *A.E.F. Ten Years Ago in France* (New York: Dodd, Mead & Co, 1928), p. 59.
4. American Battle Monuments Commission [ABMC], *2nd Division, Summary of Operations in the World War* (Washington, DC: United States Government Printing Office, 1944), p. 15.
5. USAWW, Vol. 2, p. 260.
6. E. Crozier, *American Reporters on the Western Front* (New York: Oxford Press, 1959), p. 230.
7. K. Hamburger, 'Learning Lessons in the American Expeditionary Forces CMH Pub 24–1', *United States Army Center of Military History* 24–1 (2003), p. 9.
8. Liggett, p. 51.
9. USAWW, Vol. 3, p. 254.
10. USAWW, Vol. 3, p. 262.
11. R.B. Bruce, *A Fraternity of Arms* (Lawrence: University Press of Kansas, 2003), p. 121.
12. R.A. Doughty, *Pyrrhic Victory, French Strategy and Operations in the Great War* (Cambridge, MA: Harvard University Press, 2008), p. 404.
13. Major General John A. Lejeune, Report on 2nd Division at Chateau-Thierry, 31 December 1918, National Archives and Records Administration, Record Group 120 Second Division, Box 25 Historical Decimal File 33.6.
14. Crozier, p. 212.
15. ABMC, *1st Division, Summary of Operations in the World War* (Washington, DC: United States Government Printing Office, 1944), p. 13.
16. Liggett, p. 70.
17. Ibid., pp. 380–381.
18. D. Zabecki, *The German 1918 Offensives: A Case Study in the Operational Level of War* (London: Routledge, 2009), p. 231.
19. A. Clayton, *Paths of Glory* (London: Cassell, 2003), p. 169.
20. F. Foch, *Memoirs of Marshal Foch* (Garden City, NY: Doubleday, Doran and Company, Inc., 1931), p. 381.
21. Crozier, p. 215.
22. Ibid., p. 218.
23. Ibid., p. 220.
24. Foch, p. 376.
25. USAWW, Vol. 4, pp. 225–226.
26. Zabecki, p. 231.
27. ABCM, *2nd Division*, pp. 7–8.

28. Center of Military History, *Order of Battle of the United States Land Forces in the World War [OOB] Vol. 2* (Washington, DC: United States Army, 1949), p. 277.
29. Ibid., p. 441.
30. Ministère de la Guerre, *Les Armées Français, Tome X, Vol. 2* (Paris: Imprimerie Nationale, 1924), p. 970.
31. M. Goya, *La Chair et l'Acier: L'Armée Française et l'invention de la Guerre Moderne (1914–1918)* (Paris: Tallandier, 2004); I. Sumner, *French Poilu 1914–18* (Westminster, MD: Osprey Publishing Ltd, 2009), pp. 8–20.
32. ABMC, *2nd Division*, pp. 7–8, 10.
33. Ibid., p. 11 (45).
34. D. Camp, *The Devil Dogs at Belleau Wood* (Minneapolis: Zenith Press, 2008), p. 100.
35. American Battle Monuments Commission, *American Armies and Battlefields in Europe* (Washington, DC: United States Government Printing Office, 1938), p. 103.
36. Chief of Staff Headquarters Second Division to Commanding Officer 7th Infantry, Duty with 2nd Division, 15 June 1918, National Archives and Records Administration, Record Group 120 Third Division, Box 41 Historical Decimal File: 33.6.
37. Captain J.R. Williams, Report on Operations of 1st Platoon Co. 'C' 7th Infantry in Belleau Woods June 15–21, 1918, National Archives and Records Administration, Record Group 120 Third Division, Box 41 Historical Decimal File 33.6.
38. Colonel Frank H. Adams to Major General Robert L. Howze, Report of action of First Battalion 7th U. S. Infantry in Belleau Wood, 21 June 1919, National Archives and Records Administration, Record Group 120 Third Division, Box 41 Historical Decimal File 33.6.
39. First Lieutenant Carl C. Helm, Report to Operations, 24 June 1918, National Archives and Records Administration, Record Group 120 Third Division, Box 41 Historical Decimal File 33.6. Captain J.R. Williams, Report on Operations of 1st Platoon Co. 'C' 7th Infantry in Belleau Woods June 15–21 1918, National Archives and Records Administration, Record Group 120 Third Division, Box 41 Historical Decimal File 33.6.
40. USAWW, Vol. 4, p. 538.
41. J.T. Dickman, *The Great Crusade* (New York: D. Appleton and Company, 1927), p. 56.
42. Colonel T.M. Anderson to Commanding General 3rd Division, First Endorsement, 23 June 1918, National Archives and Records Administration, Record Group 120 Third Division, Box 39 Historical Decimal File 33.6.
43. Commanding Officer 1st Battalion 7th Infantry to Commanding Officer 7th Infantry, Report of Operations at Bois de Belleau, 23 June 1918, National Archives and Records Administration, Record Group 120 Third Division, Box 39 Historical Decimal File 33.6.
44. ABCM, *2nd Division*, p. 19.
45. Ibid. USAWW, Vol. 4, p. 544. Twenty Eight Division American Expeditionary Forces, Field Orders No. 2, 22 June 1918, National Archives and Records Administration, Record Group 120 Twenty-Eighth Division Box 4 Historical Decimal File: 32.1.

46. Chief of Staff James W. McAndrew Historical Section General Staff A.E.F., Operations of the American Expeditionary Forces The Second Division at Chateau Thierry, 1918, National Archives and Records Administration, Record Group 120 Second Division, Box 5 Historical Decimal File 18.2.
47. National Archives and Records Administration, Record Group 165 French Military Mission.
48. M.E. Grotelueschen, *Doctrine Under Trial, American Artillery Employment in World War I* (Westport, CT: Greenwood Press, 2001), p. 39.
49. ABCM, *2nd Division*, p. 20.
50. USAWW, Vol. 4, p. 228.
51. Ibid., p. 656.
52. Crozier, p. 221.
53. General Mondesir to Commanding General 10th Colonial Infantry Division, Secret Communiqué No. 1438/3, 24 Juin 1918, National Archives and Records Administration, Record Group 165 French Military Mission, Box 39 Historical Decimal File 30.9.
54. Colonel Moisson, 39th Infantry Division Secret Plan of Attack, 28 June 1918, National Archives and Records Administration, Record Group 120 Second Division, Box 21 Historical Decimal File 32.7.
55. Ibid.
56. USAWW, Vol. 4, pp. 546–547.
57. National Archives and Records Administration, Record Group 165 French Military Mission, Liaison Reports.
58. Liaison Office 2nd Div. AEF to Commanding General 2nd Div. AEF, List of French Interpreters for the US 2nd Infantry Division, 29 June 1918, National Archives and Records Administration, Record Group 120 Second Division, Box 25 Historical Decimal File 35.7.
59. J. Keane, 'Uneasy Alliances: French Military Intelligence and the American Army During the First World War', *Intelligence and National Security, Vol. 13* (London: Routledge, 1998), p. 21.
60. General Pougin, Special Order No. 1129/P.C., National Archives and Records Administration, Record Group 165 French Military Mission, Box 104 Historical Decimal File 30.1, Headquarters 2nd Battalion 9th Infantry, Field Orders No. 6, 28 June 1918, National Archives and Records Administration, Record Group 120 Second Division, Box 11 Historical Decimal File 32.1.
61. USAWW, Vol. 4, p. 643.
62. Headquarters Second Division American Expeditionary Forces, Field Orders No. 9, 30 June 1918, National Archives and Records Administration, Record Group 120 Second Division, Box 11 Historical Decimal File 32.0.
63. Machine Gun Company Ninth Infantry, Report of Attack on Vaux, 29 May to 3 July 1918, National Archives and Records Administration, Record Group 120 Second Division, Box 39 Historical Decimal File 33.6. Headquarters Second Division American Expeditionary Forces, Field Orders No. 9, 30 June 1918, National Archives and Records Administration, Record Group 120 Second Division, Box 11 Historical Decimal File 32.0. According to one US account, because of the information 'gained by photos during the month of June, it was possible to assign Company, Platoons, and Squad objectives' for the attack.

64. Ibid. Headquarters Second Division American Expeditionary Forces, Field Orders No. 9, 30 June 1918, National Archives and Records Administration, Record Group 120 Second Division, Box 11 Historical Decimal File 32.0. Headquarters 2nd Battalion 9th Infantry, Field Orders No. 6, 28 June 1918, National Archives and Records Administration, Record Group 120 Second Division, Box 11 Historical Decimal File 32.1.

65. General Pougin, Memorandum on Vaux-Chateau Thierry Sector No. 1140/ C.P., National Archives and Records Administration, Record Group 165 French Military Mission, Box 104 Historical Decimal File 30.1.

66. USAWW, Vol. 4, pp. 546–547.

67. General L. Lebrun, Special Order No. 1103/3-Op, 28 June 1918, National Archives and Records Administration, Record Group 120 Second Division, Box 21 Historical Decimal File 32.7. Headquarters Second Division American Expeditionary Forces, Field Orders No. 9, 30 June 1918, National Archives and Records Administration, Record Group 120 Second Division, Box 11 Historical Decimal File 32.0. The French provided one regiment of artillery from the French 167th Infantry Division, the 37th Artillery Regiment and the 7th *Groupe* from the 107th Artillery Regiment, for a total 48 guns (47 per cent of all artillery for the US assault on Vaux). The US 2nd Infantry Division provided two full regiments of artillery from the 15th and 17th Field Artillery Regiments and half of a regiment from the 12th Field Artillery Regiment, for a total of 54 guns (53 per cent of all artillery for the US assault on Vaux).

68. General L. Lebrun, Special Order No. 1103/3-Op, 28 June 1918, National Archives and Records Administration, Record Group 120 Second Division, Box 21 Historical Decimal File 32.7.

69. Headquarters Second Division American Expeditionary Forces, Field Orders No. 9, 30 June 1918, National Archives and Records Administration, Record Group 120 Second Division, Box 11 Historical Decimal File 32.0. General Pougin, Memorandum on Vaux-Chateau Thierry Sector No. 1140/C.P., National Archives and Records Administration, Record Group 165 French Military Mission, Box 104 Historical Decimal File 30.1. 39th Infantry Division, Operations Journal 1 January to 31 March 1919, Defence Historical Service Vincennes, 26 N 335/4, p. 34. 3rd Army Corps, Operations Journal 19 December 1917 to 14 September 1918, Defence Historical Service Vincennes, 26 N 106/9, p. 59–61. When one includes the artillery from the French 39th Infantry Division (36 guns), the heavy artillery from the French 3rd and 38th Army Corps (144 guns), the 5th *Groupe* of the 107th Artillery Regiment (12 guns) and the artillery provided for the US assault on Vaux, the French army provided 240 guns for the attack. The US provided 54 guns for the attack or 22.5 per cent of all artillery for the attack.

70. USAWW, Vol. 3, pp. 254, 295.

71. G2 General Headquarters A.E.F., History of 201st Division, 10 June 1918, National Archives and Records Administration, Record Group 120 Second Division, Box 10 Historical Decimal File 22.2.

72. German Order of Battle, National Archives and Records Administration, Record Group 120 Second Division, Box 10 Historical Decimal File 22.3. Commanding Officer 2nd Battalion 9th Infantry to Commanding Officer 9th Infantry, Information secured from German Deserter, 25 June 1918,

National Archives and Records Administration, Record Group 120 Second Division, Box 36 Historical Decimal File 22.0. Notes on the Attack on the village of Vaux by American Troops July 1, 1918 taken from the statements of prisoners, 19 August 1918, National Archives and Records Administration, Record Group 120 Second Division, Box 39 Historical Decimal File 33.6. List of Interrogations, 1 July 1918, National Archives and Records Administration, Record Group 120 Second Division, Box 10 Historical Decimal File 22.3.

73. List of Interrogations, 1 July 1918, National Archives and Records Administration, Record Group 120 Second Division, Box 10 Historical Decimal File 22.3.

74. Field Messages, 1–3 July 1918, National Archives and Records Administration, Record Group 120 Second Division, Box 11 Historical Decimal File 32.16. Second Section 2nd Division A.E.F., Summary of Intelligence, 1–2 July 1918, National Archives and Records Administration, Record Group 120 Second Division, Box 8 Historical Decimal File 20.1.

75. Chief of Staff James W. McAndrew Historical Section General Staff A.E.F., Operations of the American Expeditionary Forces The Second Division at Chateau Thierry, 1918, National Archives and Records Administration, Record Group 120 Second Division, Box 5 Historical Decimal File 18.2.

76. List of Interrogations, 1 July 1918, National Archives and Records Administration, Record Group 120 Second Division, Box 10 Historical Decimal File 22.3. General Pougin, Memorandum on Vaux-Chateau Thierry Sector No. 1140/C.P., National Archives and Records Administration, Record Group 165 French Military Mission, Box 104 Historical Decimal File 30.1.

77. ABCM, *2nd Division*, p. 20.

78. Joel D. Thacker, Account of Battle, National Archives and Records Administration, Record Group 120 Second Division, Box 25 Historical Decimal File 33.6. Headquarters Second Battalion 9th Infantry, Report of Attack on Vaux and La Roche Woods, 3 July 1918, National Archives and Records Administration, Record Group 120 Second Division, Box 39 Historical Decimal File 33.6.

79. USAWW, Vol. 4, p. 727. 2nd Bureau French 10th Army, Interrogation of a Deserter of the 402nd Regiment 201st Division surrender 25 June 1918, Record Group 120 Second Division, Box 10 Historical Decimal File 22.3.

80. Headquarters Second Battalion 9th Infantry, Report of Attack on Vaux and La Roche Woods, 3 July 1918, National Archives and Records Administration, Record Group 120 Second Division, Box 39 Historical Decimal File 33.6.

81. Second Section 2nd Division A.E.F., Summary of Intelligence, 1–2 July 1918, National Archives and Records Administration, Record Group 120 Second Division, Box 8 Historical Decimal File 20.1.

82. Machine Gun Company Ninth Infantry, Report of Attack on Vaux, 29 May to 3 July 1918, National Archives and Records Administration, Record Group 120 Second Division, Box 39 Historical Decimal File 33.6. Headquarters Second Battalion 9th Infantry, Report of Attack on Vaux and La Roche Woods, 3 July 1918, National Archives and Records Administration, Record Group 120 Second Division, Box 39 Historical Decimal File 33.6.

83. Field Messages, 1–3 July 1918, National Archives and Records Administration, Record Group 120 Second Division, Box 11 Historical Decimal File 32.16.

84. Field Messages, 1–3 July 1918, National Archives and Records Administration, Record Group 120 Second Division, Box 11 Historical Decimal File 32.16.

85. USAWW, Vol. 4, p. 228.

86. Major Bourton, Field Messages, 1–2 July 1918, National Archives and Records Administration, Record Group 120 Second Division, Box 11 Historical Decimal File 32.16. German 201st Infantry Division, Battle Report, 4 July 1918, National Archives and Records Administration, Record Group 165 German Army, Box 170 Historical Decimal File 33.5.

87. 153rd Infantry Regiment, Operations Journal 1 January to 21 July 1918, Defence Historical Service Vincennes, France, 26 N 697/23, p. 45.

88. German 201st Infantry Division, Battle Report, 4 July 1918, National Archives and Records Administration, Record Group 165 German Army, Box 170 Historical Decimal File 33.5.

89. German 201st Infantry Division, Battle Report, 4 July 1918, National Archives and Records Administration, Record Group 165 German Army, Box 170 Historical Decimal File 33.5.

90. USAWW, Vol. 4, p. 729.

91. German 201st Infantry Division, Battle Report, 4 July 1918, National Archives and Records Administration, Record Group 165 German Army, Box 170 Historical Decimal File 33.5.

92. Colonel Moisson, 39th Infantry Division Secret Plan of Attack, 28 June 1918, National Archives and Records Administration, Record Group 120 Second Division, Box 21 Historical Decimal File 32.7.

93. 39th Infantry Division, Operations Journal 1 January to 31 March 1919, Defence Historical Service Vincennes, 26 N 335/4, p. 34.

94. Journal of Operations Twenty Eight Division A.E.F., National Archives and Records Administration, Record Group 120 Twenty-Eighth Division, Box 8 Historical Decimal File 33.3, pp. 1–3.

95. USAWW, Vol. 4, pp. 727–729.

96. Headquarters First Army Corps American, E. F., Report of Operations of the First Army Corps while serving under the 6th French Arm July 4 to Aug. 14 1918, National Archives and Records Administration, Record Group 120 Third Division Box 22 Historical File 33.6.

97. USAWW, Vol. 1, p. xvi.

98. Major John A. Lejeune, Report on 2nd Division at Chateau-Thierry, 31 December 1918, National Archives and Records Administration, Record Group 120 Second Division, Box 25 Historical Decimal File 33.6.

99. Liggett, p. 83.

100. Ibid.

101. Chief of the General Staff of the Field Army, Secret Report No. 15, 2 July 1918, National Archives and Records Administration, Record Group 165 German Army, Box 3 Historical Decimal File 21.8.

102. J. Eisenhower, *Yanks: The Epic Story of the American Army in World War I* (New York: The Free Press, 2001), p. 146.

12
From the *Essex* to the *Dresden*: British Grand Strategy in the South Pacific, 1814–1915

Andrew Lambert

While older naval histories, written in an age when the possibility of another great fleet battle remained, tended to focus on the activity of major fleets, placing Jutland at the core of the First World War, more recent scholarship reflects the reality that the end of the Cold War left the western sea power consortium, led by the overwhelming naval might of the United States, in complete control of the world's oceans. Today the only threats to this dominance are limited and tend to be focused in the littoral around key choke points and economic bottlenecks. The questions that need to be addressed today concern the role and value of sea power in asymmetric conflicts. Consequently, while it may be possible to adopt a short-term, local perspective on many aspects of the First World War, the naval conflict makes little sense when viewed from mid-20th century perspectives, let alone from the North Sea.

Instead, it is essential to take a long view of British policy, to understand how profoundly decision-making in 1914 had been conditioned by long-term strategic assumptions, evolved from even earlier models of global behaviour.[1] In the century between Waterloo and the First World War Britain prepared for the worst case, another major conflict, one in which the control of global sea lanes would be essential. In 1817–1818 Lord Castlereagh defined the core concerns as preventing the creation of another continental hegemon, or a Franco-Russian alliance, through diplomacy and sea power. Aside from a small area in Flanders, the stepping-off point for an invasion, Britain's main interests in Europe were peace, stability and trade.

The core problem facing British strategists was the need to defend a truly global network of shipping routes and trades, mostly dominated by

British ships, and others usually insured in London, and linked into the British commercial system by capital, markets, shipping insurance, telegraph and wireless communications, and control of steam coal stocks. In essence, Britain ran global trade, providing almost all of the essential services that facilitated the movement of raw materials and finished goods across the globe. Pre-war planners had acknowledged that the continued effective existence of this system would be essential to the development of British power in a major conflict. Key raw materials sourced in distant regions, such as Chilean nitrates for explosive and fertiliser, and Australian grain and Argentine beef to feed the troops, not to mention imperial troop reinforcements, were the first fruits of sea power. To secure them Britain would need to control the main shipping lanes, and reduce any shipping losses caused by enemy action to a negligible quantity. This would ensure confidence in the system. It would also reduce the demand for warships outside the key theatres, allowing them to be replaced by auxiliary vessels, notably armed merchant cruisers.

British strategy was conditioned by the primacy of economic and imperial concerns. The big problem remained the protection of a network of shipping routes and trades, dominated by British and other ships insured in London, linked to the British commercial system. While France, Russia and the United States no longer threatened British oceanic communications, they had been replaced by Imperial Germany. The German Navy was pinned down in the North Sea by the British Grand Fleet, leaving a handful of cruisers to patrol the sea lanes. Before 1914 the Admiralty had developed plans for rigorous application of economic warfare, using Britain's absolute dominance of global communications, shipping, shipbuilding and steam coal to smash the German economy.

This chapter will examine the development of British strategy in the South Pacific, to exemplify both the functioning of a well-prepared system and the development of long-term planning.[2] Although it lay at the opposite end of the earth, the South Pacific had been a theatre of British maritime ambition since the 1570s, requiring a permanent British naval presence since 1813. In that year the American frigate USS *Essex* inflicted significant damage on British commerce, particularly the whaling fleet. As the South American nations emerged from Spanish rule, the usual combination of British commercial interests, capital, exports, raw materials and local political instability made a fleet essential; indeed, warships and an admiral were the essential diplomatic tools to secure those interests. The South American station was formally established in 1826, evolving into the Pacific Station in 1837. Later the link with British interests in what is now British Columbia led to the establishment of the West Coast of America station. By the 1840s the squadron was following a well-practised routine: sailing from the main base at Valparaiso, where a Royal Navy Depot ship was moored in the Chilean harbour, to call on various South Pacific and north-west coast locations as occasion demanded. Occasional alarms about French land grabs in Tahiti and the Marquesas Islands, American claims on the Oregon border, and local wars drew attention to the scale of the ocean and the paucity of British resources to meet these disparate demands. Sheer distance explained why the British had been relatively confident about the security of their floating trade – as steam became an essential requirement for modern warships, only Britain had the facilities to operate in the region, using the coal stocks and mechanics of the subsidised Pacific Steam Navigation Company.[3] Even so, the station was the last to have a steam-powered flagship, and the last where auxiliary sail power was essential. A thinly settled coast, and the vast expanse of open ocean that separated Chile, Tahiti, Hawaii and Vancouver, made sails vital into the 1880s. The force on station usually comprised obsolescent vessels, including a number of smaller gunboat types, more suited to local policing than war fighting.[4]

For much of the century, naval planners envisaged that, in the event of war with a major naval power, France or the United States, Britain would occupy Juan Fernandez (better known today as Robinson Crusoe Island) as a Pacific antipode to the Falklands, or, if that proved diplomatically awkward, then one of the San Felix–San Ambrosio group further north, as a temporary naval base. These islands had been visited frequently, often to be surveyed, without the sanction of the Chilean government. British warships always took care to ensure they were not observed by Chilean vessels or settlers. The key strategic planning section of the 19th-century Admiralty, the Hydrographic Office, kept substantial files on these islands, complete with coastal perspectives, charts and information about access to water and other supplies. They were very much on the British world map, but were rarely mentioned in public. This scheme was alive and well in the 1870s, as an alternative to the development of a naval base at Esquimault in British Columbia.

The oceanic telegraph cable, steam and the local naval dominance of Chile – Britain's closest regional partner – reduced the need just as exports of nitrates began to rocket, making Chile an essential economic partner, and boosting the demand for large sailing ships to bring these noisome cargoes home to Britain, often carrying coal on the outbound leg. By 1900 this trade seemed to be secure, and the West Coast Station was greatly reduced. After the construction of an imperial dry dock at Esquimault in British Columbia in the late 1880s, configured to service the modern warships of the British squadron, it had been hoped that Canada would pick up some of the burden. Canada was far more concerned with continental issues, and, although it took over the dockyard in 1905, it left the facilities to decay, and ignored the need for Pacific naval security. Despite the failure of the Dominion, the British stood down the Pacific Station, withdrawing manpower to face Germany in European waters. This left a gaping hole in the British global trade defence system.[5] However, with Russia weak and all disputes with the United States resolved, the decision to withdraw assets to European waters seemed sound. In 1914 the defence of British imperial interests in the Pacific was determined elsewhere.

This mattered because British commercial interests in Chile peaked in 1914, and they were dominated by nitrate exports. At least 30 per cent of Chilean trade was in British hands, and this trade had been essential to the British war effort, an ample reward for the long-term effort to control both the Chilean economy and the South Pacific. When war broke out in August 1914 strong economic and political ties between London and Santiago favoured British strategic interests in the South Pacific, but this relationship had to be sustained by naval presence and the ability to secure the British network of sea control, oceanic communications, markets and supplies.

The completion of the Panama Canal in 1914 completely changed the strategic geography of the region. High-value cargoes, human and economic, would no longer need to round Cape Horn, where awe-inspiring weather crippled many a ship; those that survived usually ended their days in Port Stanley, the well-placed harbour of refuge that explained why the British had occupied the Falkland Islands in 1833.

The German challenge

For most of the 19th century, the most serious threat to British command of the sea came from an alliance of France and Russia. When this became a reality in 1893 it prompted a rapid increase in the construction of cruisers for imperial service, and new dry docks and other facilities to sustain them.[6] This enormously expensive investment shifted into a North Sea battle fleet after 1904, when Britain, France and Russia became Entente partners, in response to the hegemonic threat posed by Germany on land and sea. The concomitant removal of any lingering danger from the United States, which had been a serious threat to sea lanes and oceanic communications in the first half of the 19th century, made Britain's global situation in 1914 far better than it might have been. This was fortunate, because the level of defence in the Pacific had fallen very low indeed – only a single light cruiser for the entire South Pacific, HMS *Glasgow*.

As Sir Julian Corbett had stressed, there was no need for a battle if the enemy could not challenge that command. In 1914 Germany was unable to challenge British global naval dominance. The amusingly named 'High Seas Fleet' never left the Heligoland Bight. Corbett had been a key figure in the development and transmission of strategic ideas to the pre-war naval leadership, both as a close confidant of Admiral Sir John Fisher and as the leading educator on the Royal Navy War Course between 1904 and 1914. Corbett's cool, analytical assessment impacted on almost the entire service, creating a strategic culture that recognised 'that the primary role of the Grand Fleet in the First World War was to guarantee the ability of the merchant cruisers on the Northern Patrol to interdict German seaborne trade, rather than to engage in large set-piece battles'.[7] This highlights the point that the real task of major fleets has always been to provide cover for the real work of sea power, the exercise of command, to secure British and annihilate hostile trade and colonies.

The dramatic improvement in Britain's global naval position between 1900 and 1914 enabled Fisher to win a full-scale naval arms race against Germany by 1912 on the simplest measure: numbers of dreadnought battleships assembled in northern European waters. He was also thinking about a new system of global sea control, in which the Dominions and India made ever greater contribution to the naval defence of empire through local basing, ships and manpower. When the 1909 'Dreadnought' panic sparked New Zealand to offer a capital ship, Fisher exploited Australian political turmoil to turn a projected local defence navy into an ocean-going sea control 'Fleet Unit' of one battle cruiser and three light cruisers, along with destroyers and submarines. In 1913 the 'Fleet Unit' arrived in Australia, allowing the Royal Australian Navy to take responsibility for the area hitherto patrolled by a British squadron of the same size. The new Fleet possessed high strategic speed, and, with access to an unrivalled global network of coaling bases, dry docks, cable and wireless stations, it could be vectored in to address threats across the region as they emerged. It had been intended that similar British units would operate in the Indian Ocean and China Seas, controlling Asian waters and Asian trade. They would be supported by armed merchant cruisers, a substantial force of medium-sized cargo liners, ships of outstanding endurance and seaworthiness, which would be taken into the fleet at the outbreak of war, equipped with guns in British, Canadian, South African, Indian and Australian ports.[8] These ships would patrol the outer ocean and the distant blockade lines north of Scotland. They allowed Fisher to spend his cruiser budget on battle cruisers, which were dual-role capital ships, rather than smaller trade defence assets.

In 1913 Winston Churchill, as First Lord of the Admiralty, had so little regard for oceanic defence that he reneged on an Admiralty commitment to Australia and New Zealand that battle cruisers would be sent to the Pacific, where the Dominions were concerned by the prospect of Japanese aggression. It mattered little that their fears were borderline absurd, but it did reveal a shift of priority. After 1904, trade defence cruisers were built in miniscule numbers, far too few to replace the old trade defence fleets built between 1891 and 1904 to meet France and Russia on the broad oceans. When Fisher's battle cruisers were kept at home, the global trade defence system began to look threadbare.

War

In August 1914 the German threat was limited to a handful of regular cruisers stationed outside Europe, including the East Asia squadron of Vice Admiral Maximilian von Spee, and a well-organised armed merchant cruiser, centrally directed from Berlin. These assets did not constitute a significant danger, and there was no need for a global convoy system to deal with them. Good intelligence, communications dominance and control of the coal supply would suffice. The Germans understood the situation; they could only operate as fugitives, hiding in the distant spaces of the broad ocean. While the South Pacific coastline of Chile and Peru might appear distant and unimportant in 1914, nothing could be further from the truth. If the British Empire was going to win the war it would need to control Chilean nitrates, Argentine beef, Australian grain and global communications. Any break in the world shipping system was potentially fatal. To meet the threat posed by German cruisers, the Royal Navy needed to be strong everywhere, without weakening the North Sea battlefleet, the pivot point of the entire system. British global strategy relied on communications dominance to keep track of the handful of German ships outside European waters. However, the system was imperfect, especially in the furthest reaches of the South Pacific, between Tahiti and Chile, where there were few telegraph cables or wireless relays, and most ships still used sails. The

Germans were well aware of the enormous advantages that the British possessed, especially the submarine telegraph cable network. This was a major target for cruiser operations: it was no coincidence that both Graf Maximilian von Spee and his most successful independent cruiser were sunk while attacking cable relay stations.[9]

In 1914 von Spee moved into the vast, empty spaces of the South Pacific. Like Commodore Anson in 1741, von Spee set out to disrupt and damage a global imperial system that he could not hope to destroy. The German admiral was a skilled professional, but he would have to operate on oceans dominated by British ships, communications and coal. His force, two armoured and one light cruiser, with supporting colliers, left the German colonies around Samoa, moving east to attack French Tahiti on 22 September. Although von Spee forced the British and their Japanese allies to concentrate their heavy units, he was comprehensively outclassed by the newer, faster and substantially more powerful battle-cruiser HMAS *Australia*. Having failed to score any decisive blows in the region, and well aware that he faced a superior force, von Spee set a course for Chile, radioing his outlying light cruisers and colliers to join him at a pre-planned rendezvous.

The British had several options. Rear Admiral Patey, commanding the Royal Australian Navy, anticipated Spee's move and favoured pursuit. His superiors in London preferred to secure Australian sea lanes while troop convoys were sent to seize German Pacific colonies and to reinforce the European theatre. They kept Patey and the *Australia* patrolling round Fiji, Samoa and New Caledonia while von Spee set course for South America. Spee set a rendezvous with the light cruisers *Dresden* and *Leipzig* at Easter Island in mid-October; they brought in three colliers that had loaded at San Francisco and two prize ships, both loaded with coal. The incessant demand for fuel, and relatively secure inshore anchorages where it could be moved from collier to warship, dominated the strategy of both nations. As he headed east, Spee summoned vital colliers to meet him at Mas Afuera, the westerly unoccupied island in the Juan Fernandez group, fearing the residents of Mas a Tierra (Robinson Crusoe Island) had a working radio. In reality they did not. The coal came from commercial stocks in Chile.[10] Later it transpired the colliers were ex-German merchant ships, lately transferred to Chilean owners. Although they flew the Chilean flag, officers, crew and cargo were German. Under international law, once at war, belligerent merchant vessels could not change their ownership and registration. However, the British Foreign Office, without consulting the Admiralty, allowed the Chileans to 'buy' 25 ships, complete with German crew: the continued operation of these ships enabled von Spee to refuel.[11] Covert use of Chilean islands and a sound disinformation effort allowed Spee to cross the ocean without being located.

There was a certain irony in the indignant *Times* headline of 23 November, 'Juan Fernandez as a Base', but only because the base was 'Coaling German Warships'. The Chileans had tracked the Kosmos Company steamers *Negada* and *Luxor*, but failed to stop them clearing port. These two ships, along with the newly American-registered *Sacramento*, which had been allowed to proceed from San Francisco, supplied von Spee. The *Sacramento's* owners claim to have 'sold' the coal to the Germans looked somewhat threadbare when they landed the crew of the French barque *Valentine*, which had been sunk by the *Dresden* off Mas Afuera. Confronted with clear evidence of German malpractice and local weakness, Chile promised to uphold its neutrality, quickly despatching the armed training ship *General Baquedano* to check the islands for any residual German presence.[12]

Unaware that Spee was heading for Chile with two armoured and five light cruisers, the Admiralty had ordered Rear Admiral Sir Christopher Cradock to sweep the west coast of South America for isolated German cruisers and merchant ships on 16 September. As he stretched north from Cape Horn with his force of two armoured merchant cruisers, one light and one armed, Cradock, expecting light opposition, set a rendezvous for his own colliers at Mas a Tierra Juan Fernandez. Hurrying north to locate the enemy before they could damage British commerce, Cradock detached the old battleship HMS *Canopus* to escort the colliers to their destination. They never arrived. Cradock encountered von Spee's force off the Chilean port of Coronel late on 1 November 1914. Neither admiral had expected to meet the other in full force. Cradock felt that his orders were to fight to the end, despite heavy odds. Von Spee had more ships and heavy guns, plus the advantage of light and well-trained crews. Cradock's flagship HMS *Good Hope* blew up, as did his other armoured cruiser HMS *Monmouth*: there were no survivors. The light cruiser HMS *Glasgow* and the armed merchant cruiser HMS *Otranto* escaped.

Although they won the battle, the Germans had used half of the irreplaceable heavy-calibre ammunition of the armoured cruisers *Scharnhorst* and *Geneisenau*. After the battle von Spee visited Valparaiso, before retiring to Mas Afuera to rendezvous with the armed liner *Prinz Eitrel Friedrich*, yet more colliers and two more coal-laden prizes – one of them belonging to Cradock's force. He departed nine days later, and, after two more refuelling stops, where colliers directed by Berlin and locally won prizes helped fill his bunkers, set course through the Magellan Straits for the Falkland Islands on 6 December.

Working the system

Stunned by the defeat and galvanised by the return to office of Admiral Lord Fisher, the Admiralty despatched a suitable force to resolve the situation. On 4 November their Lordships directed a pincer movement of battlecruisers: HMS *Princess Royal* went to the Caribbean entrance of the Panama Canal, HMS *Invincible* and *Inflexible* set out for Cape Horn, and HMAS *Australia* was belatedly ordered to the west coast of Central America, to link up with British and Japanese ships, check the Panama Canal and then sweep south. *Australia* left Suva on 14 November and arrived on the coast of Mexico 12 days later. Then Admiral Patey took command of the allied squadron with orders to visit the coasts and islands of Central and South America. He began by searching the Galapagos archipelago between 4 and 6 December. The islands were clear, so he headed north-east to inspect the Gulf of Panama and follow the coast south to Guayaquil.

These movements were interrupted on 10 December, just as the *Australia* entered the Bay of Panama, by news that von Spee's force had been almost entirely destroyed by *Invincible, Inflexible* and other ships of Vice Admiral Sir Doveton Sturdee's force off the Falkland Islands two days earlier. With both German armoured cruisers sunk there was no need for British battlecruisers in the Pacific, the South Atlantic or the Caribbean.[13] Only the fugitive light cruiser *Dresden* remained at large, with a few transports and the armed merchant cruiser *Prinz Eitel Friedrich*. Surplus to requirements, Patey was directed to take his flagship through the Canal, but the Canal had been closed to heavy traffic, and new orders were sent on 12 December to make the long passage south through the Straits of Magellan. The route took in three locations where German ships had called, or were expected to call: Callao, San Felix and Valparaiso. At Valparaiso *Australia* was to rendezvous with two ships from Sturdee's force, the armoured cruiser HMS *Kent* and the armed merchant cruiser HMS *Orama*, which were working up the coast. Between calling at Callao on 18 December and reaching Valparaiso on 26 December, *Australia* stopped at San Felix. The inspection reflected more than a century of interest in these islands, dating back to James Colnett's visit. With *Australia* heading south, the Admiralty recalled Admiral Sturdee's battlecruisers, just as HMS *Inflexible* set a course for Juan Fernandez, 'which the Germans had been using so freely as a rendezvous'.[14]

After making a powerful impression on those who retained any lingering German sympathies, *Australia* left Valparaiso on 27 December, stopped off at Coronel to lay a wreath at the battlefield the following day, and entered the Magellan Straits on 31 December. After coaling at the Falklands, *Australia* captured the 5,000-tonne German supply ship *Eleonore Woermann*, which had been attempting to link up with the *Dresden*, on 6 January. Superior force, communication dominance and good cruiser work had dismantled German plans for a war on trade.

By the end of the year both Chile and Peru, recognising the extent to which Germany had abused their neutrality, had interned the German colliers, while *Prinz Eitel Friedrich*, waiting for supplies at isolated Easter Island, was obliged to leave the Pacific early in January.[15] That left the last of von Spee's warships, the light cruiser *Dresden*, hiding in the maze of inlets around the Straits of Magellan and Tierra del Fuego, violating the rights of belligerent warships to stop for 24 hours in neutral harbours. By this time the British were intercepting German radio traffic, enabling HMS *Kent* to catch *Dresden* at the rendezvous she had set for her colliers on 7 March. Once again *Dresden* escaped, only to limp into Cumberland Bay on 8 March, her boilers almost burnt out by sustained high-speed running, desperately short of coal, effectively out of ammunition, short of most stores and without any spare boiler tubes. The German ship was barely operational. Under international law the Germans had 24 hours to complete their repairs and provisions before leaving; alternatively, they could accept internment. Captain Ludecke ignored the Chilean authority on the island, the lighthouse keeper, because the Chileans had no means of enforcing their neutrality. He pressed on with boiler repairs, hoping to reach the Chilean naval base at Talcahuano before interning his ship. Ludecke sent coded signals to the Chilean ex-German colliers *Gotha* and *Santa Cordoba* to meet her in the bay on 9 March. The message was intercepted by HMS *Kent*, and relayed to the British light cruiser HMS *Glasgow*, which had a copy of the captured German codebook. While the code was incomplete, requiring a 'key' to decode messages, signals officer Lieutenant Charles Stuart managed to decode enough of the message to locate the enemy on 13 March. Using Stuart's insights, Captain John Luce of HMS *Glasgow* headed for Juan Fernandez with HMS *Kent* and the armed merchant cruiser HMS *Orama* in company.

On the morning of 14 March, *Glasgow* approached Cumberland Bay from the west; the more heavily armed *Kent* came round the eastern end of the island. They found *Dresden* still flying German colours, and getting up steam ready to sail, forewarned by lookouts on the mountain ridge. Anxious to complete his mission, Captain Luce steamed into the bay, and took his time to place the *Glasgow* in a position that ensured any shells that missed the German cruiser would not land on the solitary village of San Juan Bautista. The brief, one-sided battle began at 08.50. *Glasgow* opened fire at a range of 8,400 yards, hitting the stationary *Dresden* with her first salvo. *Kent* followed, and within three minutes Ludecke had hauled down his colours, speciously claiming the ship had already been interned, detonated the forward magazine and sent his crew scrambling ashore. The armed merchant cruiser *Orama* joined in just as Luce ordered the ceasefire. Not all the British shells hit the target; half a dozen unexploded six-inch shells remain buried in the hills behind the *Dresden*'s position. The Germans lost eight dead and 16 wounded; the latter were treated on board the *Orama*, which carried them to Valparaiso. *Dresden* sank an hour later. Her remains lie 60 metres down at the western end of the bay. Captain Luce settled local claims for damages with the lighthouse keeper and departed: 'leaving the islands to the age long loneliness from which they had been so rudely awakened by the limitless spread of the war'.[16] Any loneliness had always been more apparent than real.

After the action in Cumberland Bay, Chile protested both British and German violations of her neutrality. Britain quickly explained that German ships had been using Juan Fernandez as a base between September 1914 and March 1915, sortieing to capture and sink British and French merchant ships, and that, in the absence of any Chilean authorities on shore able to uphold their neutrality, the Royal Navy had a right to enter Chilean waters and destroy the enemy. This argument was accepted by Chile. The Germans ignored the complaint for six months, fatally damaging their case. The German crew were interned on the mainland for the rest of the war, although Wilhelm Canaris, Head of the Abwehr spy organisation in the Second World War, escaped. After the war the German community in Chile erected a memorial to the men who died in the battle; they lie in a plot that overlooks the last anchorage of the *Dresden*, only a few hundred metres from the place where they died.

Once the last German supply ships had been cleared up, peace returned to the South Pacific. It may have seemed to be no more than a minor backwater, briefly fought over – but the reality was very different. Once the last German ships had been destroyed Chilean nitrates flowed to Britain, enabling the allies to make fertiliser and high explosive. The importance of that trade to the allied war effort would be hard to overestimate, while the functioning of the entire global trading sys-tem was a matter of the utmost importance. Britain could not risk the loss of any single segment of that system. Despite the setback at Coronel, the British global system of ships, communications and coal worked: von Spee's ships, and the other German cruisers, had been hunted down and destroyed, allowing the empire to concentrate heavy naval units at home and control every significant oceanic trade route. The world-wide phase of the war was over, but it was not forgotten.

Post-war reflections

In 1918, as the diplomats gathered in Paris to settle the future of Europe, the Admiralty and the Foreign Office took the opportunity to assess ongoing strategic concerns in the South Pacific. They were strikingly well informed, building on the long-standing partnership between naval deployments and the development of navigation, geography and the ocean sciences, which had culminated in the round-the-world expe-dition of HMS *Challenger* in the late 1870s. The expedition took the enduring partnership of state, science and navy to new levels, transform-ing Britain's ability to master the great oceans for trade and strategy. The relevance of such studies to the needs of a unique global mar-itime empire was understood by the academic empire builders of late Victorian Britain.[17] This research, like so much of the British project, would enhance imperial strategic power through knowledge rather than strength. Maritime powers needed to be better informed, more intelli-gent and supremely adept if they were going to compete with larger and more populous continental powers. Victorian Britain exemplified those qualities.

The Admiralty harnessed that intellectual activity during the First World War, the Naval Intelligence Division commissioning handbooks dealing with 50 nations of strategic, economic or political interest. It was no accident that General Editor Henry Newton Dickson, Professor of Geography at Reading University, had worked on the *Challenger* data. Dickson's pre-war career in commercial geography placed him at the heart of the growing link between academic research and strategic needs of the state. His interest in the global distribution of key commodities like wheat and oil, together with the means to move them, dove-tailed perfectly with Admiralty thinking. Dickson had studied under key imperial geographical thinker Sir Halford Mackinder.[18] These con-nections harnessed the scientific foundations laid by the *Challenger* to the contemporary political/strategic imperatives of empire.

The project began in July 1915, with the battle of Cumberland Bay still fresh in the memory of its creator, Director of Naval Intelligence Admiral Reginald 'Blinker' Hall. The project was based at the Royal Geographical Society in Kensington, revealing the hitherto hidden role of the state in a major intelligence organisation that had operated for 80 years conveniently disguised as mere amateurish curiosity. The handbooks, incisive resumes of topography, communications, populations and trade, would facilitate 'the discussion of naval, military, and political problems, as distinct from the examination of the problems themselves'.[19] The key Confidential Handbook for Juan Fernandez and the San Ambrosio–San Félix Islands was printed in time for the Paris Peace Conference.

Linking Juan Fernandez and Mas Afuera with San Félix and San Ambrosio was significant.[20] Long-term British interest, the specifics of the *Dresden* affair and an enduring concern to record and assess every potential oceanic base in a vast ocean, obvious from pre-war research, visits and instructions, gave these isolated, insular fragments a significance far beyond their negligible economic utility. The Admiralty was well aware, even if the printed text did not mention the fact, that von Spee had rendezvoused at Mas Afuera, while Admiral Cradock had planned to base his colliers at Mas a Tierra. These islands were critical to coal-powered strategy in the South Pacific.

Despite 400 years of unchallenged title, the Foreign Office handbook dismissed Chilean sovereignty over the Juan Fernandez group as little more than sentiment, preferring to stress their misgovernment by the Spanish and the Chileans:

> Chilean satisfaction at the possession of these islands would probably be found, if analysed, to be mainly due to national sentiment, which in its turn is derived from their geographical propinquity and their transition from Spanish sovereignty to the dominion of the Republic at the time when its independence was achieved. Mas a Fuera is practically valueless to Chile. It has never been permanently colonised, and is still (1918) without a single inhabitant . . . . The island has no harbour; there is not even a bay or roadstead where a vessel can anchor in security; but, being more than 6,000 ft in altitude it is visible from a great distance in clear weather and serves the navigator as an unerring guide to his position . . . . Mas a Tierra also serves as a sea-mark.

Despite the implication that the islands were badly run and valueless to Chile, the Foreign Office stressed that 'the most natural, just and expedient status' would be for them to remain Chilean. However, the Confidential Handbook made a clear distinction between these islands and 'San Félix and San Ambrosio', which 'are not specifically mentioned in the first article of the Chilean Constitution, in which the boundaries of the Republic are broadly defined. The islands are still without inhabitants, and are rarely visited even by fishermen.' Furthermore, while these islands were isolated and secluded in peacetime,

> It may well be otherwise in time of war, when the belligerents are naval powers. The roadstead of San Félix affords in some respects better anchorage than any at the Juan Fernandez Islands. The holding ground is none of the best at either place, but at San Félix the bottom is more level and the depth more convenient.

Peruvian warships had refuelled at San Felix in 1865, while the possible establishment of a radio transmitter at Mas a Fuera, von Spee's rendezvous, made the advantage of the more distant islands absolute.[21]

The history of the Juan Fernandez group was largely drawn from Vicuña Mackenna's 1883 account *Juan Fernández: historia verdadera*, backed by a useful bibliography of British, American and more recent Chilean publications, among which the discrete mention of volume III of the Admiralty's own *South American Pilot* should not be missed.[22] It sat somewhat incongruously alongside the first English publication by Swedish botanist Carl Skottsberg, the analyst of the island's unique ecosystem.[23] Clearly the libraries of the Royal Geographical Society and the Admiralty Hydrographic Office were well equipped. The authors doubted Mackenna's assertion that Juan Fernandez had any strategic value for the Chilean Navy.

> Even if Chile should go to the expense of fortifying Más-á-Tierra – which is not in the least likely – this would not hinder an enemy ship from coaling at San Félix, though the latter affords no fresh water or provisions.

The threat that the Admiralty envisaged became clear as the text wound to a conclusion. Maximilian von Spee's coal-hungry cruisers were things of the past; the new danger came from large U-boats, stretching around the world to attack the shipping lanes linking Britain to Australasia:

> San Félix is also excellently adapted for a temporary base or depot for submarine vessels' stores – petrol, provisions, tanks or barrels of fresh

water, even projectiles. Petrol and few light stores might be landed at San Ambrosio in fine weather, and would be less easy of discovery by an enemy searcher than at San Félix.[24]

The published version of 1920 studiously avoided the vexed issues of sovereignty and title, simply reprinting the relevant passage of the Chilean Constitution, in Spanish and English, and, despite an editorial claim to be 'substantially as they were issued' for official use, San Félix and San Ambrosio had been entirely excised. While the commercial irrelevance of these two barren specks of land might explain the decision, the cut had a deeper purpose. The Admiralty was remarkably well informed about this group of barren islands, and the many uses to which they had been put. Passages deprecating the merits of Spanish and Chilean rule remained, although without the link to questions of sovereignty. To emphasise the distinct objectives of the two texts, the San Ambrosio group was only mentioned once in the published edition, as the only other place where the otherwise unique Juan Fernandez crayfish *Palinurus frontalis* could be found.[25] The quality of realism was emphasised by the conspicuous passage dealing with the sinking of the *Dresden*. While His Majesty's Government made a full and unreserved apology for breaching Chilean neutrality, there was another meaning to be drawn from the insertion of a Foreign Office form of words. If a British naval officer faced a similar dilemma in future he should act first, and get the Foreign Office to clear up any diplomatic fall-out later. The Admiralty Handbook exploited a wide range of sources to address the practical concerns of naval officers and diplomats: location, utility, sovereignty and resource. The next Royal Navy warships to arrive in Cumberland Bay would know that the island was Chilean territory and dirt poor; there were few resources, apart from fish. Although the next world war did not trouble the region, another, more detailed Admiralty Handbook on the Pacific Islands was produced just in case.[26]

After 1918, Britain's commanding position in the South Pacific slowly ebbed; the loss of British capital in the world war, the Great Depression and the Second World War completed the destruction of a once dominant influence. Unable to lend large sums to developing economies like Chile, Britain lost market share to the United States, an industrial heavyweight and hemispheric power. The government offered little support as market conditions turned against British interests. By contrast, the Royal Navy has retained a major presence in Chile: fully half the modern Chilean Navy consists of second-hand British frigates, while Chilean naval officers pride themselves on their British connections, and handle their ships with seamanship and skill reflecting two centuries of contact.

Conclusion

Britain entered the First World War prepared to wage global economic war, relying on naval might, communications dominance and a world-wide network of coaling stations to track and destroy German warships and merchant vessels, while seizing their overseas bases and territories. Despite a few setbacks, notably at Coronel, the system worked well, and with the sinking of the *Dresden* in March 1915 the First World War came to an end. This enabled the Entente to access and exploit colonial manpower, global food stocks, raw materials and manufactured goods to win a massive European conflict.

Notes

1. A.D. Lambert, 'Wirtschaftliche Macht, technologischer Vorsprung und Imperiale Stärke: GrossBritannien als einzigartige globale Macht: 1860 bis 1890', in M. Epkenhans and G.P. Gross (eds), *Das Militär und der Aufbruch die Moderne 1860 bis 1890* (Munich, 2003).
2. In contrast, the official history projects of Fayle, Hurd and Corbett provided analytical narratives of the commerce war, with little or no reference to the main lines of development across the 19th century.
3. This relationship has been studied in the case of the larger mail steamship companies Cunard, Royal Mail and P&O; see F. Harcourt, *Flagships of Imperialism: The P&O Company and the Politics of Empire From Its Origins to 1867* (Manchester University Press, 2006) for a case study. Founded by William Wheelwright in London in 1838, the company began operations in 1840, commissioning the steam ships *Chile* and *Peru* to carry mail. Early ports of call were Valparaíso, Coquimbo, Huasco, Copiapó, Cobija, Iquique, Arica, Islay, Pisco and Callao. In 1846 the company expanded its routes to include Huanchaco, Lambayeque, Paita, Guayaquil, Buenaventura and Panama City. In 1852 the company gained a contract for British government mail to posts in western South America. Two direct routes were established round Cape Horn – Liverpool to Callao in 1868 and London to Sydney in 1877. In 1905 the London–Sydney route was sold to the Royal Mail Steam Packet Company, which purchased the entire company in 1910.
4. W. Johnston, W.G.P. Rawling, R.H. Gimblett and J. MacFarlene, *The Seabound Coast: The Official History of the Royal Canadian Navy, 1867–1939 volume I* (Toronto: Dundurn Press, 2010), pp. 15–71.
5. Johnston et al. & 100–200 for the failure to maintain Esquimault after the transfer from British control.
6. J.T. Sumida s*In Defence of Naval Supremacy: Finance, Technology, and British Naval Policy 1889–1914* (London: Allen & Unwin, 1990).

7. S. Cobb, *Preparing for Blockade 1885–1914 Naval Contingency for Economic Warfare* (Aldershot: Ashgate Press, 2013). A.D. Lambert, 'The Naval War Course, Some Principles of Maritime Strategy and the Origins of the "British Way in Warfare"', in K. Neilson and G. Kennedy (eds.), *The British Way in Warfare: Power and the International System, 1856–195L: Essays in Honour of David French* (Farnham: Ashgate, 2010), pp. 219–256.
8. R. Osborne, H. Spong, & T. Grover, *Armed Merchant Cruisers: 1878–1945* (Faversham, World Ship Society Ltd, 2007).
9. There is a superb map in vol. I of German official history of the cruiser war that makes this absolutely clear. It displays every known cable and wireless station around the world, along with ownership, range, capacity and connections. The British cable relay on Fanning Island, the link between Canada and Australia, was cut by SMS *Nurnberg* on 6–8 September 1914. N. Hewitt, *The Kaiser's Pirates: Hunting Germany's Raiding Cruisers 1914–15* (Barnsley: Pen & Sword, 2013), p. 90.
10. J.S. Corbett, *Naval Operations vol. I* (London: Longman, 1920), pp. 344–345, 355, 406.
11. N. Lambert, *Planning Armageddon* (London: Harvard University Press, 2012), p. 248.
12. *The Times* 23 and 25 November 1914.
13. Battle cruisers had been built with the speed and firepower to destroy armoured cruisers.
14. Corbett I, pp. 365–366, 409, 435: Corbett II, p. 240.
15. A.W. Jose, *The Royal Australian Navy: The Official History of Australia in the War of 1914–1918 vol. IX* (Sydney: Angus & Robertson, 1928), pp. 124–128, 135, 262–263; D. Stevens, *The Royal Australian Navy* (Melbourne: Oxford UP, 2001), pp. 36–37. Corbett II, pp. 243–245. Hewitt, pp. 176–178, for the career of the *Prinz Eitel Friedrich.*
16. *Orama* 13,000 ton 18 knot Oriental Steam Navigation Company ship built 1911, armed with 8 six inch guns. Sunk by a U-boat 10.10.1917. Osborne, Spong and Grover, pp. 45–46, 125: quote from Corbett II, pp. 248–251.
17. For the *Challenger* and her legacy see: M. Deacon, *Scientists and the Sea: A Study of Marine Science* (London: Academic Press, 1971), pp. 306–366; H. Rozwadowski, *Fathoming the Ocean: The Discovery of the Deep Sea* (Cambridge, MA: Belknap Press, 2005), p. 28; E. Linklater, *The Voyage of the Challenger* (London: John Murray, 1972), pp. 243–249; J.Y. Buchanan, H.N. Moseley, J. Murray and T.H. Tizard, *The Report of the Scientific Results of the Exploring Voyage of HMS Challenger During the Years 1873–1876* (50 volumes were published between 1885 and 1895. The *Narrative* formed Volume 1, and even that came in two parts); Lord George Campbell, *Log Letters From the Challenger* (London: Macmillan, 1877); H.N. Moseley, *Notes by a Naturalist on HMS Challenger* (London: John Murray, 1892), pp. 466–471.
18. T.W. Freeman, *A History of Modern British Geography* (London: Longman, 1980), pp. 19–20, 56, 67, 186.
19. Rear Admiral John Godfrey (Director of Naval Intelligence, 1942): H. Clout, and C. Gosme, 'The Naval Intelligence Handbooks: A Monument in Geographical Writing', *Progress in Human Geography,* Vol. 27, No. 2 (2003), pp. 153–173 at p. 155.

20. FO Handbook 'prepared for the Peace Conference' no. 141b. June 1919: FO 373/7/14 Editorial Note.
21. FO 373/7/14 no.141b. pp. 20–22, a critical passage missing from the 1920 publication and p. 23.
22. *Juan Fernandez no. 143.* 1920, pp. 33–60, bibliography at pp. 59–60. 1,000 printed September 1920.
23. Skottsberg's article published in the American *Geographical Review* May 1918, pp. 363–383.
24. FO 373/7/14 no.141b, pp. 22–24.
25. *Juan Fernandez*, 1920 Published Handbook, p. 56.
26. *Pacific Islands: Volume II Eastern Pacific.* B.R. 519 B (Restricted) Geographical Handbook Series. November 1943, p. 46.

13
Attrition: How the War Was Fought and Won

William Philpott

It is a historical truism that the First World War was a war of attrition. Yet few, then and now, actually appreciated exactly what a war of attrition is, and what it meant for the armies and societies that fought one. Attrition is, perhaps, the other strategy of the Great War: the strategy that was engaged and worked by both coalitions after military stalemate set in, the process by which the Entente Powers engaged and defeated the Central Powers. Someone who probably did understand was Herbert Asquith, Britain's prime minister until December 1916 and the man responsible for organising Britain's war effort as the empire engaged with this novel and unexpected war of attrition. When he visited the Somme front in summer 1916, Asquith

> harped on a great deal on the fact that what the British public wanted to hear of was geographical gains of towns and territory, on a large scale, and large bags of prisoners; and that a successful fight that only involved an advance of a couple of thousand yards and the slaughter of a large number of Germans did not appeal to them. They wanted something tangible.[1]

Baldly stated by Britain's prime minister, the 'slaughter of a large number of Germans' was the central principle of attrition, one to which Lord Kitchener and Sir Douglas Haig had fully committed Britain's armies.

The problem with such a strategy, then and now, was that it involved the reciprocal 'sacrifice' of a large, and frequently greater, number of Englishmen (and of any others who took on the tactically effective German army). At some point during or after the war – perhaps during the Somme offensive itself, and certainly once disillusionment with the war set in in the late 1920s – that 'sacrifice' became 'slaughter' in its own right. The fact that, for the British army at least, for most of the war all this killing took place within a few thousand muddy yards of contested trenches no doubt contributed to growing moral outrage against attrition (which at that point was only just getting under way in earnest), as Asquith opined. There were certainly a few who protested the reciprocal slaughter in which Britain first engaged in earnest on the Somme.[2] Winston Churchill (then on the backbenches) and David Lloyd George (then Minister of War and soon to replace Asquith as prime minster) were prominent critics of the army leadership's strategy, at the time and in their later war memoirs. Their narratives became the prevailing ones (by a process that it is not possible to explain here),[3] their judgements the moral ones. Lloyd George's dismissal of Allied strategy, as enshrined in his influential yet tendentious *War Memoirs*, has ever since left attrition and those who conducted it under a shadow. He wrote in the 1930s that from 1914 to 1916 'a war of attrition was substituted for a war of intelligence', a generalisation that few would have doubted: it was echoed in the most influential history of the war, Basil Liddell Hart's *The Real War*, and added strategic substance to Churchill's earlier operational critique, 'The Blood Test'.[4] For Lloyd George (and others) intelligent strategy involved immediate mobilisation of national resources (which, as Britain found, actually took two years at least from a standing start) and attacking the supposed weak points of the Central Powers in the east and south-east.[5] (Such a strategy also seemed to deny the constraints of coalition as well as geographical, logistical and military realities. Whether Britain's Russian, Serbian, Italian and Rumanian allies – or the French for that matter – would have concurred that these were weak points was never adequately investigated, while the fact that, if threatened, Germany, which possessed the advantage of interior lines of communication, was quite capable of making them strong seemed of no account.)

The off-the-cuff judgements of a disgruntled statesman about what might have been (or, more precisely, what he argued at the time should have been) still obscure the reality and necessity of full national mobilisation and prolonged attrition to decide a war between industrialised imperial coalitions. Lloyd George and Churchill were themselves central architects of the strategy of attrition as it developed in 1915, and its mechanics from 1916 and 1917. Lloyd George was Chancellor of the Exchequer, then Minister of Munitions and of War, before becoming prime minister, during which time he found the money, munitions and men for the coalition strategy that Asquith and Kitchener (his predecessor as Minister of War) had engaged. Churchill took on the munitions

portfolio in Lloyd George's ministry in July 1917, keeping the army supplied as it engaged with and wore down the German army. The fact that
attrition's most trenchant critics are deeply implicated in its engagement
and action suggests that it was all-pervading and central to the strategic
conduct of the war. But they inhibited its workings as well as giving
it a bad press. Doubting, as Brock Millman has persuasively argued,
that Britain and her allies could ever win such a war,[6] Lloyd George,
who only had to operate effectively the British war machine mobilised
under Asquith and Kitchener's leadership, did much after he became
prime minister to undermine the effectiveness of the strategy of attrition to which it was geared. Lloyd George was like the British public:
he wanted tangible victories. Vienna, Jerusalem, Ostend and Zeebrugge
were dangled before him during 1917, distracting him from the fact that
all would fall once the enemy's armies were defeated. He deprecated,
as Lieutenant-General Sir Henry Wilson was advocating just before he
became prime minister, 'two Sommes at once' to destroy the German
army once and for all.[7] Lloyd George seemed to grasp the logic of attrition, but to despair of its practicality. After hearing Wilson's proposal,
the general recorded,

> He horrified me by saying 'we shall never beat the Boches'. I said,
> but what nonsense, because our side could produce far more men
> than the Boches. He did not agree. He said that with Bulgaria and
> Turkey and Poland the Boches would outnumber us – but this in my
> judgment is absurd.[8]

At the time Lloyd George was complaining that even after the Somme
the enemy 'had in his occupation more territory than ever before, and
he still had some four million of reserves... How then, Mr Lloyd George
asked, is the war to be brought to an end?'[9] This is a note of despair,
rather than a recognition that potentially another four million Germans
had to be slaughtered and a comparable number of Allied troops sacrificed to end the war. Indeed, Lloyd George's lengthy critique of strategy
at the end of 1916 sets out all the problems of fighting such a war
while being fanciful in its solutions.[10] Given that the Central Powers
had occupied Belgium, Serbia, Rumania and parts of Russia and France
by this point without defeating their field armies or forcing them or
their allies to the peace table, why would the defeat and occupation of
Bulgaria or Turkey that Lloyd George was pressing for bring Germany to
terms? But certainly, at the end of 1916, Lloyd George and others were

unhappy, because the reality of attrition was apparent after the Somme and Verdun, and because there was no end in sight.

> What is our policy? Has anyone mapped out a road to victory?...We must have a definite plan. I have only heard of one. People talk of hammering, and of a war of attrition. The success of hammering depends entirely upon whether you are making a greater impression on the barrier or the hammer. The success of a war of attrition depends upon the time it takes, and who can last out the longest.[11]

In that judgement Lloyd George was correct, but he was impatient and unrealistic about what was possible in a war with mass mobilisation on both sides.

The pervading perception of strategic attrition was formed in the middle of the war, when it was operating but had not yet delivered, and was being defined by those notoriously long and gruelling battles, Verdun and the Somme, both of which were ultimately successes for Allied arms. Stepping away from the trenches to look down on the organisation of societies for war, their strategies and their outcomes, allows attrition as a principle for conducting the war successfully to be unpicked from attrition as a military process, something that statesmen had trouble with while it was ongoing. It was certainly a slow-working, gradual process. Wilson assessed the military balance at the turn of 1917: 'The last day of a year of indecisive fighting. Verdun, Somme, Greece and Rumania all indecisive, both sides claiming victory; on the whole victory inclining to us, and the final decision brought nearer.' If the Germans seemed to be able to take countries while the Allied armies struggled to take villages, nevertheless, come 1917 when the Allies' war machines were fully mobilised and engaged, the war would be won, and, indeed, was already being decided, as Sir Douglas Haig's director of intelligence, Brigadier-General John Charteris, had indicated as the Somme offensive began, by 'fighting primarily to wear down the German armies and the German nation...it will be slow and costly'.[12] Notwithstanding Lloyd George's hand-wringing, by the end of 1916 Germans were finally being killed at such a rate that an attritional victory was in the Allies' grasp.

*   *   *

The war of attrition ensued after quick-victory strategies that were engaged in 1914 had failed. Germany and France–Russia sought a rapid annihilation of the enemy's armies on land. Britain expected but signally failed to deploy crushing economic warfare.[13] Attrition was, as Carter Malkassian identifies, 'in conventional warfare...the major alternative to the dominant strategy of seeking a decisive battle', which suggests that it was a default option rather than a pre-determined choice.[14] In pre-war strategic controversies in Germany, for example, attrition was represented as the unwelcome alternative to a strategy of annihilation, something which no army (or nation) wanted in the next war because of its potentially disastrous social and economic consequences.[15] This helps to explain why 1914's unrealistic war plans were geared to avoiding attrition by smashing the enemy's whole army quickly. But there is irony in the fact that, while these were the most costly campaigns of the war, 1914's early battles showed that conscription-raised multi-million-man mass armies backed by the resources of industrial capitalist societies could not be annihilated, however huge the encounter battles.

Yet there were many, foremost among them German commander-in-chief Erich von Falkenhayn and Britain's new Secretary of State of War, Lord Kitchener, who appreciated the probable form that a Great Power conflict would take.[16] Attritional warfare presented new strategic challenges. Essentially, victory in a war of attrition necessitated both outlasting and outfighting the enemy. This entailed commitment to 'a gradual and piecemeal process of destroying an enemy's military capability',[17] and acceptance that with the enemy applying the same strategic logic a reciprocal sacrifice was inevitable.

Attrition has deeper levels of complexity. An effective attritional strategy also involved applying resources efficiently to degrade those of the enemy, as well as the integration of 'positive' elements – the mobilisation of national and Allied resources: men (and women), industrial and financial capacity, and hearts and minds – with 'negative' aspects – attacking and destroying adversaries' manpower, materiel, economic stability and morale. Inevitably there was great scope for Clausewitzian friction in such an all-encompassing strategy, but, at the same time, the more closely a national or alliance war effort could approach the 'absolute', or 'total', the greater was the potential for final victory. This entailed a policy of 'all or nothing', in this instance fighting 'until the military domination of Prussia is wholly and finally destroyed', as William Robertson, Britain's Chief of the Imperial General Staff in November 1916, defined it,[18] rather than a 'limited' war approach predicated on winning battles for political ends or to secure a favourable peace, which seemed to be Lloyd George's unshakeable conception of proper strategy. Resilience, as demonstrated by armies and societies in

1914, was the third factor in attrition. Defined by Robertson as 'the staying power in men',[19] resilience also involved the staying power in economic and social strength, as well as patriotic commitment to the war. This would determine how long the war would last.

It would take a while for the principle of attrition to become established and accepted: it was clearly the guiding strategic concept by 1916, and Kitchener, Falkenhayn and French commander-in-chief Joseph Joffre had identified it as the key to victory much earlier on. Thus, it is associated with military commanders and their costly land campaigns, the necessary sacrifice that post-war reflection transmuted into 'futile slaughter'. In fact, attrition was the unifying principle of the strategic conduct of the war as a whole, not simply the method of its notorious land campaigns. These together constituted one 'front' on which the war was waged, supported by activity on four other fronts: the home front, the maritime war, the diplomatic contest, and a 'united front', the building and sustaining of coalitions.[20] The implementation and success of military attrition were facilitated by home front mobilisation, a slow, fractious process. Robertson complained towards the end of 1916, the first, faltering full year of military attrition, 'We cannot hope for a conclusion in our favour unless and until we make a full and appropriate use of all our resources.' He suggested a number of steps were essential: 'Have a full day's work from every man and woman. Make all possible use of foreign labour. Check present waste and extravagance in national life. Become as self-supporting as possible. Clearly explain to the nation the grave nature of the task in front of us.' He also advocated a more united and coordinated Allied war effort.[21] Even half way through the war, attrition was still getting into its stride.

Operational attrition was limited in its effectiveness and impact while mobilisation was still ongoing. The perception persists that operational attrition was an unwanted, if necessary, consequence of the inability to deliver on the alternative – annihilation – which seemed to be the reality in most First World War offensives. Carter Malkasian repeats the established mantra (developed by Churchill, Lloyd George and others) that attritional battles resulted from the failure of over-ambitious attempts to 'break through' and manoeuvre rather than being a central element of operational and strategic thinking: 'attrition...was less a deliberate operational strategy than the result of failed attempts at a decisive breakthrough'. Therefore, 'attrition, being gradual and indecisive, was ineffective in attaining the total aims of war'.[22] This is to misrepresent attrition as a fault in one or more campaigns, rather than the guiding principle of all.

It is certainly the case that armies' tactical and operational doctrines and systems took time to adapt to positional warfare, and to deliver attrition effectively. This required a shift from manpower to materiel-intensive offensive operations, but these were starting to become effective during 1916. Witness, for example, the operational sophistication and success of the French and Russian Armies in summer and autumn 1916, compared with 1915: the British and Italian Armies still lagged behind.[23] This time lag, during which the armies could not sit idle, led to a chaotic, unproductive, costly first year of warfare, on which perceptions of attrition's utility are usually grounded. But all armies grasped the fundamentals of operating on the fortified attritional battlefield by mid- to late 1916, even if the time lag in the industrial production cycle meant that their resources were only now catching up with commanders' more restrained operational ambitions. It should be acknowledged, however, that greater military effectiveness in itself is not going to reduce casualties in an attritional war in which final victory is a concomitant of mutual destruction, although it does make the attritional process more efficient. Statistics collated by François Cailletau suggest that the materiel-intensive combined-arms tactics developed after 1915 redressed the advantage the defence had over the offence significantly during the course of the war. While the defender always enjoyed an absolute advantage, whereas in 1915 the British and French Armies suffered two casualties to each German, that ratio was reduced to less than 1.2 to 1 by 1918.[24]

Moreover, all armies' pre-war doctrines accepted there was an attritional phase inherent in battle and warfare before the defeat of the enemy would come about: manoeuvre for position, wearing-out, the decisive blow, then exploitation, as the British army's doctrine distinguished the phases of combat.[25] 1914's campaigns proved that all these could not be conflated into one vast theatre-wide decisive battle, but would have to be played out in a series of campaigns. The early campaigns were in practice the manoeuvre for position; in which the Germans triumphed, establishing themselves in strong defensive entrenchments in French and Belgian territory, while successfully defending their own from Russia. Thereafter the war became a prolonged siege. How long it would last was impossible to predict, but the nature of the conflict was manifest in the first battle after manoeuvre ceased, the First Battle of Ypres. While on a far smaller scale than later Western Front battles, this six-week back-and-forth struggle had all the characteristics of later fights. Armies deployed along static lines cycled men and materiel into the fight in an attempt to break each other.

Although the Germans had a territorial objective – to break through to the Channel ports – and therefore conducted a costly 'manoeuvre' battle, the battle would have been decided by attrition. It was necessary to wear out the reserves the enemy could bring up to oppose any breakthrough before such territorial objectives could be pursued. As it turned out, the scale of the battle was too small and too short to wear down the enemy's forces adequately to achieve a decision, even after the cumulative losses of earlier battles. Yet the mutual scratching about for fresh reserves – cavalry formations and the first British territorial battalions were thrown into the line, while the German army notoriously deployed half-trained wartime volunteers at Langemarck – was not sufficient to force a decision. Dynamic equilibrium had been established on the Western Front. While more mobile, the situation on the Eastern Front also reflected an operational stalemate between exhausted Russian and German–Austrian armies.

For three years thereafter, as Germany's wartime martial law identified, a 'state of siege' of the Central Powers persisted, localised shifts in the front lines notwithstanding. Attritional operations would have to be prolonged and on a far greater scale to produce a decision (and, as it turned out, far greater and more prolonged than anyone anticipated at the start of 1915). This would be facilitated by fuller military and home front mobilisation, which occupied the belligerents through 1915 and into 1916. It should be noted that, even as armies engaged in long battles that were designed to wear them down, they were until 1917 deploying newly raised divisions. What the First Battle of Ypres revealed – at least to those clever enough to study it – was that the Clausewitzian centre of gravity of battle (and, by implication, the war) was the ability to furnish military reserves in a timely manner. This principle operated at all levels of warfare. Tactically, field commanders had the resources and the ability to commit local reserves to counterattack the enemy, thereby maintaining battlefront equilibrium. This was a product of the entrenched battlefield as much as anything, which allowed local reserves to be kept close at hand in relative safety for the moment when an enemy attack had to be contained and repulsed. This fundamental tactical principle operated however much defensive and offensive firepower that made the battles themselves more fluid and productive developed during the seasons of positional warfare. As Allied generalissimo Ferdinand Foch pointed out calmly as German forces buffeted the Allied lines in 1918, 'the waves diminish' as fresh reserves are deployed against tiring troops[26]: he learned this when managing the defence of Ypres in 1914. At the operational level of war, a reserve of uncommitted forces (divisions and army corps) was maintained by the theatre commander either to mount an offensive or to meet one. Having fresh reserves in hand to respond to an enemy offensive prevented the breaking of the line, and allowed operational flexibility. Germany's commanders proved skilled in using interior lines to shift operational reserves from front to front, balancing the greater coordination of Allied offensive operations on the individual fronts as the war went on. At the strategic level of war, training and deploying annual contingents of reserves to sustain the field army (and balancing military manpower demands with other calls on manpower – and womanpower – for home front production and the war at sea) determined the development and outcome of the war. Attrition was engaged against the enemy's resources on all three levels by both sides.

The principle of attrition was recognised at the beginning of 1915, in the strategic summaries drawn up by Major-General Sir Charles Callwell (director of military operations in the War Office) and Joffre's staff at *Grand Quartier Général* (French military headquarters). These were rather crude and inaccurate assessments of the existing fighting power and capacity to raise reserves of the two rival alliances. What they got wrong was their assumption that the balance of manpower and materiel would lead to an Allied victory within the year: the delusion that the war would be over quickly persisted for some months even after stalemate had set in, even while the allies were mobilising for a long war of attrition. But these papers do indicate that the exhaustion of enemy manpower was identified as the primary strategic objective at a very early point: how this could be achieved operationally had yet to be determined. Erich von Falkenhayn, who became German commander-in-chief in autumn 1914, had always anticipated a war of attrition. Falkenhayn had also identified that in a long war the balance of manpower and resources was not in Germany's favour. In the coming months he reorganised forces and tapped Germany's un-mobilised manpower reserves to maximise his army's size and staying power – intensifying German mobilisation made the Allies' task more protracted and difficult, since the army they had to destroy was getting bigger into 1916 despite casualties already inflicted on it – and adopted an 'inferiority strategy' aimed at the willpower and resources of the allies. As Malkasian suggests, attrition is an appropriate strategy for a power with inferior resources, seeking to undermine the enemy's resolve to fight on and force a peace of exhaustion.[27] Essentially, Falkenhayn accepted that Germany could not win an outright victory against a greatly superior coalition. Falkenhayn's policy was, therefore, designed to grind down the Allies in the field to the point where they realised that the cost of winning was too much and they would make a compromise peace, and it culminated in the most prolonged attritional battle against French manpower and morale, Verdun.[28]

Unfortunately for Falkenhayn and for Germany, the operational dynamics of the eastern theatre suggested that a strategy of annihilation remained viable. In 1915 Hindenburg and Ludendorff pushed the Russians out of Poland with heavy losses. To that extent, attrition on a war-wide basis worked in Germany's favour in 1915 (although in that year her main ally Austria-Hungary suffered heavy losses to the Russians and extra strain as Italy opened a new front, shifting the balance of resources further in the Allies' favour). But Russia, although worn down, was far from broken by such battles. Germany's Eastern Front leaders failed to appreciate that temporarily knocking one army out of the enemy's order of battle, or taking territory, was not decisive as long as there were operational reserves to re-establish the front and strategic reserves left to rebuild defeated armies. Russia's resurgence in 1916 demonstrated this. Also in Germany's favour in 1915 was the fact that the Allies had not yet woken up to the operational consequences of attrition. Whether it was throwing manpower blithely at German defences in France with inadequate materiel support, as France (and Britain to a more limited extent) did; sacrificing men without sufficient weapons to check a German attack, as Russia did in Poland; or sending poorly resourced and insufficient troops against Turkey, as Britain did, Allied strategy in 1915 was profligate, ill coordinated and counter-productive. The year's early and overoptimistic statistical assessments may have been partly at fault, but amateur strategy played a significant role in Germany's largely retaining the strategic initiative in 1915, even if she won little long-term advantage from this.

It took a while for statesmen to grasp the import of the war in which they had engaged their nations. While Asquith could advise Sir John French, commander-in-chief in France, when they met on 2 June 1915 that the Cabinet considered attrition to be the dominant strategic principle at that point in the war, what that entailed was as yet unclear.[29] David French has suggested that at this point in the war it was little more than Kitchener's idea that, pending the readiness of his new armies, it was a policy of active defence in the west to hold and wear down German forces, keeping them from the Eastern Front.[30] But Lord Curzon (Lord President of the Council) identified on 21 July that 'the war seems to me to be resolving itself into a question of killing Germans', with the inevitable concomitant of conscription.[31] He was not alone in waking up to the nature and potential consequences of attritional warfare.

Kitchener alone among British statesmen had perceived from the start that in the coming war Germany would fight 'to the last breath and the last horse'. It was, therefore, incumbent on the Allies to be prepared to do the same, and he intended 'to wage war on a great scale'.[32] Was he mobilising British men (and horses) both to fight the war, and, as David French suggested, to win the peace after his allies had fought themselves to a standstill in the war of attrition with Germany?[33] His later statements that the real war would only begin after two years, when Britain was fully mobilised and her troops were at the front, suggest that he appreciated that the new armies were raised to be sacrificed for ultimate victory, not simply to get one over on weakened allies in a world that had reverted to pre-war Great Power rivalries. Kitchener himself was undoubtedly learning from the war as it developed, and came better to appreciate what it entailed. Hence his conversion to supporting conscription, and opposition to the half-measure strategy of 'business as usual' advocated by some Cabinet colleagues. Attrition changed its shape, or at least its process. On 21 January 1916 Kitchener confirmed to Cabinet critics of the costly 'breakthrough' operations of 1915 (Lloyd George prominent among them) that 'he did not intend to make another heavy attack in France, but merely to pursue an intensified policy of attrition in order to use up the German reserves'.[34] The new armies' fateful encounter with the Imperial German army on the Somme was predestined.

* * *

Both sides engaged in strategic–operational attrition in the 1916 campaign. Falkenhayn planned to use local material predominance to bleed the French army white at Verdun, breaking the fighting power and will to fight on of one of his adversaries, while not weakening Germany's own forces excessively. Joffre was preparing to engage in his attritional counter-strike, the General Allied Offensive. As he was to rationalise it in his war memoirs, perhaps more cogently than he saw it at the time,

> The object we had in view was victory, and since the Germans had undertaken a war of attrition, it was for us on our side to conduct it with due economy, and turn the situation to our advantage by making attacks only when we could profitably assume the role of attackers. In this way we would cause a melting of the enemy's reserves and reduce his front to nothing more than a thin barrier

which, if we economized our own reserves, could be broken down by the combined blows of the Allies, and permit the passage of our victorious battalions. In this game it was certain that we would also suffer wastage, but the enemy would be worn down; the whole question lay in conducting our affairs with such wisdom as to enable us to last longer than he did. In war it is the final battalions that bring victory.[35]

This seems a rather stark, *post facto*, self-exculpatory summation. Yet, in practice, by 1916 Joffre's concept of attrition had evolved in response to the actual military circumstances of the war. Joffre certainly appreciated that it was a war of resources and manpower, but it took him two years to grasp that the latter was more precious than the former. His hastiness to fight and destroy the German army was perhaps over-determined by political pressures: to that extent, there is some justification in Churchill's criticism of the 'blood test' paid by Joffre's armies in the early campaigns of the war.

For the 1916 campaign he had adopted attrition concerted on all fronts as his strategic rationale. He secured Allied agreement in principle at the Chantilly Conference in early December 1915, although coordinating the General Allied Offensive in practice proved far from straightforward. The elusive strategic objective of 1916's campaign and its Anglo-French component, the Somme offensive, is to be found in the Allied plan discussed at Chantilly, and it was simple: 'the destruction of the German and Austrian armies'.[36] Politicians would endorse this objective – if with misgivings – in spring 1916.[37]

How the Allied armies might achieve this on the battlefield was becoming clearer:

> In our joint offensive on the Somme ... *we can envisage knocking out the German army on the Western Front, or at least an important part of their forces* [Haig's emphasis].
>
> ... But our experience of previous attacks indicates that, to drive the enemy from his prepared positions, we have to conduct a long drawn out battle, the final form of which it is impossible to predict.
>
> ... The plan for exploiting our success is essentially a concomitant of the level of attrition of the enemy and their dispositions, as well as our own reserves when we attain the last German position.[38]

Douglas Haig, to whom this summation was addressed, unfortunately based his operational planning on the erroneous assumption that the Battle of Verdun had largely achieved the attrition to which Joffre referred, and that his armies could be used to force the decision.[39]

This suggests that a gap existed between attrition as a strategic objective and an operational process in the early campaigns of the war, which had to be closed before attrition became effective for achieving the ends of strategy. That gap was closed during and after the Somme campaign, largely thanks to Foch's reconceptualisation of the operational level of war. Foch was the one general who rose up the operational levels of command, from army corps in 1914 to supreme command in 1918. A pre-war military theorist and teacher at the French staff college, he also possessed the theoretical understanding of war that allowed him to adapt and apply appropriate doctrine to '*la guerre actuelle*', as he termed it. How to grind down mass armies steadily and conclusively was, he identified, the task at hand: '*de quoi s'agit il*' was another of his favourite aphorisms. In 1914 Foch controlled and deployed the operational reserves provided by Joffre at the First Battle of Ypres, grasping the dynamics of the attritional battlefield. During 1915 he conducted early attritional offensives in Artois and grasped the tactical principles of attrition, judging that they needed to be carefully managed and controlled.[40] As Maxime Weygand, his chief of staff, later summarised it:

> Thus, after the attacks of May 1915 in Artois in which for the first time several lines of enemy trenches were captured, from which some concluded it was possible to secure a breakthrough and to exploit it by pushing reserves into open country, General Foch determined to show, logically, that such a conception was unrealisable on the Western Front. Although his ideas were not adopted, in the following years he continued to demonstrate the futility of such efforts, always in the same sense. At the same time, because the Marshal was essentially a builder, he forged an offensive system appropriate to the problem posed by the war: how to beat an enemy of equal strength face-to-face on a fortified front it was impossible to outflank.[41]

Effectively, warfare was transmuting into a systematic industrial process, dominated by machinery and governed by the rhythms imposed by logistical and command processes, which might be identified as modern 'operational science'. This was the 'scientific battle', a controlled, methodical engagement with the enemy's defences and forces to defeat them in the positions they held rather than pursing the chimera of breakthrough and exploitation in mobile warfare. Summing up his Artois offensives in November 1915, Foch wrote:

> Against certain particularly strong positions... persistent actions, sustained until the enemy's will is broken, ought to succeed. Not requiring large numbers of infantry, they are above all costly in artillery munitions; all the same such a form of attack should not be rejected. They should find a place in our methods.[42]

Conceptualising the system was one thing; creating the instruments to apply it and then engaging it effectively was quite another: tasks which occupied much of 1916 and 1917. Much was learned about conducting effective attrition during the Somme offensive that Foch directed in 1916, although Foch concluded that attrition of that nature was too slow and costly, and that at this pace the enemy would always be able to find reserves. A December 1916 note by Weygand summed up attrition as it had worked on the Somme: 131 enemy divisions had been engaged in five months, on average 27 per month (31 in July, 18 in August, 30 in September, 31 in October and 21 in November; 60, or 45 per cent, by the British). In addition, at Verdun 52 divisions had been engaged during the same months, ten per month. Continuing the offensive once surprise had passed clearly maintained a strong, constant *usure* (wearing-out).[43] The method of 1916 'was good in the attack, but incomplete because the enemy had reserves to play with and had not been fixed on a sufficiently long front. Only after engaging the enemy everywhere and fixing the adversary would Napoleon strike with the decisive attack.'[44] The problem was that on the Somme enemy reserve divisions were not being destroyed quickly enough, so, although the tempo of the Somme offensive was stepped up again in September, there were always enough reserves to shore up the defence.[45] In future the battle would have to be bigger and longer.[46]

Moreover, his experience directing four armies in the Battle of the Somme gave Foch the final element of his offensive system, the 'operational art' that would be applied to the whole front in 1918. He concluded that in future the attack should take place in space and not in time. An attack should be delivered on as wide a front as possible and the initial effort reduced to a few days. If there was no decisive result, the attack should recommence on another sector of the front prepared in advance, surprising the enemy where he was less well prepared defensively. The campaign would, therefore, develop as a succession of coordinated, sequenced attacks, their cumulative effect wearing down and ultimately breaking the enemy's army. In future the battle would extend wide, rather than push deep and get bogged down.

> This manoeuvre by movement [along the front] is the only way on a front on which one cannot turn the flanks, and can be managed against an enemy with inferior numbers. The enemy command will be uncertain and worried, and will be demoralised rapidly the more its reserves are committed and it suffers partial defeats. Finally, the last blow struck will find them materially and morally powerless.[47]

Here was the root of '*la bataille générale*', Foch's 1918 method of engaging and defeating the German army in an attritional battle. 'To engage in it one must have a sufficient number of engines of war of every nature, and munitions, because it must be pushed through to victory.'[48] In 1917, when Chief of Staff of the French army, Foch would encourage the development of the material resources on which attrition rested to an appropriate level. As he informed the Allied Supreme War Council in January 1918, it was his intention to 'be ready to develop [separate] actions under the form of a *combined offensive with decisive objectives* [Foch's emphasis], the moment the wearing down process, or any other favourable circumstance arising in the general situation, offers the hope of success.'[49]

The opportunity arose in July to finally defeat the German army in a high-tempo operation that rippled back and forth along the Western Front, destroying the enemy's reserves at a pace at which they could not be replaced. The *bataille générale* was more than effective tactical 'combined-arms battle' (although its success depended on the ability of all the armies now under Foch's direction to fight such battles successfully at relatively short notice).[50] It was a wide, fast, large-scale prolonged battle all along the front, one attritional blow at a time but each concerted towards the objective of destroying the German army's operational reserves. By the French intelligence staff's calculations there were still 72 fresh or reformed German reserve divisions behind the front in mid-August 1918, but only 17 come Armistice Day, 11 November. Only two of these were fresh and able to go into the line.[51] Alongside this wastage of manpower, attrition of materiel and morale was sustained: thousands of guns and other weapons were captured, while prisoners came in in their thousands on every day of the 'hundred days' advance. During this process the front moved back across France and Belgium: this was attritional 'push-back', which defeated the German army on the lines which it tried to hold, not annihilating manoeuvre warfare. 'Whatever Foch may have intended', the British official historian Sir James Edmonds wrote at the end of the 1918 volumes, 'the result was attrition, pure and simple.'[52] The elusive 'decisive battle', if it could be called such, proved to be an attritional one after all. Perhaps to 'annihilate' the enemy in modern warfare a three-month attritional campaign following on from a three-year attritional strategy was essential, rather than a three-day breakthrough!

Cumulatively over four years, battlefield attrition had eliminated Germany's strategic manpower reserves. Jack Sheldon has elaborated the manpower crisis that gripped Germany during 1917 as a consequence of the intensified attrition of 1916, only partially alleviated by the troops freed up by Russia's collapse in 1918 for a last desperate attempt at annihilating the enemy.[53] It was desperate, because by then, with full Allied mobilisation and American entry, the resource battle waged thorough home front productivity and with blockade and counter-blockade had been decisively lost.[54]

Attrition in the First World War is an elusive, mutable concept. It varies between the two sides: attritional strategies are pursued by the 'inferior' and 'superior' powers, with different purposes. But, rather than glibly dismissing the war as one of attrition (and, as is often done, therefore as a military aberration), it is necessary to consider the nature and working of the strategic principle which ties together the various theatres and elements of the war and determines warfare. Doing so enables a better understanding of the war's course and outcome.

Careful reading of the sources is needed to pick out its nature and influence, and to assess its effectiveness. Haig's despatch on the Battle of the Somme, *The Opening of the Wearing-Out Fight*, ended with the confident (and, as it was to turn out, justified) boast:

> The enemy's power has not yet been broken, nor is it yet possible to form an estimate of the time the war may last before the objects for which the Allies are fighting have been attained. But the Somme battle has placed beyond doubt the ability of the Allies to gain those objects.[55]

Haig's assessment proved perspicacious: he did understand the slow, steady but decisive effect of attrition. The enemy's power would be broken: his assessment was based on the damage his and the French army had done to the Germans in 1916. Where exactly the armies were when this happened did not matter, although the fact that demonstrating this cost Haig's troops fighting in difficult ground heavy casualties to achieve remains contentious. If Haig persisted in mounting operations that were over-ambitious for an attritional war, Foch at least grasped the principles for applying attrition at the operational level to achieve the strategic objective which had been set out at the start of 1916. He was able to apply these effectively in 1918, with Haig's army one of his instruments. Rather than operational attrition arising as an unwanted, if necessary, consequence of the inability to deliver on the alternative – 'breakthrough' and annihilation – attrition was built into the operational method of the large-scale offensive, even if a final rupture (that never actually occurred) was envisaged by many once attrition had done its work. It is fair to say that the tactical and operational systems of the armies took time to adapt to an attritional positional war, and to deliver battlefield attrition effectively; but they did so within a year or so. This required a shift from manpower-intensive to materiel-intensive operations, which was realised from 1916.

When Lloyd George first met Foch, at the height of the war's first attritional battle at Ypres, Foch had reassured him that 'there will be no more retreats'. When pressed on whether there would be any more advances, Foch had replied, after reflection: 'that depends on the men and material you will be able to throw into the battle line'.[56] That was the tenet of the attritional battle Foch was fighting in November 1914 (as well as a key precept of French coalition strategy throughout the war); but it also encapsulated the principle of attritional warfare: manpower, materiel and defeating the enemy along his battle line. On a greater scale, this was exactly how Foch brought these together in 1918 to destroy the German army along the lines which it had defended stoutly since autumn 1914.

Attrition is slow, grinding, difficult and painful, while Lloyd George was dynamic, impatient, imaginative, and wanted a quick fix. His strategic critiques reflect his personality, but not the strategic reality of 1915 to 1918. Despite his stated respect for Foch's military genius, Lloyd George probably never grasped the military principles with which the Allies won the war. He understood that the war was about manpower and materiel, but never accepted that you have to engage the enemy directly with it, or properly understood how the generals came to develop an effective operational system to do this. His practical concerns with how the war was being run in late 1916 may have some contemporary validity, but they are not a fair reflection on the conduct of the war as a whole. It would be better to study the architects of attrition, Kitchener, Asquith, Joffre and Foch, not its critics, to properly appreciate how the war was fought and won.

Notes

1. General Sir Alexander Godley, *Life of an Irish Soldier* (London: John Murray, 1939), p. 224.
2. William Philpott, *Bloody Victory: The Sacrifice on the Somme and the Making of the Twentieth Century* (London: Little, Brown, 2009), pp. 316–322 passim.
3. See Robin Prior, *Churchill's* World Crisis *as History* (Beckenham: Croom Helm, 1983) and Andrew Suttie, *Rewriting the First World War: Lloyd George, Politics and Strategy, 1914–1918* (Basingstoke: Palgrave Macmillan, 2005).
4. David Lloyd George, *War Memoirs of David Lloyd George* (London: Odhams Press, 2 vols, 1938 edition), i, p. 617; Basil Liddell Hart, *The Real War, 1914–1918* (London: Faber, 1930); Winston S. Churchill, *The World Crisis 1911–1918* (London: Odhams Press Ltd, 2 vols, 1938 edition), ii, pp. 950–973.
5. Lloyd George, op. cit., pp. 616–617.
6. Brock Millman, *Pessimism and British War Policy, 1916–1918* (London: Frank Cass, 2001).
7. Henry Wilson diary, [14] November 1916, in Major-General Sir Charles Callwell (ed.), *Field-Marshal Sir Henry Wilson, His Life and Diaries* (London: Cassell & Co., 2 vols, 1927), i, p. 296.
8. Ibid.
9. War Cabinet minutes, 3 November 1916, quoted in Lloyd George, op. cit., i, p. 541.
10. Memorandum prepared for a meeting of Allied statesmen in Paris, 15–16 November 1916, in ibid., i, pp. 545–555.
11. Ibid., p. 551.
12. 30 June 1916, Brigadier-General John Charteris, *At GHQ* (London: Cassell and Co, 1931), p. 151.
13. Nicholas A. Lambert, *Planning Armageddon: British Economic Warfare and the First World War* (Cambridge, MA: Harvard University Press, 2012).
14. Carter Malkasian, *A History of Modern Wars of Attrition* (Westport, CT: Praeger, 2002), p. 2.
15. Arden Bucholz, *Hans Delbrück and the German Military Establishment: War Images in Conflict* (Iowa City: University of Iowa Press, 1985); Robert Foley, *German Strategy and the Path to Verdun: Erich von Falkenhayn and the Development of Attrition, 1870–1916* (Cambridge: Cambridge University Press, 2005), pp. 14–81 passim.
16. Foley, op. cit., passim; George Cassar, *Kitchener's War: British Strategy from 1914 to 1916* (Washington, DC: Brassey's Inc., 2004), p. 31.
17. Malkasian, op. cit., p. 1.
18. Statement by Robertson to the War Committee, 3 November 1916, quoted in Lloyd George, *War Memoirs*, i, pp. 539–541.
19. Ibid.
20. This thesis is developed fully in William Philpott, *Attrition: Fighting the First World War* (London: Little, Brown, 2014).

21. Statement by Robertson to the War Committee, op. cit.
22. Malkasian, op. cit., p. 29.
23. The case for rapid progress and growing effectiveness is made in more recent operational studies such as Philpott, *Bloody Victory*, Timothy Dowling, *The Brusilov Offensive* (Bloomington, IN: Indiana University Press, 2008) and John Schindler, *Isonzo: The Forgotten Sacrifice of the Great War* (Westport, CT: Praeger, 2001), but the long-established counter-argument for inefficiency and ineptitude persists in, for example, Williamson Murray, 'Complex Adaptation: The Western Front 1914–1918', in Williamson Murray, *Military Adaptation in War: With Fear of Change* (Cambridge: Cambridge University Press, 2011), pp. 74–118.
24. Statistics given by François Cailleteau in *Gagner la grande guerre* (Paris: Economica, 2008), p. 106.
25. Tim Travers, *The Killing Ground: The British Army, the Western Front, and the Emergence of Modern Warfare, 1900–1918* (London: Unwin Hyman, 1990), p. 86.
26. Quoted in Major-General Sir George Aston, *The Biography of the Late Marshal Foch* (London: Hutchinson & Co., 1930), p. 226.
27. Malkasian, op. cit., p. 7.
28. Foley, op. cit., pp. 124–125.
29. 'The term [attrition] is elusive and changed in meaning over time and depending on who was using it', George Cassar notes in *Asquith as War Leader* (London: The Hambledon Press, 1994), p. 112, n. 5, although he himself does not engage with changing concepts of attrition in this study, and thereafter there is no suggestion that the British prime minister or his ministers understood or were conducting a war of attrition.
30. David French, 'The Meaning of Attrition', *The English Historical Review*, Vol. 103 (1988), pp. 385––405: 392–395.
31. Quoted in David French, *British Strategy and War Aims* (London: Allen & Unwin, 1986), p. 119.
32. Interview in *The Times*, 15 August 1914.
33. French, 'Meaning of Attrition', pp. 387–389.
34. Quoted in French, *British Strategy and War Aims*, p. 200.
35. Marshal Joseph Joffre, *The Memoirs of Marshal Joffre*, trans. T. Bentley Mott (London: Geoffrey Bles, 2 vols, 1932), ii, p. 452.
36. 'Plan of Action Proposed by France to the Coalition', in 'Written Statement of the Conference Held at Chantilly, December 6th 1915', The National Archives, Kew [TNA], WO 106/1454, Appendix 2.
37. Philpott, op. cit., p. 83.
38. Joffre to Haig, 6 June 1916, TNA, WO 158/14/121a. The sentence in italics was underlined on Haig's copy.
39. Philpott, op. cit., pp. 117–127.
40. Jonathan Krause, *Early Trench Tactics in the French Army: The Second Battle of Artois, May–June 1915* (Farnham: Ashgate, 2013).
41. 'Auprès du Maréchal Foch', speech by Weygand [26 March 1929], Papiers Foch (Fournier–Foch), *Service historique de la défense, Archives de l'armée de terre* Vincennes (AAT), 1K129/5.
42. Foch to Joffre, 6 November 1915, in *Les Armées françaises dans la grande guerre, tome III* (Paris: Imprimerie Nationale, 1926), annexes vol. 4, annexe 3056, 206–213, p. 211.

43. 'Répercussions de l'offensive de la Somme sur l'emploi des disponibilités, l'usure et la fixation des effectifs des allemands', 1 December 1916, Fonds Weygand, AAT, 1K130/J.
44. Handwritten note, 'Guerre de Position', Fonds Weygand, AAT, 1K130/14.
45. 'Répercussions de l'offensive de la Somme', op. cit.
46. Untitled and unsigned paper [winter 1916–1917], in Fonds Weygand, AAT 1K130/14.
47. Ibid.
48. 'Guerre de Position', op. cit.
49. Memorandum for the Versailles Supreme War Council, 1 January 1918, quoted in Marshal Ferdinand Foch, *The Memoirs of Marshal Foch*, trans. Colonel T. Bentley Mott (London: William Heinemann, 1931), p. 271.
50. See Jonathan Boff, *Winning and Losing on the Western Front: The British Third Army and the Defeat of Germany in 1918* (Cambridge: Cambridge University Press, 2012).
51. Philpott, op. cit., p. 532.
52. Brig.-Gen. Sir James Edmonds and R. Maxwell-Hyslop, *History of the Great War: Military Operations, France and Belgium, 1918, vol. V. 26th September– 11 November 1918: The Advance to Victory* (London: HMSO, 1947), p.604
53. Jack Sheldon, 'The German Manpower Crisis', *The Douglas Haig Fellowship Records*, Vol. 15 (2011), pp. 35–49.
54. David Stevenson, *With Our Backs to the Wall: Victory and Defeat in 1918* (London: Allen Lane, 2011).
55. 'The Opening of the Wearing-out Battle', 23 December 1916, in John Boraston (ed.), *Sir Douglas Haig's Despatches* (London: Dent, 1919), p. 58.
56. Lloyd George, op. cit., i, p. 95.

Select Bibliography

Memoirs, Diaries and Letters

Bourne, John and Sheffield, Gary (2005) *Douglas Haig War Diaries and Letters 1914–1918* (London: Weidenfeld & Nicolson)

D'Urbal, General V. (1939) *Souvenirs et Anecdotes de Guerre 1914–1916* (Paris: Berger-Levrault)

Foch, Ferdinand (1931) *Mémoires pour servir à l'histoire de la guerre de 1914–1918* (Paris: Plon)

Joffre, Joseph Jacques Césaire (1932) *Mémoires Du Maréchal Joffre (1910–1917)* (Paris: Plon)

Lloyd George, David (1938) *War Memoirs of David Lloyd George* (London: Odhams Press, 2 vols.)

Ludendorff, General (1919) *My War Memories 1914–1918* (London: Hutchinson & Co.)

Official Histories

Edmonds, James (1922) *Official History of the Great War: Military Operations France and Belgium 1914*, Vol. 1 (London: MacMillan)

France, Ministère de la Guerre, Etat-Major de l'Armée, Service Historique (1923) *Les Armées Françaises dans la Grande Guerre [AFGG]* Tome II (Paris: Imprimerie Nationale)

Johnston, W., Rawling, W.G.P., Gimblett, R.H. and MacFarlene, J. (2010) *The Seabound Coast: The Official History of the Royal Canadian Navy, 1867–1939 volume I* (Toronto: Dundurn Press)

Reichsarchiv, E.S. Mittler and Sohn, Berlin (1925) *Der Weltkrieg 1914 bis 1918, Die militärischen Operationen zu Lande, Erster Band* (Weltkrieg 1)

Secondary Sources

Anderson, Ross (2004) *The Forgotten Front: The East African Campaign 1914–1918* (Stroud: Tempus)

Bowman, Tim and Connelly, Mark (2012) *The Edwardian Army: Recruiting, Training and Deploying the British Army 1902–1914* (Oxford: University of Oxford Press)

Bruce, Robert B. (2003) *A Fraternity of Arms* (Lawrence: University Press of Kansas)

Doughty, Robert (2005) *Pyrrhic Victory: French Strategy and Operations in the Great War* (Cambridge, MA: Belknap Press of Harvard University Press)

Foley, Robert (2005) *German Strategy and the Path to Verdun: Erich von Falkenhayn and the Development of Attrition, 1870–1916* (Cambridge: Cambridge University Press)

Fritzsche, Peter (1998) *Germans Into Nazis* (Cambridge, MA: Harvard University Press)

Gooch, John (1989) *Army, State and Society in Italy, 1870–1915* (London: Macmillan)

Goren, Haim (2014) *Palestine and World War I: Grand Strategy, Military Tactics, and Culture in War* (I.B. Tauris)

Greenhalgh, Elizabeth (2011) *Foch in Command: The Forging of a First World War General* (Cambridge: Cambridge University Press)

Hernon, Ian (2000) *The Savage Empire: Forgotten Wars of the 19th Century* (Stroud: Sutton Publishing)

Holmes, Richard (2007) *Riding the Retreat: Mons to Marne 1914 Revisited* (London: Pimlico)

Hughes, Matthew (1999) *Allenby and British Strategy in the Middle East, 1917–1919* (London: Frank Cass)

Kitchen, James E. (2014) *The British Imperial Army in the Middle East: Morale and Military Identity in the Sinai and Palestine Campaigns, 1916–18* (London: Bloomsbury)

Lambert, Nicholas A. (2012) *Planning Armageddon: British Economic Warfare and the First World War* (Cambridge, MA: Harvard University Press)

Malkasian, Carter (2002) *A History of Modern Wars of Attrition* (Westport, CT: Praeger)

Millman, Brock (2001) *Pessimism and British War Policy, 1916–1918* (London: Frank Cass)

Mombauer, Annika (2001) *Helmuth Von Motlke and the Origins of the First World War* (Cambridge: Cambridge University Press)

Mulligan, William (2005) *The Creation of the Modern German Army. General Walther Reinhardt and the Weimar Republic, 1914–1930* (Oxford: Berghahn Books)

Pöhlmann, Markus (2002) *Kriegsgeschichte und Geschichtspolitik: Der Erste Weltkrieg: Die amtliche deutsche Militärgeschichtsschreibung 1914–1956* (Paderborn: Ferdinand Schöningh)

Porte, Rémy (2005) *La mobilisation industrielle?: 'premier front' de la Grande Guerre?* (Saint-Cloud: 14–18 éditions)

Samson, Anne (2013) *World War One in Africa: The Forgotten Conflict Among the European Powers* (London: IB Tauris)

Strachan, Hew (2001) *The First World War Volume One: To Arms* (Oxford: Oxford University Press)

Todman, Dan (2005) *The Great War: Myth and Memory* (London: Hambledon Continuum)

Winter, Jay and Prost, Antoine (2005) *The Great War in History: Debates and Controversies, 1914 to the Present* (Cambridge: Cambridge University Press)

Woodfin, Edward (2012) *Camp and Combat on the Sinai and Palestine Front: The Experience of the British Empire Soldier, 1916–18* (Houndmills: Palgrave Macmillan)

Zabecki, David T. (2006) *The German 1918 Offensives: A Case Study in the Operational Level of War* (London and New York: Routledge)

Index

Printed and bound by CPI Group (UK) Ltd, Croydon, CR0 4YY